on **PUBLICITY** . . .

"My life has definitely been an open book. It's been plastered across the front pages of supermarket tabloids and broadcast on the nightly news."

on **BEING A SEX SYMBOL** . . .

"By the time somebody's become a sex symbol, it's usually the time they would really like to have just one woman."

on **HOWARD HUGHES** . . .

"He knew an awful lot about me. Was he the type of man who would enjoy eavesdropping or bugging? In my mind, there's no doubt about it."

on **JOHNNY CARSON** . . .

"There's no doubt he caused me a lot of pain in my life."

on **ELVIS PRESLEY** . . .

"Anyone who was tuned in had to realize he'd had it . . . the drugs were just a way out."

on **FAITH** . . .

"The two things that I have never done in my life is lose faith in God or the American public."

Wayne Newton

ONCE BEFORE I GO

WAYNE NEWTON
— WITH —
DICK MAURICE

AVON BOOKS  NEW YORK

Photographs by Dick Maurice, Jim Laurie, Peter Kredenser, Don Ploke, David Brown, David Lee Waite, Las Vegas News Bureau, Universal Pictures Company, Inc., and the White House.

"Newton May Be Singing a Different Tune," published on October 14, 1980, used by permission of the *Chicago Sun-Times*.

AVON BOOKS
A division of
The Hearst Corporation
1350 Avenue of the Americas
New York, New York 10019

The William Morrow and Company edition contains the following Library of Congress Cataloging in Publication Data:

Newton, Wayne.
  Once before I go / Wayne Newton with Dick Maurice.
    p. cm.
1. Newton, Wayne. 2. Singers—United States—Biography.
I. Maurice, Dick.   II. Title.
ML420.N48A3   1989   89-12202
782.42164′092—dc20   CIP
[B]   MN

First Avon Books Printing: July 1991

AVON TRADEMARK REG. U.S. PAT. OFF. AND IN OTHER COUNTRIES, MARCA REGISTRADA, HECHO EN U.S.A.

Printed in the U.S.A.

RA 10 9 8 7 6 5 4 3 2 1

This book is dedicated to all those very special people in my life, both past and present: to those who are so very close to me—my loving daughter, Erin, my beloved father, Pat, and, of course, Marla; to lifelong friends that every man dreams of having—Mona, Bear, Sister Barbara, Joe Schenk, Frank Fahrenkopf, Edward Doumani, Tom Chauncey, Jay Stream, Elmer Ridenhour, June Taylor, the Doctors Jacobs, and the Reagans; to the legal brilliance of Mort Galane and the dedication of Mark Moreno; to those whom I so cherished that I will someday see again—Walter, Ricky, Bobby, Lucy, Mr. Harrah, Mr. Lastfogel, Mr. Benny, Mr. Gleason, and Elvis; to the most special person in my life—my mother; and to those very many who simply always kept the faith.

CHAPTER 1

I've had to go through that kind of hurt.
We never learn anything from the good things
that happen in our life.

IT WAS 1942, America was mobilizing for World War II, and President Franklin Roosevelt had pledged to fight to victory. That year's Oscar for Best Movie went to *Mrs. Miniver,* with Greer Garson winning Best Actress and James Cagney as Best Actor. The tune everyone was singing was Bing Crosby's "White Christmas." April 3 proved to be an important day in the lives of Doris Day, Marlon Brando, Marsha Mason, and George Jessel, and on Friday, April 3, 1942, my mother hit high C (jokey jokey) when Carson Wayne Newton was born. Would you believe as I was coming into the world a gallon of gas cost $.20, a loaf of bread was $.09, and a brand-new Ford could be driven out of the lot for $815?

Who is Wayne Newton? I've often been asked that question and, quite honestly, there are many sides to me. I think I am complex. I think any man who is aggressive is complex. It's wearing those many hats, the old cliché that we all talk so much about. I don't know that I am so complex that people would consider me difficult to get along with. I'm sure it would depend upon whom you ask and what the situation was. I'm a perfectionist. I get up early in the morning and no one talks to me because it takes me a long time to wake up. I like to start my day that way. I like to sit at the table and take a long time with my breakfast.

1

I don't like problems at home. Often I'll walk around the ranch and sit out on the side of a knoll for about an hour and watch some of the animals. Then I'll come back to the house relaxed.

I do have a temper. There are certain things that irritate me immensely. However, I don't often get angry. It takes me a long time to get there, and when you get me there, you have a lot of problems on your hands. Because with me, I'm either black or white. I can't be indifferent to people or situations. I either get involved or I'm not involved at all.

When I look back on my life, which isn't easy because I'm so busy living it, it gives me a chance to measure the successes and failures. However, I did realize a long time ago that nothing was ever going to be easy for me; none of it. I don't think it ever will be easy. I don't know why my life has had so many ups and downs, why it has been a battlefield. The only thing that has been easy has been any talent that I might have, and I can't take credit for that. I've had to work for everything. No one has handed me anything. Yet, at the darkest moments, there has always been someone there to pull my butt out of the mess. And I generally come out smelling like a rose.

While other performers are resentful when they see entertainers obtain success very easily without having to do anything for it, I feel sorry for them because I know that the day has got to come when they will have to pay the fiddler. I'd just as soon pay for it as I go because I'm more capable of dealing with it—the facts at hand rather than what I'd like them to be.

I guess you could say my life has been a series of crises. But I would prefer the word *lessons*. Now, I didn't love the little boy I was, nor do I necessarily love the man that I am. I've had to go through that kind of hurt. We never learn anything from the good things that happen in our lives. I think being happy occurs in moments. I don't know of a time when I'm the happiest. There are many times in the day when happiness comes to me for a very short period of time. It may be while walking around the ranch or having something happen onstage. One's ability to be happy depends solely on one's ability to adjust.

Once Before I Go is a story that I hope you'll like to read. I've seen it written that I'm the singer who turned ridicule into success. The story of an Indian who overcame the bows and arrows and vicious attacks to rise above it all. I've seen it written that I'm the male soprano who dropped his voice and rose to dominance in the entertainment palaces of Las Vegas. It's also been printed that I've become the highest-paid nightclub entertainer in the world, which seems unbelievable when I remember that I arrived in Las Vegas with twenty dollars in my pocket at the age of fifteen.

When people say to me, "Do you bet?" I laugh, "Only on myself." I've never been to a gaming table in my life. I'm one of those people who are terribly optimistic; the kind of guy who would take his last dollar and buy a wallet with it.

I don't like bad news. Nobody likes bad news. I also try not to cross bridges before I get to them. And when I feel it's time to be sad, that's soon enough because it's real. So I try not to make a lot of sadness for others as well as myself. I have had three attributes in my life: a great faith in the man upstairs, a great faith in the public, and the ability to just kind of pull back my energies when I feel I'm getting close to the burnout, and go sit down somewhere and let the chips fall where they may.

I am my own worst critic. No, I'm not my own best friend, I'm a lot harder on me than anybody else is. It really doesn't matter how hard someone is on me when I feel that I've done something wrong or failed at something. There's nothing that anyone can say or do to make me feel better about it.

My life has definitely been an open book. It's been plastered across the front pages of supermarket tabloids and broadcast on the nightly news. There's no doubt that I've been a headline maker, though not by choice. But no paternity suits yet. Controversy has been my middle name, over whether I was willing to take on Johnny Carson over his gay jokes, and when I was willing to pay the price at the risk of changing my life to go against one of the top networks for attacking me. I have no regrets about my defamation suit against NBC when they broadcast in 1980 that I was linked to reputed mob figures. If I had to do it again, I would. Even knowing what I know now—the pain, the hurt, the suffering, and the price—I'd still do it.

Yes, it took its toll. But not to have taken them on would have been an admission that they were correct in what they had said. I can just tell you that when it was over and the dust settled, there were an awful lot of surprised people. Can you imagine challenging a network? If I were guilty of anything at all, I would have had to be the dumbest person in the world to take them on. I was told right up front by my attorney that there was a chance I would lose my family over their lies. It was a fishbowl, and it was vicious.

So would I do it over again? Once before I go I'd have to do it over again.

There have been disappointments along the way and many times I've cried a lot. However, it's always been me alone. When I'm superdisappointed or superhurt, I prefer to be alone.

Love has played a very important part in my life. It's a necessity for me to be in love. It has been since I was very young. I recognize that in myself, and I believe the need to love and to be loved is in all of us.

I like my life now. I'll change a few things about it one of these days, but on a scale of one to ten, I'll give it an eight. I would be less than candid if I said the most important thing in life is living. I don't believe that. The most important thing in life is the quality of life.

Let me tell you a quick story. There are two people I know who flunked Ted Mack's *Original Amateur Hour* audition: Elvis Presley and me. I can understand Elvis, but not me. Jokey jokey! Ted Mack came to see me six months before he passed away. I introduced him onstage, and I said I'd always be grateful to him because people handle rejection in one of two ways: It either destroys them or motivates them to say, "Damn it! I'm going to do it!" The fact that I didn't make his audition was motivating to me. Early in my career, I was one of those people who are never really accepted by their peers. I was always the guy who was the brunt of the jokes. I believe part of the reason I've succeeded is a result of all that rejection. It didn't make me tough so much as determined. If you do what I do twice a night—walk out onstage and open yourself up—you make yourself vulnerable. I had to survive. What's the alternative?

So who is Wayne Newton? I can't sum up what I am— only what I hope to be. If you were wondering who I am—I am a man. A man who is special dares to dream and pursues it, using his head for himself and his heart for others. A man who is special strives to leave the world better than he found it. I guess that's what I hope to do.

CHAPTER 2

☆

Threatening me with the word orphanage *was a way of keeping me in line.*

IF ANYONE MENTIONS the word *orphanage,* I cringe. My parents used to say to me that there was an orphanage not too far from our home, and if I didn't behave myself, they were going to leave me there. That was devastating to me. It has lasted all my life and I react to it to this day. Threatening me with the word *orphanage* was a way of keeping me in line. I was a hyper kid. When my dad used to take his belt off and threaten to spank me, it didn't bother me nearly as much as when he made me sit in a chair.

It's left its impact. If someone says, "I'm going to leave you," my attitude is, "Go right ahead. The sooner the better. If you're going to stay with me, then stay with me. If you're going to threaten to leave, then go now." I know this reaction derives from that threat as a child.

My brother was never as frightened by the orphanage as I was. It hurt my feelings more. My brother let it roll off his back. He was a great deal more capable of being insensitive about that than I was. Maybe that's one of the reasons why I went into show business, but I'll never know.

Unless you're Judy Garland, born in a trunk, I'm not sure that anyone who goes into show business wants to be in show biz as a kid. I'm not even sure I knew then what show biz was. The first time I remember singing I couldn't have been more than three years old. I sat out on the porch of my aunt's farmhouse in a little rocking chair that wasn't too far from the pigpen. I don't remember whom I learned it from, but there I was, singing my heart out to the tune "Blues in My Mind." At the age of four, my parents took me to the Grand Ole Opry road show that came through Roanoke, Virginia. I was starry-eyed watching Hank Williams and Kitty Wells. At the end of the show I said to my mom, "This is what I want to do." She said, "What?" and I said, pointing to the stage, "That!"

That was my first recollection of a performance. I really never knew it as show business. But from that moment on I started to bug my parents to give me music lessons. Here I was, this four-year-old walking around the house with a broom, pretending it was a guitar. Finally they decided to give in and took me to a woman piano teacher. They dropped me off at her house and I went inside very timidly. A woman in her early forties was seated at the piano. She said, "Come over here and sit down." As I sat down, she barely looked at me. She was scribbling something on a piece of paper. She looked up and said to me, "You know your ABCs?" And I said, "No, ma'am, I don't." She snapped, "You don't know your ABCs?" I repeated, frightened, "No ma'am." She went berserk. She started to pound the piano with her fist, yelling and screaming. She jumped up from the piano stool and, pointing her finger at me, said, "You wait right here." I was scared to death.

She went into the kitchen and I thought she was going to kill me. I saw her take out a big knife and a piece of string. She ripped off a piece of paper and began to write on it. She cut off a piece of string and angrily walked into the room. After punching two holes in the paper, she placed it around my neck. Grabbing me by the collar, she yelled, "Now you can wait out on the porch until your parents come back!" I went out on the porch and sat there for what seemed an eternity. There I sat, devastated and all alone. I wondered what I had done wrong. When my parents drove up, they saw me sitting there with a sign around my neck that read, HOW DARE YOU SEND THIS CHILD TO LEARN MUSIC WHEN HE DOESN'T EVEN KNOW HIS ABCS?

My parents realized that a terrible thing had happened to me in terms of rejection. For about the next two weeks, they kept saying, "We'll find you another teacher." And I cried, "I don't want to do that." I hated the piano. I hated piano until I became an adult and realized that it wasn't the instrument I hated but the way the piano teacher had treated me.

It took them about a month to talk me into going to another teacher, and then, after they said, "Your brother will go with you," I felt that as long as I had my older brother with me it would be all right.

That's when Elmer Ridenhour came into my life. We walked into his little studio and he said, "Well, what do you boys want to play?" Of course, the two of us wanted to play guitar. And he laughed, "Well, that doesn't make any sense," and suggested that one of us take up steel guitar and the other one try rhythm guitar. Jerry and I both wanted to play rhythm guitar. My mother and father said, "Look, Jerry's the oldest. He gets his choice. So Wayne, you play the steel guitar."

I started to take my first lesson when the teacher said those famous, dreaded words. "Do you know your ABCs?"

I thought, *Oh, God, here we go again,* and stepped behind Jerry. I said, "No, sir, I don't," as the fear rushed to my eyes.

Quickly he asked, "Can you count to twelve?"

And I said, "Yes, sir."

And he said, "I will teach you by numbers."

Each week he would play the song that he wanted us to learn for the next week's lesson. It was a year before he found out that we were playing by ear. We would never rehearse the things that we were supposed to practice. We'd just play around. When we'd go back for our next lesson, I'd play it for him the way he had played it for me.

When the teacher discovered that we were playing by ear, he didn't go berserk. In fact, he was amused by it and said, "Well, someday, sometime, you'll probably have to learn to read music the correct way. But right now, it doesn't seem to be a problem for you. So just keep up the good work."

There was never a moment when he was less than encouraging. He was a very gentle man and was an inspiration to me. I credit him with a lot of insight, caring, and sensitivity that many teachers never possess.

That was my formal education in music. The most I could wish for is that everybody should have a music teacher like Elmer Ridenhour.

It was at a Christmas party for the AFL-CIO union where I made my stage debut. I played steel guitar and sang for five dollars.

My brother and I wanted to be Roy Rogers and Gene Autry. My mother told us, "There's only one of them, you know. So if you're going to make it, you have to develop your own style." My parents never pushed us into anything. And I remember that it was my mother who discovered that we were playing by ear long before my music teacher did. We'd been taking music lessons for a year, and she observed that we rarely practiced but always played right when we went to our music lesson. One night she surprised my brother and me when we played the song for our teacher and didn't miss a note. He was proud of us and said, "They're really doing great!" That's when my mother announced, "Well, I'll tell you something. They're not reading the music. They're playing by ear." My teacher told my mom, "Take them out of music school for a while." So she did. And we kept right on playing by ear.

As I look back, I was really a happy kid. I always had lots of animals and I could occupy myself for hours when I was alone. Jerry, being eighteen months older, went to school, and I used to play with my dog and cats. My parents raised chickens in those days and I helped with the farm chores. I lived a farm boy existence. There are still things that stand out in my memory. One was the slaughter of the hogs. I remember running from that. I remember my dad and my uncle slitting the hog's throat and hearing the squeal, which is a terrible memory. I remember that a puppy I had started sucking eggs, and once a dog starts that, there is no way to break the habit. My uncle threw him up in the air and batted him with a baseball bat. I happened to be coming around the corner of the barn and saw the puppy die. I was devastated. Ever since then, I cannot forgive someone who is cruel to an animal.

I felt closer to my mother than to my dad. My dad was gone all day because he was an auto mechanic.

My brother was absolutely the apple of my mother's eye. I mean, unquestionably, it was the Smothers Brothers syndrome: "Mother always liked you best." There was no question about it. Even though she never admitted it, my brother could do no wrong in her eyes. Anywhere, anytime, until the day she passed away, he was her pet, but I don't remember the favoritism surfacing until after the music lessons. I was more outgoing with regard to the music and not afraid of being onstage. My brother was never afraid, but it was something he never liked.

I earned a great deal of attention because of the music, and that could have been the real reason for my parents feeling that they had to compensate my brother. I don't remember that love was ever the issue. I felt loved, but I wasn't allowed to outshine my brother. I remember that he got a bicycle for Christmas and it took him four days to learn how to ride it. He kept falling off, and I was standing around, until the one time I got on the bike and just went my way. My brother got very angry and my parents chewed me out because I rode my brother's bicycle.

One time my parents went into business with another woman to open a restaurant in Fredericksburg. I wasn't even in school then. After eight months, my mother had a nervous breakdown. There were times when we would have all the drapes down to prevent light from coming into the house in the daytime. She would cry all the time. My dad would take her to different doctors to seek help. Finally it was determined that it was low blood sugar. Her illness was definitely a crisis and I felt insecure.

My parents had their spats like any other couple. There was one in particular that was devastating to me. They were having a verbal fight and my dad stormed into my brother's and my bedroom. My brother was out playing and my dad said, "I'm going to leave your mother and you come with me." Just the thought of it was frightening.

By no means were we wealthy. But I don't remember wanting for anything. I'm sure everything is comparative. When you grow up in the ghetto, you have to get out of the ghetto to realize that it was the ghetto that you were in. My parents moved a lot from town to town—from Fredericksburg to Roanoke, back to Fredericksburg, and back to Roanoke.

It was on station WDBJ in Roanoke that I first hit the airwaves. I was six years old. I would do a radio show at six o'clock in the morning before going to school. It lasted for about a year. I also entertained in church two or three times a month. I did a couple of assemblies in school. In one of them I played Steven Foster with a guitar. On weekends, my brother and I would tour with any of the Grand Old Opry road shows that had come through Roanoke, and we played any private parties that came up. We traveled to Bristol, Tennessee, where we performed three songs as a preview to movies in a theater.

Our town used to have what was known as community sings. They'd put on a little show in the middle of the park and my brother and I were always a part of them.

When I was eight, Jerry and I entered a contest in Fredericksburg where we won a chance to audition for Ted Mack. My dad took a day off from work and we drove from Virginia to New York. I was shocked at the rudeness in that city. We auditioned, but Mack didn't even bother to tell us if we had made it or flunked. They simply said, "Don't call us, we'll call you!" We never heard anything from them.

The first real recollection I have of school was in the third grade. I was in love with my third grade teacher, Miss Ward, but I was also in love with a little girl in my class by the name of Betty Ferguson, whose father owned a drive-in theater. I used to sit in Betty's car with her parents and watch the movie. Once her father found out that Gene Autry was coming to Roanoke. Autry was flying his own plane and was going to stop there for fuel. We all piled into Betty's dad's car and went to the airport. When Autry came off the plane we were all excited. He autographed pictures, and when he came to me he said, "I don't have any more pictures." I said, heartbroken, "It's okay, sir." Autry said, "But I'll send you one." I've never gotten it, but I'm still waiting.

In third grade I formed a gang, and at recess we would play cowboys and Indians. I was always the Indian chief and the Indians always won. Many times I would be called into the principal's office because of my mischievous activities. We didn't destroy any property or anything, but my insistence that the Indians win didn't always make for a happy playground. We were always on the warpath ready to scalp and beat up the cowboys. Finally, the principal figured out that if she made me leader of the junior patrol on the bus, she could probably direct some of those pow-wow energies. She did, and I came upon the side of law and order.

In the fourth grade I had a teacher who I thought was an opera star. Although I didn't know exactly what opera was, I knew she sang differently from the way I sang. She always put the music in keys that I couldn't reach. That was pretty hard, because I had a high voice. She had a real resentment of me, which didn't bother me a lot because I didn't like her either. One day in class she looked at me and said, "I don't know what it is about you Newtons"—my brother had been there two years before me—

"but all of you seem to have a problem with my music."
I said, "That's because my mother taught me to bark, not
howl." That was one of the serious times I got sent to the
principal's office.

I was a very sickly baby. I was born with a jaundiced
look about me, and until I was ten months old I would lie
in the crib and whimper. Then they discovered I was al-
lergic to milk. My diet was changed, and I was okay after
that.

Illness became a way of life. It kept me out of school a
lot. They didn't put a name on my illness—asthma—until
I was about seven. The minute winter set in, I would get
sick. Maybe that's when my parents started to pay more
attention to my brother. They may have felt they should
show my brother more notice since they spent so much
time nursing me. No matter what I did, it led to illness.
Finally the doctors told my parents that if they wanted me
to live, they had better get me to a dry climate. It was a
do-or-die situation. For my parents, it meant tearing up
their roots and leaving everything they had known behind.

Even though the hurt was never verbalized, I felt it. It
was as if I were a burden. At night I would lie in bed and
think how they were giving up everything they ever wanted
because of me.

We went to Phoenix, Arizona, because my mother had
a brother there. My father searched for work for seven
weeks and came up with nothing. In the meantime, my
health cleared up and I didn't have a problem at all. It was
during that time that my brother and I auditioned for a
local producer in Phoenix, Lew King, for the "Lew King
Ranger Show." But with my dad being unable to find
work, and with my health improved, my parents risked
moving to Newark, Ohio, where my dad's sister lived.

Jerry and I worked on Sundays at a place called Hill
Billy Park, where they headlined all the big country acts.
Everything was fine during the summer and my parents
even bought a home. They put fifteen hundred dollars
down, and along with the house came a cocker spaniel.

The previous owners of the house left it behind, and I couldn't have been more thrilled. Winter set in just as we were about to move in and I became deathly ill. The doctor told my parents, "If you can get him back to Arizona, you had better take him."

They forfeited their down payment, which was all the money they could beg, borrow, or steal, and we moved back to Arizona.

I remember watching my mother try to sell whatever she could. Most of the stuff she had to give away. She gave away the furniture that had been left to her by her grandmother; we could only take so much in the little canvas-covered utility trailer. As we drove to Arizona, our entire world was in that trailer.

CHAPTER 3

⭐

*I realized that my dad's problem with being Indian was
his fear of the Southern prejudice about blacks.*

MY DAD, PATRICK Newton, was born on November 30,
1915. His father was pure-blooded Indian and his mother
was as Irish as a shamrock. As a youngster, my dad truly
knew what it meant to be poor. He was one of thirteen
children and remembers well the hungry years. He tells of
catching sparrows, which the family cooked with pota-
toes. He often went to school barefoot, and in the winter,
in order to keep his feet from freezing, he wore his sister's
high-buttoned shoes, which had to be laced up with a cro-
chet needle.

If there's anyone to whom I give credit for teaching me
to have the courage to fight, it's my father. He always lived
by the motto "If I'm right I'm going to fight to the end."
My father has a country way of saying things. He is the
type of man who will look you straight in the eye and say,
"They need their butts kicked, those liars."

My mother, Evelyn Marie Smith, was born on July 6,
1922, in Alabama. Actually, her surname was Plasters, but
her father had had some problems with the draft during
World War I and changed his name to Smith. As a little
boy I kept asking, "Why is your uncle named Plasters and
you were a Smith?" Finally, when I got older, she explained it. But as far as she knew, from the time she was
a little girl her name was Smith. She was raised in West

Virginia until she was sixteen years old, and then moved to Virginia.

Her mother was pure-blooded Cherokee and her dad was as German as apple strudel. So, I'm half Indian, a quarter Irish, and a quarter German.

I remember asking my dad about the Indian chief that I had heard about in our family. As a youngster I was fascinated about Indians. My dad said, "The child is half Negro." Many years later I realized that my dad's problem with being Indian was his fear of the Southern prejudice about blacks. He feared that if he told anybody he was half Indian they might have considered him the next thing to being black. My dad never admitted his Indian heritage until he was almost seventy years old. Now he's proud of it.

Phoenix was the first place where I realized that prejudice existed. I hadn't really mentioned to anyone that I was half Indian because it was no big thing to me. It's not something that was prevalent in my mind or theirs. It all started because I was doing a television show. My teacher in the fifth grade, Mr. Carter, said to the class, "We have a new kid in class and I want you all to know that just because he's on television, it does not mean that you should treat him any differently than you would anybody else." I was shocked. It had never occurred to me that they would treat me differently. I surely didn't take the teacher telling these other kids that they ought to be nice to me as a compliment.

In the seventh grade I experienced the same thing. This time it was in my music class. The teacher said, "We have a student who is in show business and on television, but I will not favor him over any other student." I hated to be singled out that way. When she saw me holding back the tears, at the end of class she asked me to stay. She called me up to her desk and whispered, "You won't appreciate what I did today, Wayne. It hurt your feelings, but one day you'll understand it." She reached out and held my hand. She said, "I took away any malice that any of the students might feel for any kind of favoritism that I might show you because I enjoy what you do.''

I got along so well with the kids at school that when my parents couldn't afford fifteen cents a day for lemonade, someone would come to our rescue. My brother and I carried our lunch to school every day in a brown bag. One of the kids would always walk up to me and say, ''What are you drinking?'' and knowing that we couldn't afford it, they'd either buy me a lemonade or say, ''Share mine.'' I got along famously with the kids. It was the teachers that I had problems with. Not all of them, but most. I was sophomore class president, junior class president, and had been elected student body president when I quit. I got called in by my counselor right before the election for junior class president. He rudely said, ''I called you in here to tell you that, basically, the rest of the faculty and I would appreciate it if you didn't run for junior class president.'' Because he hurt my feelings, I asked why. He said, ''We don't feel that you represent the kind of image that we would like to have our student government officers portray to the rest of the city.''

The teachers resented that I was in show business. It didn't seem to matter that I maintained a B average while doing my television show, that I raised more money with class projects when I was sophomore class president. I used my show-biz connections to produce rock 'n' roll rumbles. I called in friends of mine, performers like Dwayne Eddie and Marty Robbins. We'd charge something like twenty-five cents per seat in the school auditorium. It was sold out for two shows.

When the counselor asked me not to run, my feelings were so hurt that I withdrew from the race. It was two days before the election. But it didn't seem to matter because I felt that maybe the kids shared the teachers' feelings. It was my own insecurity showing again. The day of the election, I didn't even go to school. The morning after the election, the first three or four kids I saw didn't say anything, and I didn't want to be obvious and ask who won. Finally, a girl walked up and said, "Wayne, congratulations!" I said, "For what?" She said, "For being junior class president." I thought that maybe she hadn't heard that I withdrew. What had happened was that I had won overwhelmingly with a write-in vote.

As a result of being on television, I was invited to St. John's Indian Mission outside Phoenix. It was a Christmas program and I had been invited by the coach at the school, who wanted me to sing a few songs. He had seen me on television and had noticed my extremely dark eyes and high cheekbones. Through the producer of the television show, he had found out that I was half Indian. My parents and I drove out there. I got out of the car and looked around and saw a poor Indian mission. But I was taken at how polite the kids were. Even though I had much lighter hair I felt something, some kinship.

I remember many times, as a child, asking my dad about Pocahontas and my Indian heritage. He'd simply shut me up by snapping, "I don't know anything about our family tree." When I questioned him further he became annoyed. He'd say, "I never looked at it for fear we'd find a goddamn monkey." Little did I realize that my dad had a real problem with the fact that his sister had married a full-blooded Indian chief from the reservation right outside Fredericksburg, Virginia.

As I stood there surrounded by Indian kids, I felt something with those people that I had never felt before. And I couldn't even explain it. Because I had my own television show there were bound to be kids who would throw a few catcalls in my direction. But at the mission, there was a total quiet when I walked in. The kids were very respectful. It was eerie to me. My brother and I sang three songs, and I felt such a closeness with those kids. Their poverty was obvious, but the intimacy of the tribe was something that stuck out. They were from western tribes, so their skin was much darker than mine. They were, for the most part, purebloods.

When I went home I said to my mother, "I want to do

something for those kids." And she said, "Like what?" After thinking for a moment I answered, "Well, I want to do something for Christmas."

I got a group of kids together at school, and with the help of my brother, Jerry, who was two years ahead of me in high school, we did do something. He got the ROTC unit and I got a bunch of kids and we went from door to door collecting canned foods and old clothes. We ended up with a truckload and we drove it out there. That was my first involvement with St. John's and I've been involved ever since.

After Christmas vacation, I went back to school and started to admit, because I was proud of it, that I was part Indian. I was in the eighth grade and in student government. One kid started a fight with me. He called me a half-breed and mimicked an Indian dance. After he was done I said, "I don't want to fight you because if I do I will be kicked out of student government. But what is a half-breed?"

He said, "It's one step lower than a Mexican."

From then on I realized there was a real problem with being a half-breed, and I became terribly involved with the Indian school. There was a gentleness and pride about all those people with whom I could identify.

In my sophomore year I decided to become a member of the public-speaking team, and for a competition I wrote a speech called "Nobody Loves a Drunken Indian." In the speech I described why there's a drinking problem on the reservation—because anytime you take a person's pride away from them without giving them the training and education of a vocation, what else is there to do but drink? I may have been just a kid, but I meant every word. I felt as if I were talking about my brother and sister.

By now, my class and my school knew all about my Indian background. After the speech I learned to deal with it by adopting a tongue-in-cheek approach. I was a member of a team sent to the University of Arizona for a public-speaking contest. When I finished my speech the judges rated it the second-best speech they had ever heard. Then they went on to say to my teacher that they felt the subject matter was something less than desirable and that I should be discouraged from delivering speeches of that kind in the future. So I learned something new about prejudice: It speaks out of both sides of the mouth.

My parents did not discourage me from my passion for the Indians, but they didn't encourage it either. My brother, at that time, realized the kind of prejudice that he had been up against, so I was bringing heat on him without realizing it, and it became a real problem. We had a great many confrontations about it and usually wound up in a fistfight.

I've often asked myself, ''Why did I do it?'' Well, probably one reason was the fact that I really believed one should stand up to bigotry. I was also proud of my Indian blood, but that became incidental at that point. I think the fact that it irritated my brother probably spurred me on. In all candor I would like to say it was altruistic at that point. It wasn't! It started out to be that way, but the fact was that I was irritating many people, and I took a certain pleasure in it, and, you know, a rebel-with-a-cause approach.

When I was in high school I had an old broken-down car that didn't have a gas gauge. My mother was very much against me driving. She kept envisioning two renegade teenage boys getting stuck and running out of gas. It was my dad who went out and cut off a broomstick and proudly announced, ''You really don't need a gauge. If you just stick this down in the tank, it will tell you if you have enough gas. If it gets wet, you've got gas.'' Sometimes my dad would really come across for me.

I will always remember the look on his face when I acquired my first horse. I sold my bicycle and picked up pop bottles in alleys and sold them for two cents apiece. A girl in school sold me the horse for twenty dollars.

Two weeks before my junior year ended, an agent by the name of Bookie Levin came through Phoenix. He was

quite a nice man who booked lounges in Nevada. Bookie
had seen my brother and me on television and had contacted a gentleman he had done some fair dates and concerts for throughout Arizona. I was at home when we got
a call around nine o'clock at night to ask if we would
come over to this gentleman's apartment and audition for
an agent.

Bookie was like a Damon Runyon character. He must
have been around sixty-five in those days. He had something like seven children. His appearance was disheveled,
and he had a little dandruff on the lapels. After listening
to two or three songs, the elderly gentleman asked, ''Do
you sing 'Danny Boy'?'' And I said, ''No, sir.''

''Well, learn it!''

With that, he just got up and walked out. My brother
and I kind of looked at each other and said, ''Well, that
takes care of that!'' While we were packing up, the Phoenix agent came back into the living room and said,
''Bookie's going to see if he can arrange an audition for
you in Vegas, the problem being that you're too young.''
I was fifteen then. He added, ''In order to work lounges
in Nevada you have to be twenty-one years old. So even
if the audition is successful, I don't know if I can get a
work permit for you.''

My brother and I boarded a bus and rode the long trip
through the desert to Las Vegas all alone because my dad
was working and couldn't afford to take any time off. We
auditioned at the Fremont Hotel for Eddie Torres. We set
up our instruments in the huge ballroom. There we were,
in this huge ballroom with just Eddie Torres and the
agent, Bookie Levin, and entertainment director Ricky
Moreno, who was to remain a lifelong friend and booster,
a wonderful man.

After singing three songs it was just like déjà vu. Eddie
Torres got up and walked out of the ballroom. My brother
and I did a double take and said, ''Well, that takes care
of that!''

Just as we were packing our instruments to go back to

Phoenix, Bookie stuck his head back in and said, ''Well, if he can get a permit for you to work, he'll hire you for two weeks. Stay over till tomorrow and we'll let you know.'' Ricky looked at us and winked and said, ''I'll look out for you kids. Everything will be all right.''

There we were in Las Vegas. We had our bus ticket and twenty dollars total in our pockets. We stayed in a place called the Monte Carlo Motel.

I'll always remember Bookie. He was your typical totally absentminded professor. The clothes were expensive; they just didn't fit. He would drive his car around the Strip and park to see somebody, and he'd have to catch a cab when he came out because he had forgotten where he had left his car. So we would be driving him around at two in the morning looking for his car. The same with his coat or his tie. He was always leaving them someplace. I was awfully fond of Bookie.

That first night in Vegas, we simply went back to the room and watched television. We were both under age, and even though I was fifteen, I looked nine. So we just stayed there till we heard from the agent the next day.

When the phone rang, my heart was beating so fast I could hear it. My voice went even higher than it was when I answered the phone. Bookie was able to obtain a work permit, and the work permit stated that I could work on-stage; this simply meant that after each show I would have to go outside or to the dressing room or to the coffee shop. We had to promise not to go into the casino. But we had a guarantee of two whole weeks and they weren't to start for another two months.

We returned to Phoenix. For me there was no question but that we should go back to Arizona. Jerry was concerned because he had just graduated from high school. He was making his plans as to which college he was going to attend. He was going to work for a year as a sales clerk in a clothing store to earn the money for it.

I was worried about how I was going to tell my girlfriend that I might be leaving town. I had fallen madly in love with the prettiest thing I had ever seen in my life. My brother and I were taking a walk between taping our television shows when I'd spotted her. Although we were both very shy, I was more aggressive. I introduced myself and asked her if she would come and watch us perform on one of our TV shows, and she said she couldn't because her parents were picking her up. I asked her for her number and she gave it to me. We went out together until I left for Las Vegas. And then, at the age of sixteen, she went to New York and became a top fashion model. She was the Brooke Shields of that time. In Phoenix, her name was Linda Whitehead. Later on she would marry an actor and become Linda Day George. She's also a fine actress.

Once we had gotten the job I sat in my bedroom and went into a deep depression. My parents came in and sat on the bed and my mother very lovingly said, "What's wrong?" With the tears flowing, I said, "How are you going to get along without us?" Neither of us had ever been away from home before. I didn't see how my parents were going to handle it because we had always been there. But they didn't take it the way I thought they would. They were excited because we had the Vegas opportunity. And while they said they were going to miss us, they were not as openly emotional about it, which hurt my feelings even more.

I never really analyzed it before, but, in retrospect, I must have been a somewhat overly emotional child. My parents didn't get upset when I got upset, including that night. Perhaps they thought that it was an extension of my being sick all my life, or that it was an attention-getting thing. But it wasn't at all. I was truly devastated, really worried about what was going to happen to them. My brother didn't give a damn. To him it was just another move. Finally it was agreed upon that Vegas was where we were headed.

I decided I was going to ride my horse Sheik as much as possible before I left. He had never been ridden or broke. At first I was doing fine. He and I got along great.

I was riding in back of the stable area and one of the horses in the stall kicked the wall as we rode by. The horse shied and I fell off and broke my wrist.

I drove myself to the hospital. I had only a learner's permit, and wasn't supposed to be driving without a licensed driver with me. My parents weren't home, so when I arrived at the hospital, being under age, the doctors wouldn't touch me. The wrist was dislocated in addition to being broken. Finally they reached my dad. When my parents arrived in the emergency room, needless to say, they were upset. My brother was livid, just livid. I wasn't getting much sympathy. My mother said, "Well, there goes Las Vegas. That's the end of that hope and dream."

When I got home, I could still move my fingers. So I grabbed the neck of my guitar while my cast was still wet and kept squeezing it into the cast until I finally was able to carve out a place for it. I was determined not to let the dream die.

CHAPTER 4

*I was propositioned a lot,
but I was too naïve to know it.*

I'M A HIGH school dropout. I quit high school in Phoenix in 1959, two weeks before my junior year was up, and headed to Glitter Gulch, known as downtown Las Vegas, Nevada.

Our opening night in Vegas was just Jerry and me. My mom and dad didn't drive up to Vegas from Phoenix for our opening at the Fremont. I was hurt by it. We had been there about a week before they came up. Their excuse was that they would have been just too nervous to sit through it. It seems like, for one reason or another, my parents missed some of the major shows of my life.

In addition to being disappointed over that, I was equally disappointed in Las Vegas. I thought the Dunes Hotel should have been big sandhills with a door. I thought the Flamingo should have been a big bird with the elevator going up the leg. At least the Showboat should have been a real showboat in water.

When we opened at the Fremont, we worked the five-to-eleven shift. We would do six shows: one at five, one at six, one at seven, and one from eight to eight-forty; then another group would alternate twice with us. They had four lounge acts at the Fremont. There were Glenn Smith and the Fables, the Jets, the Makebelievers, and the Newton Brothers. Those were pretty much the mainstays. A lot of groups came and went.

One group, called Buddy Michael and the Satellites, was from Philadelphia. Talk about an education in show business; it was the first time I had ever seen a group that performed choreography while wearing tight pants and padded crotches. Thanks to Fabian, Frankie Avalon, and Dick Clark, the Philadelphia groups were the hottest rage. I would sit backstage and peek through the curtain and watch them hour after hour because I was so taken by that style of performing. It was high energy! I couldn't believe my eyes. After all, my trademark was "Danny Boy." Can you imagine an Indian having an Irish hit as his trademark?

The Fremont taught me a lot of lessons. At times the crowd could be brutal. One night a woman threw her beer bottle at us. She was drunk and thought we were being sacrilegious by singing "He's Got the Whole World in His Hands" in a bar. She kept pelting us until she was taken away.

The stage was on a high platform, with the bartender standing below us mixing drinks, and the audience sat looking up at us. Some women would sit there at the bar and open up the tops of their dresses. We were the only ones who could see it. I was propositioned a lot, but I was too naïve to know it. It never occurred to me that any of the flirting was being directed at me. I always thought it was for my brother because he was older and enjoyed the attention.

When I wasn't looking down the fronts of ladies' dresses, I was trying to finish high school by correspondence during the first year or two, an effort that didn't prove too successful. My brother and I, as a duo, made $280 a week. We sent half of it home and $80 of it went to the union. At the end of the first two weeks Eddie Torres asked us to stay on, and the two-week engagement turned into a forty-six-week booking.

For the first six months we stayed at the Monte Carlo Motel. I had a pet skunk. I always somehow ended up with an animal. We lived in one big room at the motel, with one couch, one bed, and my pet skunk who loved to wander at night. I didn't get to keep it very long because Jerry didn't like it.

It was at the Fremont that I started to get heavy. I think it was because of frustration. My whole life had become work. I didn't have enough energy to do anything else after performing six to eight hours six days a week. Forget about doing anything on your day off! You just died. So I'd go to the restaurant and eat strawberry shortcake and I'd go to the movie house on my breaks and eat popcorn. There was a soda fountain across the street and that became my hangout. There you'd find me eating. It was my total reward. Because I wasn't allowed in the casino, I'd spend most of my time in the coffee shop. All the waitresses mothered me, knowing my brother and I were away from home. Those nice women were forever slipping me an extra piece of pie.

Eight months after we started playing in Vegas, we moved my parents to Nevada. We then rented a little, dinky two-bedroom apartment on New York Avenue, which was behind the Monte Carlo, and stayed there a year or two.

After about three years at the Fremont, my brother and I were still just two guitar players. We were coming up against groups in the Fremont lounge that were seven- and eight-piece ensembles. What made that so devastating was that the Fremont had a revolving stage with a partition down the center of it. So the group that was appearing to the audience would be in front of the partition and the group that would follow would set up immediately behind it. Someone would push a button and the stage would revolve, not unlike a saucer, and you were out there.

So there was a direct difference, we felt, between two guitars and the six-, seven-, and eight-piece groups. When people started to get up and leave the showroom, we realized that we'd be out of work if that continued. We were busting our asses by alternating with these larger groups. We knew that if we didn't do something, we wouldn't be able to keep our audience or get a raise.

We were beginning to play the Nevada circuit—Ely, Elko, Winnemucca, Battle Mountain, Jackpot, Tahoe, and Reno. In 1961 we were in Reno playing the Riverside Hotel. Minsky's Follies was in the main showroom and we worked opposite a group called the Kay Stevens Trio. Kay was married to a really neat guy, Tommy Amato. We came to find out that they were going through a divorce and Tommy was having a real tough time. Kay had a new boyfriend and one day he beat Tommy up in the parking lot while she watched. It was very messy. I don't know whether Tommy suggested it or it was kind of a mutual agreement since he played bass, but we agreed to add a bass player to our show. He had done a fine job managing the Kay Stevens Trio, so it was agreed that Tommy Amato would manage us as well. We added a drummer named Jimmy Rose, and overnight we became a quartet instead of a duo.

The billing remained the same—the Newton Brothers. While we sounded good, we were worried that Eddie Torres at the Fremont wouldn't be interested in paying for a quartet. So a vote was taken and the general consensus from my brother and Tommy was that I should call Torres and tell him we wanted to add two pieces and see if he was willing to double our salary.

My hands were trembling as I stood in the lobby of the Silver Top Motel while they paged Torres. I was scared to death because I've always had great respect for authority, and I've always felt somewhat inferior because of it. It had taken me hours to get up the nerve to call. I paced back and forth. Finally, he came on the phone. "Mr. Torres," I said, my voice almost cracking. "Yes, Wayne. How are you?" I said, "I'm fine. Are you working hard?" Torres, annoyed, said, "Wayne, what do you want?" I said, "Mr. Torres, my brother and I want to add two pieces to the group—a bass player and a drummer. And we want to know if we could get enough money in a raise to do that." He said, "I'll pay for one, and if that's not sufficient, then forget it.'' So that's what he did and that's how we made $540 a week for the next two years.

Playing downtown in those days was the kiss of death. If you performed downtown you never had a prayer of even playing a lounge on the Las Vegas Strip. There was a caste system for entertainers. If you played a lounge on the Strip, you never had a prayer of playing a main room. The Kim Sisters were the only ones to break out of that in the early days of Vegas. Once you became important to them downtown, that's were you stayed forever.

I didn't have to be a soothsayer or have my fortune told to know that if I ever was going to get ahead it was going to take a big break. My break came from a real biggy—Mr. Jackie Gleason.

CHAPTER 5

☆

*Mr. Gleason had become like a father figure to me,
and I felt bad about hurting his feelings.*

I GOT A call from Tom Chauncey, the owner of the local
CBS television station I had worked at in Phoenix. He
went into some lengthy discussion about the fact that Jackie
Gleason was going back on the CBS television network.

"The Great One" refused to fly in airplanes, so whenever he traveled he would have his own private train car.
To promote his return to national television, he took a
group of press people with him on a train from New York
to Los Angeles. Gleason planned on stopping in Phoenix
on the way back. Tom Chauncey was in charge of arrang-
ing a luncheon and asked me if I would come to Phoenix
to entertain. Since the luncheon was at eleven in the morning, we packed up the car after doing six shows at the
Fremont, and my brother, manager, drummer, and I drove
to Phoenix. It was in Phoenix that Mr. Gleason stood up
in front of everyone at the end of my show and said, "My
God, don't go on any other television show till you do
mine."

Tom Chauncey told me years later that while we were
performing Mr. Gleason had asked him, "Is this kid for
real?" When Mr. Chauncey said I was, Mr. Gleason told
him he was going to have me on his show.

But before Mr. Gleason made his announcement, his
manager said, "Jack, you cannot do this." Mr. Gleason
turned to his manager and snapped, "You take care of

business and I'll take care of the show." It was then that
Mr. Gleason stood up and made the announcement. Well,
I was in shock because the chances of that happening were
a million to one. No one had ever heard of me. I'd never
been on national television and I didn't have a hit record.

After the luncheon we went to a cocktail party and met
Mr. Gleason. It was a brief meeting, but he couldn't have
been nicer. Puffing away on his cigarette, Mr. Gleason
smiled and said, "Boy, I'll be seeing you in New York
and somebody will be contacting you," continuing as he
pointed, "This guy over here." Mr. Gleason's manager
was bent out of shape. You could feel a cold draft coming
from him and I prayed that deep down inside it would all
come to pass. As we drove back to Vegas, I prayed a lot
and hoped that Gleason really would keep his promise.

For three months we heard nothing. Every time Tommy
Amato would call Gleason's manager, he would do a tap
dance about having us on the show. Without saying it in
so many words, he let my manager know that he was the
true power structure, and without his approval it wouldn't
happen.

I don't know what changed—maybe an order from Mr.
Gleason—but we finally got booked, almost as an afterthought.
He told us we had to be at rehearsals on such-and-such a
day and asked where we were staying.

We all piled in the Cadillac, and filled an aluminum-
covered utility trailer with new instruments borrowed from
the Fender Instrument Company because ours were pretty
beaten up. We drove fifty-two hours nonstop to New York
and checked into the Park Sheraton. We were living high,
and we didn't care what it cost. We just wanted to look
good. Jokey jokey. We were floating on a cloud, only it
was a rain cloud about to pour.

In the morning my brother went down to the car. He
came back to the room shouting, "We have been robbed!"
Everybody thought it was a joke and started to laugh. But
when Jerry kept yelling I took off and ran down to the
street. There was a cop standing at the car giving us a

ticket. I said, "Why are you giving us a ticket?" He looked up from his pad and smirked. "Because you are not supposed to be parked here after a certain time." And I stated, "But we've been robbed!" He said, "Not my problem."

Welcome to New York. I didn't have the nerve to call my folks and tell them what happened. I felt sick about two things: How were we going to tell the Fender Instrument Company, and how were we going to pay for those instruments? They were worth four thousand dollars. How could we possibly ever afford to buy new amplifiers, basses, and guitars? Then I was worried that the company might think we had sold them just to have the cash. When Tommy Amato telephoned the artist representative from the Fender Instrument Company—Tom Walker was his name—he was incredibly nice. It's those kind of people who make a difference in your life. Mr. Walker said, "Fellas, don't worry about it. These things happen. We're covered by insurance. The most important thing is, what are you going to do about the show?" Tommy said, "I don't know." Mr. Walker said, "Tommy, we have another factory outlet in New Jersey. I'll call the guy and get you brand-new instruments." And he did.

Then the decision had to be made about who was going to call the Gleason show and tell them what had happened because we were supposed to be in rehearsals. June Taylor was kind and reassuring. She said, "As soon as you get your instruments, we'll begin rehearsals. We have rehearsals every day and we've still got time. We've got two weeks before the show airs."

As if we didn't have enough trouble already, we discovered that our drummer had a drinking problem. That night, when we went back to the Park Sheraton, he said he was going out for a while just to look around. About two in the morning he still wasn't back. I went to bed. Tommy and my brother started to roam the streets of New York looking for our drummer. They found him drunk on the street hassling with, shall we say, a lady of the evening and the police. Tommy and Jerry got him out of that jam and back to the hotel. The problem was keeping him sober since we now realized that he went on these drunken binges frequently. How we ever got through that first show I'll never know.

We began rehearsing in a large rehearsal hall with June Taylor and her dancers. She had choreographed a production number around the song "Love Makes the World Go 'Round." The set was a big carousel covered with beautiful girls. We rehearsed for ten days before we ever saw Mr. Gleason, one week before the show. He was very pleasant. He sent me to his tailor to have some suits made and, my God, they cost around six hundred dollars each. We were used to casual attire. The tailor realized that we didn't have the money to pay him, but he kindly told us we could pay off the four suits a little at a time.

One reason why Mr. Gleason had sent me to this particular tailor was because he could make suits for heavyset people that made them appear slimmer. I'd ballooned up to 270 pounds. Another reason why he had sent me there, and he discussed it in front of me, was because my legs were so deformed. I have what is called in horses offset cannon bones. You will find that any kid who has had a weight problem generally has knees that end with the bottom part of the leg going out. When you're that heavy it's the body's way of distributing the weight. Mr. Gleason was concerned that I would look distorted on television, so he sent me to his tailor, who knew how to handle that particular problem.

Being live on national television didn't bother me as much as being in Mr. Gleason's presence and not wanting to let him down. That was more important to me than anything in the world. He was giving us a chance. It was a gift from God because there was nothing we could do for him. We had to be good because we could never pay him for the opportunity he was giving us.

During the days of rehearsals I was constantly afraid that, being typically male and chasing anything with a skirt on, both my brother and Tommy would get into trouble; I was concerned that they would take to one of the Gleason show girls and there would be a big problem. A BIG problem. My fear was that Mr. Gleason would get angry with them for going after the girls. In a strange way, it was total paranoia.

The big night came. Mr. Gleason introduced me by saying that on his train ride through Arizona, this kid had entertained him at a luncheon. And he wanted people to remember the name and write it down because the kid was going to be a big, big star. It all seemed to happen so fast. All those days of rehearsing, and in nothing flat it was over.

After we did the show, Mr. Gleason was coming down in the elevator as I was going up, and he said, "Good job, kid." And I looked at him and thought, *Is that it? Is that all there is?* Now I realize that his mind must have been on the show, but I was looking for more than a few words of encouragement. We went back upstairs to our dressing rooms and just sat. It seemed like the worst letdown in the world to come off that high of performing and then to get the quick pat on the back: "Good job, go home."

After the show was over, we packed up and I said, "We should go by and thank Mr. Gleason." We walked into his dressing room and he was sitting there wearing a smoking jacket, asking someone to get him a hamburger. I said, "Mr. Gleason, I don't know how to thank you." And he said, "It's not necessary. You did a great job." As I thanked him again, our conversation kind of died and I mumbled, "Well, we're going to go now." I was all the way out the door when Gleason said, "Kid, I'll see you next week. Don't be late for next week's rehearsals."

Needless to say, the cloud that had seemed to be over us when we first arrived in New York had a silver lining. I was bursting with excitement. The first thing I wanted to do was telephone my folks. Like my Vegas opening, they had missed my first appearance on national television. For some reason, something happened that night in Phoenix and the show was blacked out.

We received eleven hundred dollars, which we split four ways. I paid our hotel bill and we moved out. We were running very low on money, and it became apparent that in order to stay in New York to do the Gleason shows, we were going to have to find more work. So Mr. Gleason called the Copacabana and put me in the lounge there, which is how I ended up at the world-famous nightclub.

While I didn't know much about the Copacabana, I did know that its main room was famous for presenting the best performers in the world.

I appeared in the lounge. It wasn't a big room, and in the right-hand corner there was a triangle-shaped stage where no more than four musicians could fit. There was a large oblong bar where people stood. The main showroom was downtown and to the left. One hundred fifty people, seated and standing, could fit in the lounge, while the main showroom seated eight hundred.

I mixed very little with the patrons. I guess the reason was a throwback to my Vegas days when I wasn't allowed in the casinos. I just kind of got in the habit of leaving when I went offstage. The Copacabana, like other nightclubs, wanted the talent to mingle with the patrons. I remember hearing stories about show girls whose contracts stated that they had to mingle with the patrons in the lounges. The reason was to keep the customers there as long as they could. Management wanted the performers to mingle because it built a following, which meant repeat business. In those years, in order to stay in the lounge you had to buy a fifty-cent drink. That was it. You could sit there as long as you wanted to until that drink was gone.

It was at the Copa where I met someone special—Nat King Cole. While I was working in the lounge he was appearing downstairs in the main room. I would go there every night to watch him open his show because, not only did I love his music, I was fascinated with his cordless mike, which I had never seen before. The mike was under his shirt, and he gave the impression that his magnificent voice was coming from nowhere. I admired the way he worked and the smoothness with which he performed. As I watched him each night, I had no idea that I would ever meet him. Then he started to come upstairs to the lounge between his shows, and he would sit there night after night and watch me perform. He was very gentle, very soft-spoken. He spoke the way he sang, with that same kind of velvet quality. Unlike some performers who are quick to give you advice, never at any time did he offer words of wisdom; nor do I remember asking for any. We became friends.

To know Nat King Cole was to love him. He was the most gentle person I ever met. When he passed away his widow sent me his makeup kit and the watch he was wearing when he died. I still treasure them.

The Newton Brothers had finally made it. We were at the Copacabana and appearing on *The Jackie Gleason Show.* But had we made it? We were earning seven hundred dollars a week to be split between four guys. Out of that came 10 percent for the agency we were assigned to, the cut for the musicians' union, and my brother and I were sending half of whatever we ended up with home to our parents. We might have had fifty dollars left between us.

We lived on West Seventy-second street at the Ruxton Hotel, where no decent cockroach would stay. It contained a living room, one bedroom, and three couches. We became experts at surviving in New York. I'd often take ketchup, put hot water in it, and make Newton's famous tomato soup. We'd buy loaves of bread and bologna, and that became our one big meal for the day. Once a week, if we were lucky, we'd get invited to a restaurant or to someone's home by people who had come to the Copa and were fans.

My brother was dating one of the girls from the Gleason show who had a great deal more money than the rest of us. However, he'd leave us all and go to her apartment and usually have something to eat there. Sometimes he'd bring home a loaf of bread. One night at the Copa I was so hungry that I almost passed out. Tommy Amato went to the owner, Julie Podell, and asked him if we could have Chinese food and take it out of our check at the end of the week because we were broke. Although I ate it all because I was so hungry, I was terribly embarrassed by having to ask.

Mia Kim of the Kim Sisters, who were a successful nightclub act in Vegas and had appeared countless times on *The Ed Sullivan Show,* came to New York and we went out on a date. She had wanted to see the movie *Lawrence of Arabia.* I had ten dollars left from my weekly allotment and, being stupid, I figured that if we walked to the theater we wouldn't have to worry about spending money on a cab. I thought the movie tickets would cost three dollars each, which would have left me with four dollars. I conned Mia into walking to the theater under the pretense that I needed some exercise. When I walked up to the box office I was in shock. The tickets to the movie were four dollars and fifty cents each! It left me with a dollar. As we walked in I said, "Do you want some popcorn?" all the time hoping she'd say no. Just as she said no and I'd sighed with relief, she said, "I'll have some bonbons." I thought, *How much can candy cost?* Well, it was ninety cents, leaving one dime to my name.

After the movie, as we were leaving the theater, she announced, "I'm real hungry." So I looked across the street and saw a Howard Johnson's. And I thought, *Great! I have a credit card on me. Surely, Howard Johnson's takes credit cards.* We sat down and ordered hamburgers. When the waitress came with the food I asked, "What cards do you take?" Then I died: "We don't accept credit cards." As I sat there in shock, people kept coming up saying that they had seen me on *The Jackie Gleason Show,* asking for my autograph. I sat there signing autographs, thinking, *If these people only knew how broke I am!* Now, I could have told Mia, "I've lost my wallet," or

"I've spent all my money," or, even worse, the truth. But my pride would not let that happen. Instead, I excused myself under the pretense of going to the bathroom. I went downstairs to where the pay phones were and called the hotel. I realized that the hotel had a switchboard, so if my brother or Tommy were not in the room I would have lost my last dime. Luckily, my brother was there and I asked, "Have you got any money?" Jerry, realizing the urgency in my voice, responded, "I've got the money we have to pay the agency commission, but if you need it, I've got it." In panic I pleaded, "Please bring me some money." He asked, "Where are you?" And I said, "Howard Johnson's. You know, the one in Times Square."

Then I went back to the table with the weight of the world off my shoulders. Ten minutes went by and no brother. Then an hour went by and still Jerry hadn't shown up. I started ordering more food. I told him on the phone, "Slip it to me; pretend you're just passing by, sit down for a minute, and then leave." Two hours later, after I'd tried every one of Howard Johnson's fifty flavors of ice cream, he showed up. I was ready to kill him but I couldn't show it. He followed my instructions, slipping me the money and leaving.

When I arrived back at our hotel after dropping Mia off at her hotel, I looked at Jerry. "What the hell happened to you?" He said, "Did you realize that there was a Howard Johnson's on every corner in Times Square? There were four and some of them were double stories. I had to go through every single one of them, and of course the one that you were in was the last one!"

The last person I ever expected to find sitting in the audience at the Copa lounge was Bobby Darin. I had been a big fan of his ever since I'd first heard his music, and had sung a lot of his songs in the Fremont lounge. He had seen me on the Gleason show and came into the Copa and sat in the corner. I wasn't even aware that he was there. When I came offstage he sent a waiter to ask me to come over. Darin took off his glasses and introduced himself. He said he had seen me on *The Jackie Gleason Show.* He asked if I was recording and I told him I wasn't. Darin, with that Cheshire cat grin of his, smiled. "We will." I just looked at him and didn't know what to say. I was mesmerized. Darin must have thought that either I wasn't from this planet or I wasn't understanding him. He looked at me, cocked his head, and announced, "I'll produce you. I've got a deal at Capitol Records and I have a production deal. So come by my office at one tomorrow."

Interestingly enough, Mr. Gleason had recently said to me, "I'm bringing out the people at Capitol Records. I think that maybe we can get a record for you." So when Darin announced his plans, I just said, "I'm not recording, but Mr. Gleason had said that some people from Capitol Records were interested." Darin just shrugged it off. "Well, I'm with Capitol Records. So we don't have a problem."

The next day we showed up for our appointment and signed with Bobby Darin's production company. I was so excited. Then I called Mr. Gleason's office and asked to see him. We walked over, and when we arrived he was sitting behind a big desk. I told him that Bobby Darin had come to see me at the Copa and wanted to record me. I explained to him that Darin had a production deal with Capitol, and though I really didn't understand what it meant, I was just thrilled that Bobby Darin wanted to record me. And God, that was wonderful. Then I looked at Mr. Gleason's face. It was like I had just stabbed him in the back. Naturally, I thought he would be thrilled. Gleason leaned back in his chair, pulled out a cigarette, lit it, and after one puff snapped, "Well, why would you want to do that? As I told you, the people from Capitol Records were coming out to see you. You'll have a deal directly with Capitol. You don't need to go through Bobby Darin." I could tell there was no love lost between them, although I don't know to this day what the problem was between Mr. Gleason and Bobby. So I thought to myself, *Self, you've done it again.* Mr. Gleason pushed his chair back and stood up, as if to dismiss me. I started to apologize. "Well, Mr. Gleason, I realize that, but I've given my word." Mr. Gleason was not pleased. As he shuffled the papers on his desk, I began to talk as fast as I knew how. "I really hope it won't affect our relationship in any way, because had I known you felt this way about it, I certainly wouldn't have gone this far with it." He was definitely irritated. He said, "I don't know why you'd make that kind of deal. But since it's done, all the luck in the world. Good day." Well, then I thought, *God, maybe he'll cancel me from his show.* He didn't. But Mr. Gleason had become like a father figure to me, and I felt bad about hurting his feelings. What I didn't know was that coming into my life was a man who would become like a brother. His name was Bobby Darin.

CHAPTER 6

The night Bobby Kennedy was assassinated, Bobby
Darin telephoned me. . . . He was getting rid of all his
worldly goods.

BOBBY DARIN WAS absolutely like the older brother I had
always wanted. All the tantrums and bad behavior that I
had heard about Bobby I never saw. He never, ever, at any
time, showed me that side of him.

Bobby represented to me the epitome of what I considered a recording artist to be, as did Nat King Cole. To
me, a record was just a prelude to being onstage and winning an audience. Darin knew that I had been in a recording studio before and that it made me terribly nervous and
uncomfortable. Therefore, there was always a lack of success in my attempt to make a hit record. I thought it was
impossible. I was sure I would never have a hit.

The first record I ever made was in 1953 for ABC Paramount. I was eleven years old. It was recorded in Spring-
field, Missouri, and I think it sold three copies. Long
before Bobby Darin, I had other records released one at a
time on different labels. Then I'd get a short letter saying,
"Thank you, but our releasing schedule next year does
not include you." I was sure I was never going to have a
hit record, which is why I put so much energy and effort
into stage performing.

Darin had a different opinion. He said, "We'll set up
the studio just like it's a nightclub and we'll record you as
if it's a live performance."

When I walked into the recording studio I saw that Darin

41

had kept his word. It looked like a small nightclub and my group—brother Jerry, Tommy Amato, a drummer, and I—went in and recorded. But it was just a warmup—it was never released. The next night Bobby found a song called "Heart." We went into the session and we did the song. After the first run-through, Darin said, "That's a take." Wayne Newton and the Newton Brothers had a top-twenty record across the nation.

After that record Bobby called my brother, Tommy Amato, and me into his office. He said, "I'm gonna suggest something. In fact, I'm going to insist on it from this point forward. It's gonna irritate everybody and most of all Wayne." Now, I didn't have the slightest idea of what he was talking about and I was worried. I'm the type who's always waiting for the world to end at those meetings. Anytime somebody calls me and says, "I want to have a meeting with you," I know there's never going to be good news. Well, my heart stopped and I was wondering what Bobby was going to say next. Without batting an eye he said, "What I have to say is not open for discussion. The name of the show, the name that's going to be on records, and the name that you guys will live with from now on will simply be 'Wayne Newton.' " Well, I think it broke my brother's heart. I went into temporary paralysis. Tommy Amato just sat there with his mouth open even though, deep down inside, he agreed with Bobby's decision. Before anyone could say anything, Darin explained. "Now I'm going to tell you why. Jerry and Tommy, it has absolutely nothing to do with the two of you. There is no brother act, or, for that matter, sister act or group, that ever achieves the heights of a single performer. You just can't direct people's attention in too many directions."

When Jerry began to squirm in his chair, Darin challenged him. "If you can name one act that is as big as a single performer, then we will discuss it. But as far as I'm concerned, this discussion ends."

The next time Bobby and I came face-to-face was when he was appearing at the Flamingo in Las Vegas and we were back in the lounge at the Fremont. He would come downtown and bring other performers to catch our act. One night he telephoned and said, "Come over to my apartment. There's a song I want you to hear." In those days, behind the Flamingo Hotel there was a little house the performers stayed in. So I went over to see him and he said, "I've got this acetate demo record. It's recorded by a baritone German singer. I'm going to show you the way it's going to sound when you record it." It may sound like a show-business lie, but it was the absolute truth. Darin took the 33⅓ acetate demo record and sped it up to 78. And that's the first time I heard "Danke Schoen." At the time I didn't know that it was written by Bert Kaempfert, Kurt Schwabach, and Milt Gabler, who wanted Bobby to sing it because of its likeness to his hit "Mack the Knife." So when Bobby told them that he wasn't going to do it and that he was going to have somebody he was producing do it, they went nuts. They threatened to pull the song. Bobby stood firm. He said, "If you do that, I will never record anything from your publishing company again." At the time he was really hot. So they didn't want to take that chance.

Naturally, we thought that Eddie Torres and the Fremont Hotel would be excited about our recording opportunity. They weren't. When I cut my first album, *Danke Schoen*, Torres gave me an extra day off at the Fremont. I did the entire album in one day. Torres made us do nine shows a night for the next week to make up for that one day off.

When the song was released we were appearing in Reno, staying at a place called the Silver Top Motel. Bobby Darin telephoned to ask me what it felt like to have a hit record, and my shouts of joy could be heard through the streets of Reno.

After "Danke Schoen" had finished its run as a hit, Bobby hired two young producers. One was a kid by the name of Terry Melcher, who was Doris Day's son, and the other was Bruce Johnston, who became one of the

Beach Boys. Bobby said he had gotten very busy with his own career and thought that maybe a little different sound might be achieved by having these two young guys produce me. At the next recording session, they gave me a song called "Comin' On Too Strong." I had very few lines to sing. It was basically a sound similar to the Beach Boys. While it sounded wonderful, it just wasn't me. When it was released, it was an instantaneous hit. Such acceptance you couldn't believe. When I heard it on the air I called Bobby and said, "You're gonna think I'm crazy but you've got to pull that record." Bobby thought I was nuts. "Wayne, it's a hit!" I said, "Yes, I know that and that's the problem." Bobby laughed, "We should all have such problems." I tried to explain: "I can't sing that song. I'm going to have to walk onstage and try to sing that song in front of a live audience. There's no way I can make it sound like the recording." There was dead silence on the other end of the phone. Finally, after a minute, Bobby said two words. "You're right." He pulled the record.

Two weeks later I was in New York City appearing on *The Jackie Gleason Show* and I went to visit the publisher of "Danke Schoen." He said, "I want you to hear something," and he put on Bert Kaempfert's record of "Red Roses." It was an instrumental. Little did I know that he had also sent it to Bobby. When I called Bobby from New York I was so excited. He could hear it in my voice. "I heard a song today and we've got to set a recording session right away." Bobby said, "What's the song?" Excitedly I told him, "Red Roses for a Blue Lady." Again silence. Finally, he spoke. "When can you come to Los Angeles and be available for a recording session?" When I told him he said, "Okay, I'll set it." He did. He didn't tell me until later that he had planned on recording the tune himself. Nor did anybody tell me that they had sent it to him.

During the recording session of "Red Roses for a Blue Lady," a promotion man from Capitol Records heard us and went out and told another singer what I was up to. Within three days, a kid by the name of Vic Dana was out with a new record entitled "Red Roses for a Blue Lady." There was quite a fight between the two records for about a month. And then mine went on to become the number-one record.

By that time everyone thought that, with two hits like "Danke Schoen" and "Red Roses for a Blue Lady," I was financially wealthy. The truth is, by the time I saw any money from "Danke Schoen" as a hit record, we had so many recording costs built up as a result of the album and other singles, I don't think I ever got a check or saw a single penny from that hit. You have to remember that a lot of time is spent in recording sessions recording tunes that never even get released. You keep building the tab at the recording company. The only money I got from any record, no matter how big a hit it was, was from "Daddy Don't You Walk So Fast." We had sold more than five million copies worldwide and I received a total of eighty thousand dollars for it.

I think Bobby Darin made money from my recordings, not necessarily off the sales of the records but by being the publishing company. He did write some of the B sides and some of the album cuts, so maybe from that standpoint he received a check. However, he was certainly far from taking advantage of me as a new artist.

There's always a price for success, as I discovered. One night I went to see Bobby at the Flamingo. Because he was my hero, I would visit him for inspiration. I went into his dressing room, which in those days was about the size of a closet. He was sitting there with his head down, his hand on his forehead. He looked like a beaten man. I thought, *What in the world could he be sad about?* I stood behind him for a moment and finally, trying to break the depression that I could feel in the room, said, "What's bothering you?" He looked up in the mirror with tears in his eyes. "One day you'll understand," he said. He started to wipe the tears away and apply his makeup. Without saying another word I went out to sit in the showroom to wait for the show to start.

Bobby was right. One day I did understand. I know the burden and the responsibility of having your own heart breaking and dying inside and yet knowing you've got to go out there and be a clown. You've got to make the world smile because people in the audience are suffering from the same thing. I loved Bobby Darin and I always will.

This is not a story that is known by too many people. It's certainly not one I've ever discussed. When things started to go well for my career and Bobby's career had stalled, we didn't talk for two years—not because I wanted it that way or because there was a problem with our friendship. It was just that Bobby's pride would not allow it. I would try to reach him and he would never take my phone calls. Someone would always get on the telephone and come up with an excuse. They would say, "Wayne, he's tied up," or, "He just went onstage." It was apparent that Bobby was avoiding me. So I'd say, "Well, I don't want to bother him. I just want to tell him hello." On one of my albums, entitled *How I Got This Way*, which sold maybe two copies, there's a song called "Where Is My Friend?" It was written with Bobby Darin in mind; it was a way for me to express my feelings.

One night at the Dunes Hotel, Sammy Davis, Jr., and his opening act, Gladys Knight and the Pips, were performing a show at two in the morning for the show kids. From up and down the Strip the dancers and show girls had come to see this special performance. I arrived kind of late and was seated in a booth.

The booths were constructed in such a way that it was impossible to see who was in them unless you walked up and stood directly in front of them. Sammy began to introduce the guests seated in the audience. Protocol was such that the biggest names were introduced last. Sammy introduced Bobby Darin before me and saved me till last, which was a supreme compliment, but I wish it hadn't happened. Bobby was in the booth on the other side of the aisle and I didn't know he was there. Although I had tried to call and visit with him backstage, he was never available. After Sammy had introduced me, I stood up and took my bow. As the lights went down and the show continued, I quietly left my booth to say hello to Bobby. But before I reached him he had slipped out.

It was on the night Bobby Kennedy was assassinated that I heard from Bobby. He called me at three in the morning to tell me that he was getting rid of all of his "worldly goods" and that he wanted me to have his briefcase telephone. Kennedy's death was devastating to him. It was the turning point that drove him over the edge. He was determined to rid himself of all personal possessions. All Bobby Darin wanted to do was wear blue jeans, throw away his toupee, move to Big Sur, and demand that everyone who spoke to him call him Bob Darin. He became a recluse.

After cutting himself off from the world he came back and was following my engagement at Harrah's in Reno. This was the first time in three years that Bobby Darin stood in the spotlight of a nightclub stage. He came in to see me on my closing night. And when he came backstage, it was as if he had never been away. As he embraced me he whispered in my ear, "You know I love you as a friend." I smiled. "Yeah, I know." As Bobby sat down he said, "I had some things I had to work out. I needed to spend some time pulling my life together."

During our visit there was something in his eyes that was searching. So I knew that I had to spend more time with him. I said, "Bobby, why don't we have dinner together tomorrow night?" And he said, "You'll stay over for my opening?" I told him that I had to go back to Vegas the next day, but that I would fly up and join him for dinner. Bobby said, "You wouldn't do that." But I promised him that I would and I kept the promise.

That night while we were having dinner I was under the assumption that he had been signed for an engagement in Vegas. It seemed so natural since he had been away so long from the Entertainment Capital of the World. So when I asked, "When do you open in Vegas?" I was stunned

that he replied, "I don't have any dates in Vegas." I said,
"What do you mean you don't have any dates in Vegas?"
I wasn't prodding him, and I realize now that it must have
sounded cruel, but I just couldn't comprehend how a star
of his magnitude would not have any Vegas bookings.
Darin pushed away from the table. "Nobody will touch
me there with a ten-foot pole. Wayne, I probably am paying for some of the dumb things that I did in my past.
People haven't forgotten about my throwing chairs through
windows, and everybody thinks I'm a risk. I doubt if I'll
ever play Vegas again."

"Well," I said, "would you mind if I mentioned you
to some people?" Softly Bobby smiled. "No, I'd be grateful."

So when I went back to Vegas I called the newly appointed entertainment director of the Summa Howard
Hughes Corporation. He was a white-haired older man
whom Howard Hughes had sent to Vegas to run the entertainment for his hotels. We didn't hit it off at first. I thought
he was a smooth operator and I didn't trust him. In fact,
till the day he died, Walter Kane was an old smoothy—
but by then he had long been family to me.

So I called Walter and asked if I could see him. He was
terribly gracious, which he always was, and I said, "I
need a favor. I'm not good at asking favors, but I need
this one. As much as it is a favor to me, it's going to turn
out to be a favor for the Hughes Corporation." Well, now
I had him really intrigued. So I figured he'd be delighted
when I asked him to hire Bobby Darin. At just the mention
of Bobby's name, Walter Kane's face went white, as if he'd
seen a ghost. "Oh, God, Wayne! Ask me anything, but
don't ask me to hire Bobby Darin." Before Walter could
say more I went into a song and dance. "He's great,
there are no problems. I saw the show and it's incredible, and he looks wonderful." Walter shook his head.
"Wayne, anything but that." "Mr. Kane," I said, "I need
this." The old man was quiet a while, then said, "Well,
you've got it. What do you want me to pay him?" I didn't

know what to say, so I told Mr. Kane, "I don't want to get into that. I don't know how much he makes but I'll have his manager call you." Then Mr. Kane surprised me by asking, "How many weeks do you want him to have?" I quickly responded, "I want him to play between eight and twelve weeks per year for two years." Walter lived up to everything he promised and Bobby came back to Vegas and started to do terrific business. He was filling showrooms again.

With one more engagement left to his two-year contract with the Howard Hughes organization, Bobby's manager made a deal with the Hilton. Bobby called me and said, "I don't know how to tell you this. I'm not going to stay with Summa." I said, "Okay. Have you told Walter?" Bobby admitted that he hadn't. "I love Walter and the money's great, but I know they'll never match my new deal. And inasmuch as you initiated this, I thought maybe you'd want to tell Walter." He took me off guard when he said, "I have to make this move, Wayne, because I don't know how long I'm gonna be around." "What do you mean by that?" I asked. "Well, you know, physically. I'm not talking careerwise. But I don't know how many nights I have left." As we ended our conversation I said, "Will you cut the crap? You're gonna live forever."

It was decided that Bobby should call Walter Kane. I told him he wouldn't have a problem with Walter, that Walter would want the best for Bobby, and the fact that he had succeeded would be payment enough. It turned out to be exactly the way Walter took it. I went to see Walter right after Bobby called him and he laughed and said, "I remember your words to me, Grandson. You said Bobby Darin would be a winner again and you were right. That's one gamble that paid off."

It's not too many times in life that you have the opportunity to repay someone who helped you along the way. That's how Bobby came back to Las Vegas, and he died while he was signed at the Hilton.

It seems like only yesterday that he died. My mother

had received the call but decided not to wake me. The first thing I do when I get up is walk around the ranch. As I passed my ranch foreman he said, "Gee, I'm really sorry about that." I said, "What?" And he said, "About your friend Bobby Darin dying this morning."

It was not a great surprise. Bobby had called me about two months before his operation. He was appearing at the Hilton and I was at the Sands. "Let's go to Mount Charleston and have a picnic," Bobby kidded. I was delighted. It would be a chance to spend time with him because I had heard stories that he was having a tough time breathing onstage. So, with my wife and his lady, we drove up to Mount Charleston for the day. I quickly discovered that he was having serious health problems. He could walk only about ten feet. Then he'd have to stop, gasping for breath. I had no idea of the severity of his heart problem. I knew he had had rheumatic fever as a child and that he had undergone open-heart surgery, but I thought that had corrected the problem. At least that's what everyone told me. Bobby and I both knew that this was a special day for us. As we talked he would say things like, "You know what would really be a kick? Would you ever work onstage with me?" "You bet," I told him. "Name the time and the place. There's nothing in the world I would love more." But we never did. The sun was setting as we drove back, and I had an eerie feeling that this would be the last time I would ever see Bobby.

Bobby had his psychiatrist call his manager and tell him that he wanted out of their contract and wanted to end their relationship. They had been together since the early days of "Mack the Knife," on and off. That same day the psychiatrist also telephoned Bobby's wife and told her that Bobby wanted a divorce. Bobby Darin was severing ties with everyone he loved, and he wanted to do this all before the operation. Medically, there was no reason for him to die. I'm told the operation was a success. He simply willed himself to die. These are my words and no one else's. When he eliminated from his life the people he loved, it was Bobby's way of trying to ease their pain after he was gone. He wanted to make them angry in preparation for what was coming. He just plain quit living.

Bobby Darin lived with a tremendous inner trauma. He had been told as a child that his mother had died giving birth to him, when, in reality, the woman who had raised him claiming to be his sister was really his mother. He didn't know the truth until he was an adult, and it was devastating to him.

Bobby was an extremely emotional person. He used to tell me stories about the pain and hardship that had left their emotional scars. When a youngster he shined shoes in New York City. A guy once gave him five bucks for a shoeshine that only cost ten cents. Bobby looked up and said, "I don't have any change." The guy looked down at this little kid and said, "I'm not expecting any change. Take the money and get your face fixed."

Bobby was absolutely Clark Gable's biggest fan in the world. One time when Bobby's birthday was coming up and I didn't know what to get him, I went to a publicist who had handled Clark Gable. I told him that I wanted something personal of Mr. Gable's. The publicist said, "Let me see what I can do." He invited me to take a ride out to Mr. Gable's ranch, where I met his widow, Kay. She presented me with some of Mr. Gable's silk handkerchiefs that were monogrammed. When I gave them to Bobby Darin, you would have thought that I had given him the world. While I was a big fan of Clark Gable, it was nothing compared to Bobby's feelings for the legendary film giant. Bobby Darin had a copy of every film Clark Gable ever appeared in. He had studied everything Mr. Gable had ever done.

Bobby Darin was the most consummate talent I've ever known. I suspect that the only person who could rival him would probably be Sammy Davis, Jr. Sammy Davis gave Bobby Darin his first break, but they did not remain close.

When Bobby died, it was sad. He was a Catholic, but he didn't have a funeral. He had contributed his body to science and there wasn't even a memorial service. He had asked that it not be done. I believe it was his way of shedding anything at all to do with this earth. He left no one but his son, whom he loved and who is an absolute reincarnation. When I hear Bobby's music, tears come to my eyes every single time; tears of sadness and of joy. You can't love somebody as a friend and see him suffer and not suffer along with him. But the thing that affects me most when I hear Bobby Darin's music is how far ahead of everything it was and how it has sustained the years. It's as good today as it was then, if not better. The memory of Bobby Darin will always live on through his music.

I'll always be grateful to Bobby for his belief in me to record "Danke Schoen," and I remember the first time I heard it on the radio. I was in Los Angeles and a disk jockey on KFWB—I still can recall the station—said, "Here's a brand-new record that's an absolute smash, and it's supposedly being sung by a guy named Wayne Newton, but I happen to know it's Margaret Whiting recording under a different name." That broke my heart, and I can't begin to tell you the kind of rejection I then went through at the hands of the entertainment industry. I had the number-one hit record in the country, I had Michael Jackson's voice—I was a boy soprano—but back then all it brought me were attacks of vitriolic humor. I was the joke of the industry.

But one man never laughed. He was a giant among men. He was Bobby Darin and he was my friend.

CHAPTER 7

☆

*... They were betting up and down the Las Vegas Strip
that Wayne Newton was going to be the bomb of the
Nevada test site.*

I DECIDED THAT I had done enough lounge work to last
me the rest of my life. I couldn't take it anymore. My
voice couldn't take it anymore. I kept learning to play new
instruments simply to give my voice some relief. So when
we played our last weeks at the Fremont, I vowed that was
the last lounge I'd ever play. We had the opportunity to
perform in Sydney, Australia, and in mid-1964 we packed
up our instruments, lugged our luggage, and traveled to
Sydney. There we were, the desert rats: my brother, my
drummer, Tommy Amato, and I invading the land of the
kangaroos. We appeared at a place called the Chevron
Hilton Hotel.

Now, in my entire career I was never fired. But I came
close to it in Australia! The hotel management was fighting with the agent who had booked the showroom. Little
did I realize that he had been fired for the booking because
we had no name recognition since we had never played
there before. The management of the Chevron Hilton was
convinced that I was going to bomb. They were so sure,
they had an act hired to replace me the next night. Little
did I know that my opening night was also going to be
my closing night.

When we arrived at the hotel I couldn't understand it,
but the hotel manager looked like the cat who swallowed
the canary when he said, "Well, welcome. We're glad

you're here." At the time I said to Tommy Amato, "Something's strange here." So, as luck would have it, as I was going to my room before the opening show, a beautiful girl from Hawaii got on the elevator and I struck up a conversation. "What are you doing here?" I asked. And she said, "Well, we're opening tomorrow night." Curious me asked, "Where?" She smiled. "The Silver Spade here at the hotel." She then said, "What are you doing here?" And like a Marx Brothers comedy I laughed, "I'm opening the Silver Spade also." As it turned out, by the grace of God and the Australian people, the place became packed. The hotel paid the other act off, which I wasn't too thrilled about because it meant she had to leave.

The next night, Mr. Jack Benny came to see my show and came backstage. He invited me to see his concert the next day and I went with my brother and Tommy. At the end of his performance, Mr. Benny invited us backstage and asked me if I would consider working with him. I said I'd be thrilled. During that year, we were turning down a considerable amount of money in Nevada lounges—up to ten thousand dollars a week.

The first place Mr. Benny wanted me to appear was at Lake Tahoe at Harrah's. I explained to Mr. Benny that I had worked at Harrah's in the lounge and that they didn't want to have me in the show as a performer. He said, "If they don't take you, they don't want me." I tried to explain to Mr. Benny that I didn't want to get in the middle of his relationship with Harrah's, but I wanted to let him know that I wouldn't be welcomed at Harrah's in the main showroom. As it turned out, Harrah's was not thrilled; but because Mr. Benny was a gigantic star, they bowed to his wishes. So in 1964 we played Harrah's, and it was my first time in a main showroom in Nevada.

Thanks to the success of that booking I toured with Mr. Benny for almost three years. The first year and a half we made fifteen hundred dollars a week. It was a far cry from the ten thousand dollars a week we had turned down to play the lounges.

I so admired him that I always called him Mr. Benny. We had a real problem with him about that. He kept saying, "Call me Jack," and I'd just shake my head. "I can't do that, Mr. Benny, because I have such tremendous respect for you. You're one of my idols and to call you by your first name would be the height of disrespect." It really had to do with my Southern upbringing. I was brought up to show respect for my elders by calling them Mr. or Mrs.

One day I was walking through the parking lot of Harrah's when I caught Mr. Benny out of the corner of my eye. He was headed for the backstage area and I shouted, "Hello, Mr. Benny." He shouted back, "Hello, schmuck!" Of course, I didn't even know what *schmuck* meant, but I sure knew it wasn't a compliment. As I got closer to him he must have seen the confused look on my face and he laughed. "If I can call you schmuck, you can call me Jack." After several minutes of friendly arguing we came to a compromise. I said, "Could we agree on Uncle Jack?" and he said, "I'll accept that." So that's what I called him.

We had a lot of fun on- and offstage. He was always coming up with hilarious bits to put in the act. I still laugh about one of them. Uncle Jack would call me on stage and the two of us would begin to chat. I would say, "Mr. Benny, I want you to know that I'm your biggest fan in the world, and when I'm not onstage, I always stand in the wings and watch the way you use your hands and the way you walk." Of course the audience would laugh because Mr. Benny walked a little effeminately. Then Uncle Jack would put his hands up to his face, like he was posing, and say, "Oh, you do?" As the audience would roar, I'd say, "Yes," and then Mr. Benny would put his hands on his hips and stand in an effeminate pose and say, "Well, Wayne, I must tell you. I have worked with a lot of young singers before and they invariably try to steal my mannerisms, you know—they way I move my hands and the way I walk. You never have." I'd just stand there and, with a very serious look on my face, reply, "With my voice, I wouldn't dare!" The audience would scream. We were disarming people by saying what they might have already been thinking.

Mr. Benny was one of the most gentle souls I have ever known. In the years that I was traveling with him, literally on a day-to-day and night-to-night basis, I never once saw him angry. I never once heard him say anything unkind. That's just the way he was. I'll never forget one night at the Tropicana. It was the last time he played in Las Vegas and Mrs. Benny came into the dressing room and said, "Damn it, Jack, you're sitting around in your tux pants." Without missing a beat he looked at her, got up out of his chair, took off his pants, and sat back down, not once letting it interrupt the story he was telling.

After I played Lake Tahoe with Jack Benny, I was supposed to play the Flamingo Hotel on the Las Vegas Strip as a supporting act for Jack Carter. The General Artists Corporation had locked in the booking, but I said to my manager, "I don't really want to play that date and I don't want to play supporting act anymore." There was no rhyme or reason for this except that I thought to be a supporting act to somebody other than Mr. Benny just wasn't where it was at. After all, in my mind, Jack Benny was the epitome of entertainment.

I asked Tommy to tell Morris Landsberg, who owned the Flamingo and several hotels in Florida, that I would headline. Tommy became unglued. "He'll sue us, he'll sue us if you don't play that date!" I just shrugged my shoulders and laughed, "Well, we've got nothing." After all, we had turned down ten thousand dollars a week in the lounges because I wouldn't play them anymore and went in with Mr. Benny in the main room for fifteen hundred bucks. So in my mind it made sense to take a risk. Tommy kept shaking his head, saying, "We're going to turn down ten grand as a supporting act at the Flamingo to Jack Carter and we're going to get sued on top of it? You must be crazy!" Tommy looked doubly surprised when I said, "Tell Mr. Landsberg that I'll play headlining twice for the same money he was going to pay us as a supporting act."

Tommy Amato, with hat in hand, did just as he was told. He repeated my words to Morris Landsberg, who laughed in his face. Landsberg said, "Surely this is a joke. You've got to be kidding us. Wayne Newton headlining the Flamingo in Las Vegas? Are you crazy?" Although Tommy thought so too, he never let it show. He said, "No, that's what Wayne said and that's what he'll do." After Morris Landsberg stopped laughing, he said, "I'll tell you what I'll do. Anyone with those kind of balls I will headline." Tommy jumped with joy. He had pulled off the coup of the century until he arrived back and told me that Landsberg had agreed to headline us in November. Well, in those years, you could shoot a cannon off in November and not hit a single soul on the Strip. From mid-October until after Christmas the desert city of Las Vegas turned into Death Valley. There was just absolutely no business. Tommy said, "I guess it's good news and bad news." My response was, "We'll play it!"

In November 1964, the only thing they were betting up and down the Las Vegas Strip was that Wayne Newton, at the age of twenty-four, was going to be the bomb of the Nevada test site. The odds-makers had predicted I was going to flop. The only thing that none of them counted on was the local people. The night we opened they came out in droves and totally saved my career. We broke all attendance records at the Flamingo in November. And that's how I ended up headlining the Las Vegas Strip the first time.

That opening night, when I sneaked a peek out into the showroom and saw all those faces, it was the greatest feeling in the world. The only thing that ever came close to it was the Fourth of July concert in Washington years later.

When I realized all of a sudden, in one moment, that my entire career was on the line, and if it didn't work it was over, that's when the people of Las Vegas came to my rescue. The local people of Las Vegas have saved Wayne Newton from drowning time after time. More than once, the good people of Las Vegas have picked me up by the straps and pulled me out. With the grace of the good man upstairs, and the love and support of the people, I have become whatever it is that I am.

We were making twenty-five thousand dollars a week. Because Mr. Landsberg owned the Dovall in Miami Beach, it was a dual deal: If you played one you played the other. It seemed a natural.

The Great One, Jackie Gleason, had moved his entire show and production facility to Miami. It became a very integral part of the economy of Miami Beach. So, in addition to appearing at the Dovall and the Eden Roc, I did some guest shots on the Gleason show.

We played that circuit for three years, and then Kirk Kerkorian bought the Flamingo. This was long before he built the International Hotel and later the MGM Grand. The Flamingo was his first hotel.

Kerkorian had two gentlemen running the hotel: Alex Shufy and Jerry Gordon. And they were not happy with my attitude, especially when I told them, "Wait a minute. You cannot sell my contract." I didn't mind that Kirk Kerkorian had bought the hotel, but my contract was not assignable. Therefore, I didn't think it was right for my contract to become part of the assets of that resort. My feeling was that my contract should be renegotiated. Mr. Kerkorian's attitude was that, since he had bought the hotel, the contracts came along with the furniture and should stay in place. At that time he had Bill Cosby, Diana Ross and the Supremes, Bobby Darin, and yours truly under contract.

Six months after Kirk Kerkorian took charge, I still hadn't met him. But I'd heard many nice things about him. So one night, while I was appearing in Reno, I picked up the telephone and called him. "Mr. Kerkorian, could I visit with you? I'll fly down from Reno." The Flamingo Hotel owner said, "Hell, Wayne, you don't have to do that. I'll come up there." It confirmed my suspicions that he was indeed a nice man. So I laughed, "Well, no, it gives me an excuse to come home."

The reason why I wanted to meet him face-to-face was because we had been offered a job at the Frontier for twice what we were making at the Flamingo. My contract was ending at the Flamingo. We'd made a deal at the Frontier, but we hadn't firmed it. I felt that Kirk Kerkorian deserved to hear it from me first. So I flew down and met him in one of the back rooms of the Flamingo. I got right to the point: "I realize that there might have been some tension with regard to my visit today, but I wanted you to know that any disagreement with anybody at this hotel is not personal. It's just that I felt I'm being taken advantage of with the contract." Kirk Kerkorian just listened, nodding his head. When I was through, he said, "Wayne, I understand. Let me show you what we're doing here." He showed me all the plans for the exciting brand-new International Hotel. As Mr. Kerkorian proudly displayed the art renderings, he confessed, "You know, this is my first hotel and I'm gonna own others. I certainly don't want to fight with you. I really appreciate your coming here and telling me about this offer from the Frontier. So why don't we do this: If you really want to stay, and I want you to stay, why don't I just match the other offer and we'll all be happy." I extended my hand and said, "There's nothing I'd like more." We became instant friends.

Three weeks later I had finished my engagement in northern Nevada and come back to Las Vegas. One evening Mr. Kerkorian and his wife and my girlfriend, who was later to become my wife, were having dinner at the Dunes. Mr. Kerkorian didn't mince his words. "Wayne, I've got a problem. There are people in my organization who tell me you've already signed with the Frontier and that you used our conversation as leverage to get more money over there." Tears came to my eyes because I was so shocked—not at the fact that somebody would say something like that but that, even for a second, he would think something like that. I said, "I can tell you, Mr. K., that this is not true. And I will face whoever it is that said it. The true fact of the matter is that we'll probably end up taking less there than you are willing to pay us because they simply will not let us out of our verbal commitment." This was the truth. I firmly stated, "It has nothing to do with using you as a wedge." I called the people responsible and told them and Mr. Kerkorian, "I'll blow the whole thing. I will end up in a lawsuit before I will have my dignity and honor questioned that way." Mr. Kerkorian found out, after talking to those people, that I was telling the truth: The real reason why we were going to the Frontier was that they were holding us to a verbal commitment because Howard Hughes was interested in buying the hotel.

Hughes, in fact, did buy the Frontier and owned it before I ever played my first date there. There were no hard feelings with Kirk Kerkorian. He later gave me my wedding reception and we have been friends all these years.

I was never one to read newspapers. So I never knew when I worked at the Flamingo that Morris Landsberg and his associates had problems. I had never heard reports about hidden interests at casinos where I had played. I didn't even know the circumstances under which Howard Hughes had come to purchase the Frontier. I was unaware that organized-crime figures were being caught in Las Vegas by the sheriff's office and forced out of the Frontier for holding hidden interest. I didn't know about the unusual circumstances immediately preceding Mr. Hughes's purchase of the hotel. The only thing I remember is the story of how Howard Hughes came to buy the Silver Slipper.

According to stories, Mr. Hughes lived on the top floor of the Desert Inn and he enjoyed sleeping with the drapes opened. But he discovered that the lights on the big revolving slipper shone right into his window. So he telephoned the owners one morning and asked if they would remove the slipper, or at least move it away a few hundred yards. The owners laughed, thinking he was just an eccentric millionaire. Mr. Hughes was not amused. That afternoon he purchased the Silver Slipper and by nightfall the slipper was not as brightly lit.

CHAPTER 8

*The Lucy decision helped prompt the breach of my
relationships with my brother and my manager.*

I'VE BEEN VERY lucky to have the help of some wonderful
people in show business. One was the last of the red-hot
mammas and the other was a redhead.

Everyone loves a clown, and if the whole world loves a
clown, then everyone loved Lucy. She will always be the
"Queen of Television." For instance, have you ever
thought of how many Americans don't even remember a
world B.L. (Before Lucy)? For more than twenty-five
years, one had only to flip on the television dial to see that
laughable, lovable, irrepressible redhead bring laughter
into one's own living room. She was proud of being a
professional in her craft. And she went to great lengths to
deserve that laughter from her adoring audiences. She'd
been coated with chocolate, had her fake clown's nose
catch fire while the cameras were rolling, and almost frozen to death while filming her television series. She even
managed to get me to sing to a cow!

Appearing with Lucille Ball on *The Lucy Show* as a
country bumpkin may be the part that I will be best remembered for on television, for it has been seen around
the world hundreds of times. Because I am so closely related to that show, and have had to live down that character, it has been tough for me to appreciate the huge
effect it had on my life and career.

Lucy used to fly to Vegas from Hollywood all the time.

On weekends she would stay at the Sands and she'd come and catch my show. One night she came backstage and asked, "Would you do one of my shows?" Of course I was thrilled to be asked and accepted gladly. I know that the part was written especially for me and I performed on twelve of her television shows over a four-year period.

When it came to being a perfectionist, nobody could top Lucy. She and Mr. Gleason were both the absolute personification of perfection in terms of what they did. They cared about every detail; Lucy was there for the first script reading. She had hands-on control. She made every decision. We would rehearse it, rehearse it, and rehearse it. And then we would tape two shows—one at five and one at eight in front of a live audience.

My country-bumpkin character caught fire right away. It was so successful that at one point Lucy brought the head of CBS to Vegas because she wanted to produce a TV series around that character. After all, Gomer Pyle's TV series, starring Jim Nabors, had been such a big hit. I was really excited about the idea. Lucy was staying at the Sands Hotel and I went over to have a meeting with her about the show. Lucy said, "You know, if you want to do this series, Wayne, then we'll do it. The network wants you and we'll produce it at Desilu. But I want to tell you something." The redhead paused and raised her eyebrow and gave me that "Lucy look." "Wayne, I want you to know that if you do this, you're going to live with that character." She puzzled me, so I replied, "I'm not sure that I understand." She grinned. "That's going to be the people's conception of Wayne Newton. You know Jim Nabors. Everyone thinks of him as Gomer Pyle. He may have an operatic voice, but the only thing that's remembered is Gomer saying, 'Golleee.' That's how Jim Nabors is going to go down in history."

My brother and my manager were excited and said it was wonderful. Not convinced, I thought it over at home that night because Lucy said, "Come back to me tomorrow. Think this thing over." After the second show at the club, I sat Tommy and Jerry down and told them, "I can't do it. That's not me; that's not what I am. I can play the part and I can make it believable because I know that guy, but that's not me. I don't want to be known as that for the rest of my life." They were livid! They didn't even want to go to the meeting with Lucy the next day. When I gave her the news she was understanding. "I'm disappointed and I'm thrilled," she admitted. "From a business standpoint I'm truly disappointed, but from a personal standpoint I wouldn't have had the conscience to not point out the pitfalls."

Lucille Ball was truly special. And I have been grateful for that guidance ever since.

The Lucy decision helped prompt the breach of my relationships with my brother and my manager. There were other major factors that finally forced me to make a decision: I had to go it alone.

One of those factors was a multimillion-dollar Wall Street corporation that conceived an idea to buy some of the world's biggest entertainers. They approached us. They said, "We will give you ten million dollars now, up front, and for that ten million dollars you will work the next ten years. The checks will come to the corporation but we will give you all the money you will personally receive up front. You will guarantee us so many weeks a year. Everything you make will come to the corporation and will be disseminated among the stockholders."

My brother and Tommy flipped. They both said, "Absolutely! Draw up the papers!" I said, "Hold it! Let me tell you what the problem with this is. It's called white slavery. What they're taking away from us is not our earning capacity, but our incentive to earn."

The Wall Street broker quickly added, "Well, I'll build incentive into the program. If you start making X amount of dollars over what we've paid you, then you'll get a percentage of it." My brother and Tommy were even more anxious to sign on the dotted line. They were yelling, "Go! Go! Go!" When I raised my hand and said, "No," I realized something about myself, and about Jerry and Tommy: We were not coming from the same place. It was the beginning of the end.

There was an inner show-biz circle whose members played a very important part in Wayne Newton's professional life. That group consisted of Lucille Ball, Danny Thomas, Jack Benny, Jackie Gleason, Bobby Darin, and George Burns. They saw something in me that I think most other people in the entertainment industry did not. Few could understand why these stars at the peak of their careers went so far out of their way to help me. My agents didn't even believe it. General Artists Corporation never could understand why I enjoyed such acceptance by such great people.

When I opened at the Fairmont in San Francisco, a young agent, David Gerber, who went on to become a successful producer, flew up to catch the show. As my agent, he was thrilled when I was a hit. He came to my room after the show and insisted on calling the president of GAC to tell him what had happened. In front of me, he got him on the phone and had a conversation on which, I'm sure, he's reflected many times. Gerber kept saying, "You will not believe what has happened here tonight. I am not lying to you. Honest to God, it was just sensational!" But I could tell by the look on David's face and the tone of his voice that the president didn't believe it and lacked confidence in me. As he tried to convince the president, I realized that David was the only one at the agency who had any belief in me at all. To the General Artists Corporation, Wayne Newton represented 10 percent, that's all. But I'll always remember how David put himself on the line for me with that call, and I'll always be grateful.

Danny Thomas was very much an integral part of my career. Whenever he did a big show on television, such as *The Follies,* he would include me so that I could benefit from the national exposure. He always made me a part of the St. Jude's fund-raiser.

Surprisingly, that whole group was so tight and helpful,

one has to begin to wonder if maybe it was some master plan. When they would talk among themselves they would say, "If you can use the kid on something, use him." It was wonderful because I had nothing to contribute to them. But I think they saw an anachronism: I was a fish out of water because my contemporaries were the Beatles and the Rolling Stones. There was Elvis before I came along, and I was not doing the kind of music that was part of the trend. I didn't look like any of the hot recording artists. Musically, I would have fit in somewhere between the twenties and the thirties and certainly no later than the forties. But they believed in me, and because they did, I believed in me.

I may never have had the opportunity of working with Jayne Mansfield or Sophie Tucker if it wasn't for my un- happiness with the owner of the Copa.

We left the Copacabana under somewhat adverse con- ditions after we had been performing there about six months. We got into a disagreement with its owner, Julie Podell. I say a disagreement. It really wasn't. In retro- spect, it was nothing. It was just that when Mr. Podell drank a lot everything became too loud for him. So when he felt that things were getting too loud he would go through two swinging doors in the back of the lounge and turn down the microphone one notch. The more he would drink, the more he would lower the sound. Night after night, he would blast through those doors to go by the kitchen and turn down the microphone one notch, notch after notch. It got so bad that when I came offstage I was so hoarse I couldn't talk. My brother became furious and so did my manager, Tommy Amato.

Mr. Podell had the gravelly kind of voice that you get from drinking and he wore a huge star sapphire ring that he would pound on the table when he got angry. I watched him be terribly rude to Sammy Davis, Jr., one night. In those years, Sammy was the biggest star in the world. But "frankly Scarlett" Podell didn't give a damn. Sammy was running overtime in the show and he walked up to the edge of the stage and said, "Nigger, get off my stage."

I'm told that when Johnny Ray was appearing there at the height of his career, Mr. Podell got angry at the singer and actually locked him in a walk-in freezer and forgot he was there. Johnny Ray ended up with pneumonia.

Depending on what part of the evening it was and how much booze he had consumed, if he didn't like you, or if you spoke to him the wrong way, he would go on a power surge. It was fun to watch guys come in who wanted to impress their girls. They'd slap Julie Podell on the shoulder and say, "Hey, Julie, how you doing?" In his raspy voice that everyone could hear, Mr. Podell would answer, "Get the f____ away from me, ass____."

Many times Podell would hit his ring on the table and whisper in a guy's ear. Then all of a sudden a table would disappear and then the customers would be picked up in their chairs and carried out the door. He was Napoléon and Mussolini without the charm.

The Copa was to play an even more important part in my life than just being a place to perform. Two weeks after I opened at the Copa in 1963 I met a man who years later would change my life forever. While I was onstage doing my show, a guy walked in with a group of people. He sat down ringside and wasn't necessarily interested in what we were doing onstage. He was busy talking and laughing. Finally he reached into his pocket and took out a hundred-dollar bill and began waving it in the air, yelling out, "You're Nobody Till Somebody Loves You." So I looked at him and then turned away. He kept holding the hundred-dollar bill in the air as if I were supposed to dance or bark or sit up. He looked like most other people who came to the Copa. He had on a suit and glasses and there wasn't anything special about his looks.

It might have been the following night when I noticed that the same gentleman who had offered me the hundred dollars was seated in a booth by himself. My brother and my manager were very angry with me for not taking the hundred-dollar bill when he first waved it because we could have used it for food.

After the first show, as I stepped off the stage, out of my peripheral vision I could see him motioning me to come over. I ignored him, and went out the back door and up to the locker room. When I came back in forty minutes for my next show, he was still seated there, alone. This time when I came offstage I ignored him again, but I wasn't going to get away that easy. He called over the maître d' and asked him to summon me.

So I went back to his table and sat down and his opening line was, ''Why did you refuse the money?'' I said, ''I'm sorry.'' He was very irritated and said, ''You heard me, kid. Why did you refuse the money?'' It was then that I realized that I had humiliated him by refusing his gratuity. So I tried to explain to him, ''I get paid for what I do. I get paid for singing. So I don't need your money. If you have a request, and if I know it, I'll be happy to sing it.''

He didn't seem to buy my response and admitted that I was the first entertainer who had ever refused money from him. I explained to him that it wasn't meant to offend him in any form or fashion. It's just that I have my pride and dignity also.

I couldn't tell you if he spoke with an Italian accent. I have a problem discerning an Italian accent from a New York accent. To me they're one and the same. Having been born in Virginia, I was never around ethnic groups of any kind. I didn't really know a Jewish holiday from an Italian holiday, or an Indian holiday. We were just Virginians, and most of us are mixed-bloods, and so, to me, the accent was simply New York.

After that Guido Penosi would come into the Copa periodically, maybe twice a week, and generally with other people. Trying to give me a hundred-dollar bill became a little running joke with him. I found out later that he told his friends about the entertainer who wouldn't take money from people. He would even bet people to see if I would

take the hundred-dollar bill. He always won for he knew
I wouldn't.

At that time, "Guido" was the only name I knew him
by. Seventeen years later I would discover a lot more about
my own naïveté.

One night, I had a stomachful of Mr. Podell and his
turning down the sound. So I just stood onstage and lip-
synched. I moved my lips but nothing came out. He became very angry and called us to a meeting, at which
point my brother explained to him that we were not used
to being treated that way, and that it would be best if we
left.

The other disagreement that I personally had with Mr.
Podell was over our tailor-made, beautiful blue mohair
suits, which we wore with blue bow ties. We thought the
suits were sharp. But Mr. Podell went nuts. He started
screaming, "Get upstairs and put on a tux or get out." It
ended up being a big scene. So that, along with Mr. Podell
calling us everything but gentlemen, was a sign that our
days at the Copa were destined to end.

Mr. Podell always called me Winn. He never knew my
real name. At our last argument, he said, "What do you
got to say for yourself, Winn, you son of a bitch?" And I
said, "Mr. Podell, you don't even know my name. I don't
like that, or the way you talk to me. So we can either
finish tonight, or we can finish this week. But we are leaving." I hoped he'd say, "Stay the week," because we
needed to eat.

Two weeks later, we shuffled off to Buffalo. The first
time, the agent booked us with Jayne Mansfield. I was the
opening act, or supporting act, which is pretty interesting
when you consider that I was with Jayne Mansfield.
Though the showroom was big, the backstage area was
very small and you had to walk through the star's dressing
room to get on and off the stage. The club was right off
an amusement park and Jayne Mansfield arrived every
night looking like she just came off the roller coaster. You
could count on squaw having too much firewater.

On Sunday afternoon we were to do a matinee and the place was loaded with kids. Jayne Mansfield, as part of her act, would do a mock striptease. She would strip down to a very conservative bathing suit, but in those days it was still a little risqué. She would bump and grind and peel off a little of her clothing. But this one afternoon she was so drunk that when she grabbed the buttons to undo the long part of the outfit, her whole top came off. I was standing backstage and I couldn't believe my eyes. There she stood, bosoms totally exposed in front of a jam-packed audience filled with families. The light man killed the lights and there was a total blackout as the audience started to boo. The owner came running backstage and said to two guys, "Get out there and get her off." The guys rushed out and threw a raincoat around her and pulled her backstage. The owner looked at me and shouted, "Get out there, kid."

I was stunned. I asked, "And do what?" He screamed, "Do anything, but get the hell out there."

So fools rush in where wise men never go. I ran out there and the audience was beating on the tables screaming catcalls, booing, and hissing. I looked at my conductor and said, "Play 'Danny Boy.' " He didn't even hear me because it was total bedlam. So I started to sing. It was as if I were not even there. There were things flying through the air, and I was so nervous that the microphone slipped out of my hands. I was afraid to bend over for fear that I would be hit by a flying object, and my voice was already high enough. So I just continued to sing, and soon, in less than a minute, you could hear a pin drop. So when you talk about learning tricks of the trade, it was that moment that taught me you can outshout an audience.

By the time I had finished the song, the audience was standing and applauding. Everybody had forgotten Jayne Mansfield's boobs but me. God were they pretty. After performing another twenty minutes, I walked offstage. There wasn't even a thank-you from the owner. It was

like, "That's what you are here for, so go do it." I guess
he was right.

The next time I played that same place, it was with
Sophie Tucker. It was the year before she passed away,
and the second night she called me into her dressing room.
She sat there looking very much like the legend of the last
of the red-hot mammas. She wore feathers in her hair and
a full-length sequined gown. As I passed her dressing-
room door, she invited me in with a raspy voice. "Come
in here, young man, and sit down." As I walked through
the door and before I could even sit, she asked, "Where
are you from?" I smiled. "Virginia." In her best "Some
of These Days" voice, she asked, "How the hell did you
wind up here?" Being polite I said, "The agency,
ma'am." She howled, "I don't mean working here. I mean
New York."

She intimidated me. That was a problem I always had
with New Yorkers. I found them kind of aggressive because of their loud attack form of speech. I still do. I
mean, if anybody comes at me that way, it always takes
me aback. I've learned to respond to it better than I did
then, but Sophie Tucker scared me to death.

CHAPTER 9

✩

*I've got to leave. I don't know whether you've
outgrown me or I've outgrown you.*

BILL HARRAH WAS a wonderful man. He looked like a
Baptist preacher. He was very thin and tall and soft-
spoken. I never saw him angry at any time. I heard of
things that supposedly happened as a result of his irrita-
tion, but I personally never witnessed them.

On one hand, he was terribly smart about people; he
was one of the few to realize that performers are people
and not trained seals, who knew that we think, we hurt,
we bleed, we cry, we get angry. On the other hand, Bill
Harrah was also the guy who made sure the stage manager
called the Denver Conservatory on time to make sure that
the show went on not one second before eight o'clock and
not one second after. Harrah insisted that they log when
the show started and ended to the second. If you said
"damn" or "hell" onstage, Harrah gave you a pink slip,
which was a warning not to do it again.

Bill Harrah wanted the shows to be an hour and ten
minutes long. Sammy Davis, Jr., and myself were allowed
to do an hour and twenty. That's really how I started not
having an opening act. Most headliners have an opening
or supporting act. Sometimes it's a comic or a singer, but
two acts usually share the bill. It was because of Bill Harrah and his obsession with time that I decided to cut my
opening act.

In the beginning I tried to get along with Harrah and

live within his time frame. But I've always leaned to the audience to tell me what kind of show to do. With Bill Harrah, I said, "Okay, I will try it your way. I will keep the shows to an hour and twenty." I lived up to my commitment for the first ten days of my engagement. Then I started to get letters from people in the audience saying, "We came to see your show last week. We're sorry you weren't feeling well. It wasn't the kind of show that we're used to." Others wrote, "We never thought we'd see Wayne Newton looking at his watch."

I couldn't ignore my fans. I called the Harrah's people and asked for a meeting, where I told them, "I've got to leave." "Why?" "Well," I said, "because I can't go on. I don't know whether you've outgrown me or I've outgrown you. But I know we're no longer compatible. I've tried it your way and it does not work for me. And it doesn't work for my audiences. If I have to lose anything it's going to have to be this association rather than my audience." I knew that either way I lost.

I care very much about my audience. I found out one thing a long time ago, and that is that people go through an awful lot to get to a show. It costs them a small fortune; they stand in line for hours; they're hassled; and after being hit upon for a tip to get a decent seat, it takes the performer twenty minutes to get them over their frustration. The audience doesn't understand, sitting in the showroom, that Wayne Newton does not set the entertainment policy. They don't understand when they're standing in line that Wayne Newton has nothing at all to do with the line or how it goes through the casino or which slot machines it goes by or what employee is rude to them. They don't understand that Wayne Newton has absolutely nothing to do with whether they can bring their cameras or where they're seated. Because the first thing a showroom employee will say when someone says "I want to sit there" is, "We're holding that for Mr. Newton's guest." In reality I have nothing to do with it.

Aside from Bill Harrah's obsession with time, he was

one of the most likable, kind, and generous men you'd want to meet. Once after an engagement I said to Pat France, who was the entertainment director in those years, "The Rolls-Royce I'm driving—are you considering selling it?" My manager at the time, Jay Stream, wanted to buy that particular car for his wife. Well, I didn't feel it necessary to go into details to Pat that Jay wanted the car; instead, I simply asked if the car was for sale. He said he'd check with Bill. On my closing day I got a call from Pat France and he said, "Wayne, I checked the car with Bill to find out if it was for sale. And Bill said to tell you it's not for sale, it's yours. Bill wants you to have it." Well, now my mouth was down to the ground and I couldn't say, "Tell Bill it's not for me, it's for my manager." So I went to Jay and told him, "Look, this is what happened." He said, "My God, you've got to keep it, otherwise it would be offensive to Bill if you turn around and sell it to me for my wife." He was right.

Jay started off as a friend I had met in the horse business and was literally responsible for getting me through the whole turmoil and breakup with my brother and former manager. When Jay took over I had about thirty-eight lawsuits against me for bad investments that had been made by my former manager. Jay did a great job in straightening everything out.

Once I confessed to Bill Harrah that I was crazy about Duesenbergs. He had nine in his collection. So I asked if I could buy one of them. Harrah said, "No, they're not for sale, but I'll find you one." A year or two went by and I'd forgotten all about it. One day I got a call from Harrah. He said, "Wayne, I found a Duesenberg. It belonged to Howard Hughes. Now, this was even before I was working for the Summa hotels and for Howard Hughes. So I said, "Okay." Then Harrah told me the price. "It's forty thousand dollars." When I heard how much it was I took a big gulp and a deep breath and said "Great!" knowing I couldn't afford it but would rather die than tell him.

So they delivered the car and I puttered around with it for three months before deciding that I wanted to have the spoke wheels chromed. So I called the man who was in charge of Harrah's car collection. When I asked if I could have him pick up my car and chrome the wheels he checked with Bill Harrah, and a week later Harrah sent a man to pick up the car. Four months passed and I still hadn't heard anything about my Duesenberg. I thought to myself, *How long does it take to chrome wheels?* I figured it was probably due to a backlog of work, and since I was appearing at Harrah's in a month, I thought, *Ah, hell, I'll wait until I get there.* So when I arrived at the hotel I telephoned Bill and said, "I'm going out to see my car." Harrah agreed to meet me. When both of us strolled into the shop, I didn't see my car anywhere. When I said, "Bill, where's my car?" he smiled and started pointing. "Well, those are your wheels hanging there, and there's your fenders on that wall, and there's the chassis over there." I nearly died. Mr. Harrah just smiled and walked out the door saying, "We're restoring it for you." They restored the car from the bolts up. I paid forty thousand dollars for the car with a bank loan, and the car today is worth a lot of money. It looks like it just rolled off the showroom floor. It's magnificent. Bill Harrah was not the kind of guy to do anything halfway.

CHAPTER 10

*Sometimes I wonder if underneath it all Howard
Hughes wasn't pulling the strings. He was the puppeteer
and we were the puppets.*

TO SUPERSTARS, HE was a wheeler-dealer, he was the man
who sat at the right hand of Howard Hughes. He was Walter Kane, but to me he'll always be just Grandfather. For
Walter Kane, Las Vegas was a grand proving ground of
entertainment. He manipulated the showrooms and the
lounges of Howard Hughes's Summa Corporation like the
ringmaster at an unforgettable three-ring circus. Born November 27, 1900, in Dallas, Walter grew up in New York.
He danced for pennies on sidewalks and appeared onstage
for the first time at age four in *Ten Nights in a Barroom*.
Walter was born to entertainment. His mother, Frankie
Kane, taught him to sing; she was a star in the *Klaw and
Erlanger show*, a predecessor to the famed *Ziegfeld Follies*. She died when he was nine. He then lived with his
father and stepmother but did not get along with them, so
he ran away to become a vaudeville performer while still
a child. Years later, when asked what university he attended, Walter replied, "The University of Broadway."

He served in the navy during World War I and enlisted
in the coast guard during World War II, being cited
for bravery after the invasions of Eniwetok, Saipan, and
Taiwan.

Walter was grateful for his natural talents. He once re-
vealed to me, "I had a good voice. Instead of stealing, I
could go into a place and sing songs and have them throw

76

quarters and dimes at me.'' He became president of Harry
Webber, Inc., in 1932, then one of America's largest theatrical agencies. He joined Zeppo Marx, Inc., film agency
as vice-president in 1934. When he opened his own talent
agency four years later, he represented a galaxy of Hollywood stars: Lana Turner, Mickey Rooney, Ray Milland,
Joan Fontaine, Lucille Ball, Barbara Stanwyck, Clark Gable, and Fred MacMurray. He also represented writers
like George S. Kaufman, Moss Hart, Morrie Ryskin, Norman Krasna, and Bella and Sam Spewack.

After buying RKO for Howard Hughes in 1948, Walter
Kane took over as executive for creative talent at the studios in 1950 and later talent executive for Hughes Produc-
tions.

Walter met Howard in 1927 in a New York society
restaurant. That same year Kane arrived by train in Las
Vegas, a place he remembered only because there was a
windstorm in the desert on a whistle-stop to Los Angeles.
In those days, Las Vegas wasn't much more than a place
for planes and trains to stop for refueling.

In 1970 he moved to Vegas, which he called, ''the
greatest town in the world.'' He arrived in the aftermath
of a power struggle in the Hughes organization and
promptly recommended Sands executive Jack Entratter be
appointed as entertainment director for all of Hughes's hotels. But Entratter died in March 1971, and Walter accepted the job of entertainment director for Hughes's
renamed company, Summa Corporation.

In Las Vegas, Walter was instrumental in the careers of
many stars, including Debbie Reynolds and Rich Little.
The two of us became close personal friends and Walter
never tired of boasting about my contribution to the success of the Sands, Frontier, and Desert Inn showrooms.

Walter was the gray-haired man in the dark suit with
the dandruff on the shoulders. People both feared and
loved him.

''No one knew Howard Hughes as well as I,'' Walter
once said. ''Sometimes we were together as much as eigh-

teen or twenty hours a day.'' He described the late indus-
trialist as a big, tall, handsome man with a wonderful sense
of humor.

Walter also remembered his ex-boss as being a hard
worker. "I never met anyone who could work harder or
put in longer hours than Howard. Sometimes he would go
as long as seventy hours without sleep, except for a couple
of naps that only lasted a few minutes.''

It was Walter who noticed the first indications that Mr.
Hughes wanted to withdraw from life. According to Walter, one night Howard said, "I'm not going out tonight,
Walter. I seem to have a lot of friends in town since I
bought that movie studio. People keep asking me for jobs,
and I don't like to say no, so I think I'll start staying in."

Walter said his friend withdrew from the social spotlight
even more after his marriage to Jean Peters, and by the
sixties was completely reclusive. Walter attributes the final, total withdrawal to a nervous breakdown. "His brain
was so active—he was always under pressure," said Walter. "Howard Hughes was literally a one-man organization." Walter once noted that Howard was the only
individual ever to own and develop a major airline—Trans
World Airlines—from a local to an international carrier.
He was also the only individual ever to own outright a
motion-picture studio.

Long before Howard Hughes moved to the ninth floor
and reigned from his penthouse of the Desert Inn in 1966,
the billionaire was a Las Vegas booster. "He loved Las
Vegas. He wanted to own the town; it was the greatest
tonic in the world to him," Walter once told me.

How was it that the man who I mistrusted as a shrewd
operator when I first met him would become my closest
and dearest friend?

Walter Kane was shrewd, cunning, kind, sensitive, and
insecure. For someone who is oversensitive to criticism,
Walter Kane knew how to wrap me around his little finger.
He knew of my immense dissatisfaction with most every

show. I'm sure that every perfectionist is insecure. And Walter Kane always knew how to approach criticism from a different way. If he thought I was doing a line that was demeaning to someone, it would come up in conversation totally out of context. It had nothing to do with the show or show business, but Walter knew that I was sensitive enough to pick up on what he was talking about. He was never demeaning and there was never a time when he tried to take away my dignity. Even when he thought I was wrong and I refused to change, he would look at me and say, "You got to do what you got to do, and if that's the way you feel about it, then don't ever change your feelings about it. You stick with it." Then he would add, "But if you approach it from this way, your chances are better at getting it on or being understood." Walter Kane had a great ability to get to the heart of the matter without being heartless.

I especially remember him telling me, "I used to think I was broke 'cause I had no money. But I realized I wasn't broke. I was just out of ideas." He knew me better than I did. And he knew that I was bullheaded. Walter was so cagey at times, he'd say, "Wayne, I'm going to have to talk to your tailor because he didn't do a very good job. You know that suit you were wearing last week, well it doesn't fit quite right." In reality, what he was saying was, "Wayne you're putting on weight." He had a great charm that way.

But only after the Bobby Darin incident, when Walter Kane had stuck his neck out and hired Bobby, did I realize what a gentleman Walter was. I said to him, "Walter, I'm embarrassed." Walter scratched his head. "Then you don't have a lot to worry about, do you?" I asked, "What do you mean?" Kane smiled. "Wayne, I know you had nothing to do with that. And if you love Bobby the way that you say you do, and I know you do, then you have to want what's best for him. Maybe that's what's best for him." When Walter noticed a look in my eyes, he embraced me. "I'm sorry we lost him and I'm sorry that we couldn't continue on that basis. But he's going to make more money and I think he's going to be happy. I know you'd want him to be happy.'' It took a big man to do that, but, then, Walter Kane was a giant.

Walter wanted me to grow, and he knew that growth would not happen if he held my hand. But he also understood that he had to be right there before I went over Niagara Falls. He was my safety net. I never really knew either of my grandparents. I vaguely remember them when I was about four. And so here was this gray-haired man who treated me like a grandson. He and Tom Chauncey filled that void of never having known my grandparents. Walter listened to my excitements and didn't make fun of my mistakes; he offered counsel and advice, and because of his wisdom I was drawn to him. Other than him and Tom Chauncey, I never had anybody older whom I could talk to. He had lived life long enough to give advice and he knew that time takes care of most things. He became a grandfather to me, and I was like a grandson to him. I would talk to him about everything. He knew me so well and he knew what was important to my dignity.

He also taught me the meaning of love. One night he called me to his suite at the Sands. He had had prostate surgery and they had put a catheter in him. As I sat next to him, he took my hand and said, ''Grandson, I want you to talk to Dr. Ted Jacobs. I want an operation and I want this catheter out of me.'' I tried to explain why that was impossible, but he just shook his head. I said, ''Grandfather, you know what the problem is. It's you heart.'' ''Do you love me?'' he asked. I answered, ''How could you ask me that? You know I do.'' He squeezed my hand as hard as he could. ''I don't want to live if this is the way I have to live. It is the quality of life that's important to me. And not the quantity. I don't care what you have to do to convince your friend Dr. Jacobs to give me that operation, 'cause I want it. And if anyone can convince him, and I know how much you love me, I know you'll do it.'' I told him I would talk to Ted, knowing full well

Ted would ultimately do what was best medically for Walter.

All the way home I had a big lump in my throat. What should I do? Should I ask Dr. Jacobs about operating and chance losing Grandfather? Or did I want Grandfather to continue to suffer and be unhappy? That night I prayed for God to give me a sign. The next day I realized that it was not my decision. Dr. Jacobs would do what was correct for Grandfather's health and safety. I approached Dr. Jacobs. "Grandfather wants the operation." Jacobs repeated several times, "Not a chance." He took his glasses off and pointed at me. "Life is better than no life." That's when I said, "Come on, Ted, you don't believe that? If it were me, and I said to you I would rather die than live like this, would you really want me to live that way?" Dr. Jacobs put his hands in his white doctor's coat and looked down at the floor. It seemed like hours were passing. My heart was beating and I was praying, *Please say yes*. Ted looked up within seconds and said, "You realize the risk. Does Walter realize?" I assured him that he did. Ted looked at me and said, "Okay, I'll schedule it."

So I went to the operating room with Walter Kane. I held his hand as they gave him the anesthesia. Just before they started the actual surgery, I was asked to leave. I kissed him on the cheek, told him that I loved him, and left the room. It was touch and go after that for about four days, but he came through the operation with flying colors. It was during that crisis, while he was fighting for his life, that his heart was broken. The Howard Hughes organization was in a turmoil and the new regime wanted him out after fifty years of service. That has become corporate practice almost everywhere where they forget about the individual, only caring about doing away with liabilities as they perceive them at that moment in time. Welcome to the real world. It was sad. But I could give Walter a certain amount of protection, not that Walter needed my protection at all in the beginning. But toward the end, when I was still packing people into the Summa Howard

Hughes hotels, I could protect Grandfather in a way. The corporation was reluctant to do anything against Walter because they knew I would react to it strongly.

I was not in town when Grandfather passed away in May 1983. I was performing in London and I knew that he would die while I was there. I would not be with him. Now, that must sound strange and dramatic, but Grandfather came close to passing away no less than twelve times. The doctors would call me and say he has an hour to live. I'd go rushing to his suite and pray with him and Walter would always get that extra bit of strength, and somehow he'd come out of it. Just before I went to London, Walter said to me, ''I don't want you to watch me go.'' I knew what Walter Kane had planned as his last headlining engagement. Dream-maker Walter Kane, who brought the superstars to Las Vegas, died at 12:10 A.M. at Sunrise Hospital from heart and kidney failure.

Walter Kane and Howard Hughes came into my life at a crucial time in my career. Hughes had just moved into Las Vegas and I had just moved out of adolescence. Hughes was trying to put a Mr. Clean front on the reputation of Vegas practices. And I was trying to make the transition from novelty act and lounge performer to mainroom headliner.

According to Walter, Howard took a keen interest in the kind of entertainment being offered at the casinos he'd been buying up. Walter once told me that he paid special attention to me. I believe that Howard Hughes watched me on TV monitors or above the stage from the light booth. The invincible emperor began in his own particular way to communicate with me. Up in his Desert Inn suite, he'd drill one of his Mormon attendants on messages he wanted memorized and delivered to me. Many nights there would come a knock on the door and a guy would appear in my dressing room and say to me, ''Mr. Hughes wants you to know he knows what you're doing and he's proud of the kind of entertainment you're representing. He's happy that you're a member of his family.''

In 1975, Howard Hughes gave his blessing to the Wayne Newton/Howard Hughes Festival Week. It was publicized all over the country. It was the only time that Howard Hughes had ever allowed his name to be used on a marquee, and then in a secondary position. Howard himself authorized the sequence of national publicity.

There are those who say that Walter Kane did more for my career than anyone else. He probably did more for me personally because there were so few people I could really talk to. One could say that Walter's interest in me was less than altruistic, and that was probably true in the beginning. But it ended up not being true. I can tell you that if there were people who maligned me in any way, they also made an enemy of Walter Kane. One who experienced Walter's wrath because of the way he treated me was Jan Murray.

Early on in my career, before I even knew Walter Kane, Jan Murray gave me a rough time while we were playing together at the Palmer House in Chicago. I have just appeared on the Gleason show and was Jan Murray's supporting act. One night Sammy Spear, who was Jackie Gleason's musical conductor, had come in to see me at the Palmer House. I knew it was not the opening act's place to introduce people in the audience. It's just an unwritten rule that the headliner does the introductions, and I've always known it. Yet I didn't want to ignore Sammy Spear to the extent that I would pretend he wasn't there. While I didn't officially introduce him, I casually remarked that there was a friend of mine named Mr. Spear sitting out there in the audience. I didn't even say Sammy Spear was Mr. Gleason's musical conductor and I quickly went right into the next song. When I came offstage Jan Murray pushed me up against the wall. He put his finger in my face and started to chew me out. He shouted that he was the headliner and said, ''Who the hell do you think you are? Don't you ever introduce a celebrity when you're working with a star. You're nothing more than an opening act and don't forget I'm the star."

For a long time Jan Murray, Vic Damone, and Jack Carter believed that I had blacklisted and kept them from working in Las Vegas. In fact, it wasn't like that at all. It was Walter who saw that they weren't hired after he heard stories about them and me. To Walter, if they were saying bad things about me, they were saying them about him.

Sometimes I wonder if underneath it all Howard Hughes wasn't pulling the strings. He was the puppeteer and we were the puppets. Was my dressing room bugged? Were there hidden TV cameras? Or did Hughes simply sit secretly watching my show and others every night? Walter knew the secret and he always promised to tell me how Howard Hughes kept tabs on Wayne Newton. Unfortunately, that secret, like so many, died with Walter.

It's spooky, but Howard Hughes knew an awful lot about me. He knew too much about my growing process, what kind of person I was, what my beliefs and habits were. Was Howard Hughes the type of man who would enjoy eavesdropping or bugging? In my mind, there's no doubt about it.

It didn't take long for the word to get up and down the Strip that the unpredictable Howard Hughes was buying up Las Vegas and had adopted Wayne Newton. Suddenly entertainment directors all over town wanted me and were bidding up my price. Emperor Hughes had made me the pride of Las Vegas and put me in his stall of fame. Walter once told me that Howard Hughes saw a lot of similarities between himself and me. God help me! I would love to know what they were, but I guess I never will.

Oddly enough, when Howard Hughes was in trouble, I could sense it. Call it what you may, but I would wake up in the middle of the night and Howard Hughes would flash into my mind. One incident involved Walter Kane. Howard Hughes was in the Bahamas and Walter got a call from one of Mr. Hughes's aides. He said that Mr. Hughes wanted to see Walter and they had a JetStar waiting at

Hughes Airport to fly him to the Bahamas. Walter was curious and asked, "Why does Mr. Hughes want to see me?" The raspy voice said, "We don't know. But he wants to see you."

Right before I was about to go onstage, Walter came to visit me backstage and said, "Wayne, I'm going to be gone for a couple of days. The old man wants to see me." (Kane always referred to Howard Hughes as "the old man.") Then Walter told me that he was flying to the Bahamas. When I asked when he planned on returning, Walter seemed very vague. "It might be two or three days. I don't know." He slipped a piece of paper into my tuxedo jacket and on it was the number of the hotel where he could be reached. Then he pulled out an envelope from the inside of his black suit. As Walter handed it to me, he said, "Now, don't open this. I just don't want to leave it in the safety deposit box here at the hotel. That's why I put your name on it. I'll pick it up from you when I get back."

I had a little safe in the dressing room and I immediately placed the envelope there. I thought nothing about it. Several days passed and I was halfway through the show at the Sands Hotel when I noticed Walter standing in the wings. At the first opportunity, after singing a song and getting a round of applause, I walked to the side of the stage. Walter grabbed me on the arm and I could feel him shaking. "Wayne, I have to talk to you. It's urgent."

So I went back onstage and with each song I sang my mind kept flashing on Walter and what could be so urgent. After finishing the show, we went to the back of the dressing room, and it was quite clear to me that the elderly man was visibly shaken and there was something wrong. Walter, in fear that the room was bugged, wanted us to speak only in whispers. Quietly, he said, "I went down there and the aide said to me that the old man wanted me to go to Mexico and get him some dope." Startled, I said in a loud voice, "Dope?" Walter quickly put his finger to his mouth as I whispered to him, "What do you know about dope?'' Of course, Walter explained that he knew absolutely nothing about dope and he told me he realized that Howard Hughes's top aides were trying to set him up. Walter confronted them and demanded to see Howard Hughes right away. They refused to give him access to Hughes, claiming, ''He can't see you now. He will see you tomorrow.'' Walter, realizing that tomorrow might never come, yelled so loud that his voice was clearly heard down the hallway of the hotel. ''He'll see me now or you have the JetStar waiting 'cause I'm on the way back to the airport.'' Hughes's top boys assured him in no uncertain terms that Walter Kane was not going to leave the Bahamas. That's when Walter told them the facts.

''I'm going to tell you guys something. You're screwing with the wrong guy. I left a sealed letter with my grandson, and if anything should happen to me, it's to be opened. In addition, I left a sealed letter with Hank Greenspun, publisher of the *Las Vegas Sun*. Now, if I'm not back by tonight, those letters are going to be opened and you're in deep shit.'' They knew that Kane would carry out his threat. They sent him back to the airport and put him on the JetStar. He came immediately to my dressing room.

About three weeks later, Walter was contacted by the CIA. They knew he had gone down to the Bahamas supposedly to meet with Howard Hughes. They had wiretapped the telephone calls, and continued to tap them in the Bahamas, which he found out later.

One night when Grandfather and I were discussing Hughes, he became terribly defensive. He said that Howard Hughes wasn't on drugs like we think of them. It wasn't cocaine or marijuana or any of that kind of stuff. He blamed it on the plane crash and said that Hughes was on morphine. According to Grandfather, Howard was so broken up after the plane crash that he was in constant pain. So in order to kill the pain, he was regularly given morphine. One of the reasons why Walter became so suspicious when Hughes's insiders asked him to go into Mexico to bring back drugs was that Howard had two doctors with him at all times. That was what tipped him off that Howard was not safe.

As for Walter Kane's relationship with Howard Hughes, it was rumored that Walter would go out and find young starlets all over the country and then bring them back to Tinseltown for Howard's pleasure. Certainly, as head of RKO he would definitely be scouting for new talent. Walter would discover these young girls, so the story goes. They would be brought to Hollywood; their families would not be allowed to see them for six months; and during that rehearsal period, they would literally be cut off from the world. At the end of the six months of isolation, Howard Hughes would arrive with a little poodle under his arm and it was time for the young lady to pay up.

But I firmly believe, knowing Grandfather the way I do, that that is just another discrediting tale of the Howard Hughes legend.

Walter was simply a very close friend of Mr. Hughes—the man whom Howard could count on to be loyal and discreet.

There is no question that Hughes had strange phobias and at times could be very demanding. He would often arrive at Walter's Los Angeles apartment in the middle of the night and say, "Listen, I moved out of the Beverly Hills Hotel. Can I spend the night here?" Walter would pack his bags and get himself a room at a hotel. The next day, when Walter would come back, he'd find that Howard had moved all of Walter's luggage and clothes out into the hallway. And for the next six months Walter Kane's apartment became Howard Hughes's residence.

Hughes was a friend. If Walter Kane felt guilty about anything, it was about the way Howard Hughes died. It broke his heart. And if he said to me once, he said it to me one hundred times: "Why didn't Howard Hughes call me? I'd have been there. Maybe I could have stopped it."

He's not the only one who felt guilty or upset over the death of Howard Hughes. I think that Hughes's passing and his final physical deterioration is one of the great crimes of our time. When one considers what Howard Hughes contributed to mankind, and realizes that he was held hostage by his own people and died from malnutrition and morphine, it's a crime that defied definition.

But Howard might have brought upon himself his own isolation when he limited his inner circle to six people. It's incredible to think that Howard Hughes was the man who went into London, England, without even a passport. There he was, living in a hotel, buying hotels in Nevada, and was not present when he was licensed to operate casinos in hotels in the Silver State. The former governor of the state, Mike O'Callaghan, and Senator Paul Laxalt went to London to verify that there was a living Howard Hughes.

It was a love-hate affair that Mr. Hughes felt for Nevada. He had a true affection for the state, while at the same time he hated the test site. He felt that the radioactive material that came from it would eventually destroy the desert he loved.

Walter was secretive, but he sometimes would sit in his tall director's chair in my dressing room and tell Howard Hughes stories. He told me about the time when Howard was going with an actress and then met someone else whom he liked better. He stood up the actress to take out the other woman. Finally, when he finished his date with the new woman, Hughes went running down to the corner where he was to meet the actress and she wasn't there. So he went back to his place. Well, what had happened was that the actress had left when Hughes didn't show and went to his bungalow at the Beverly Hills Hotel. She got a glimpse of the other girl as she was leaving. Howard had gone out the back door and driven away to meet her. When he returned, actress Terry Moore was standing there fuming. Howard looked at her and said, "It takes a lot of guts to stand me up that way." And Terry Moore beat the crap out of him with her purse. It was those kinds of stories that Walter loved to tell. Walter would grin and laugh and joke, "Wayne, you and Howard are so much alike."

It wasn't that we were alike. It was that Walter needed

to think we were. Mr. Hughes and I were both tall and dark and liked women immensely. Grandpa used to kid, "You're never going to die a natural death. You're going to be shot. Yup, someday you're going to meet up with some husband or boyfriend." Walter took great pride in our "similarity." I think it was because he was so fond of us both.

Ironically, maybe Grandfather did have a crystal ball. Because as I become older, I'm becoming more reclusive. I enjoy it. I still love people, but I believe that my reclusiveness is a guard against burnout. It's almost a mechanism that I've developed, and when I feel like I'm getting deluged from every direction, I quickly pull back. I hold back my energies. It's almost a self-preservation thing. Let's face it, that's what being a recluse is. According to Walter, Hughes left the country literally because of the nuisance suits. People knew that he would not go to court. So they sued him. That's the reason he packed his bags and said good-bye to the country he loved. People living in the public eye are sitting ducks for nuisance suits. I said to Walter after we watched a film about Howard, "Grandfather, how much of that was really like him?" And he leaned over to me and said, "They missed the most important ingredient. His sense of humor. Howard Hughes had an incredible, outrageous sense of humor that has never been portrayed. Howard Hughes had an incredible spirit that books and movies will *never* be able to capture."

Grandfather used to tell me that I had a sense of humor like Howard Hughes's. I could never understand why, because I have a bizarre sense of humor. I'm not exactly sure how even to define humor. Quite frankly, I often find myself laughing alone. I find things funny that a lot of people are not amused by.

I could never understand why Walter worked twenty-eight hours a day for the Summa Corporation. It was definitely for his love of Howard Hughes and pride of doing

a job well. There were a few raised eyebrows when I announced that Walter Kane's name should be on every
Howard Hughes hotel marquee. After all, he was the director of entertainment. So I had it placed and proudly
displayed. It announced in bold letters, WALTER KANE
PRESENTS.

I had that done out of respect. It was just my way of
paying tribute to a show-business giant. Every night before I walked onstage, the announcer would say, "Ladies
and gentlemen, Walter Kane proudly presents Wayne
Newton."

Walter wasn't the only one to set records in Las Vegas.
I may have been the only entertainer in the history of the
Entertainment Capitol of the World ever to do five shows
in one night. It's known as the entertainment marathon.
Not only did I do my own shows, but I ran across the
street and filled in for Robert Goulet, then, down the Strip,
I went onstage for Debbie Reynolds. I was not exhausted
physically while I was doing it. It was kind of like running
track. In fact, there's a certain amount of charging of the
batteries involved. When you come offstage you're far from
being tired, and you know you have to run across the street
to do another show. It becomes an exciting challenge. I
put my show on early and my comedian followed me,
while at the same time other comedians were onstage at
Robert Goulet's and Debbie Reynold's shows. I always
managed to walk through the backstage door just as they
were telling their last joke. And somehow we were able
to work it out to stagger those shows. That's probably the
record for showrooms on any given night. I did thirty-six
hundred people between the five shows in one night.

The nicest thing about it all is that Walter Kane never
directly asked me or expected me to put myself through
that show-business Olympics, although Walter would say,
"Gee, Wayne, I've got a problem. Goulet's ill [or Debbie's
hurt her leg, or Jimmy Durante can't make it back from
L.A. in time from performing at a tribute for Sinatra]. I
guess we're going to have to call the shows off and send

the audience home.'' Of course, Walter was being a cagey old cat; he knew that if he went into his song and dance, I would say, ''You want me to do it?''

Walter Kane and the Summa hotels and Howard Hughes were my family. Howard Hughes may have been in charge, but Grandfather was the genius who made Las Vegas truly the Entertainment Capital of the World. So many stars should look to the heavens each day and be thankful and say a blessing to Walter Kane.

So many times I reflect back on the discussions Walter and I had. There must have been hundreds, and even today I'm able to draw upon Walter's knowledge and wisdom. Believe me, he's still not gone from me. There have been many times when I've sat in the dressing room remembering Walter giving me some advice or telling me a wonderful show-business story. He's just always there with me, every day. He's never left me.

Walter will always be king in my eyes. And sometimes the court jester. During an arbitration hearing I had with an ex-manager, Walter was subpoenaed to testify. The opposing attorney asked him a question that, with my recent experience with lawsuits and the law, I now know left the lawyer wide open. You never ask a question you don't know the answer to. Well, this young attorney had not learned this first rule of interrogation. So he asked Walter a question and Walter answered it, much to the dislike of the attorney. The young attorney's temper grew angrier as he said to the elderly statesman of entertainment, ''Mr. Kane, I'm not sure you understood my question. So let me rephrase it and I'll ask it again.'' Walter just sat there with his hands folded as the young lawyer rephrased the question. Walter answered it as if he were reading a script. It was the same answer verbatim that he had given several times before. The attorney disliked the answer and became increasingly upset. Finally, he walked up to Walter and point-blank said, ''Mr. Kane, forgive me. I mean no disrespect to your stature in this industry or to your age. But I don't think you're understanding what I'm asking. So let me rephrase it again.'' Walter didn't blink and the attorney rephrased the question again. Walter answered it as if it were an instantaneous replay. The attorney, now totally exasperated, shouted, ''Mr. Kane, I'm not sure you understand what I'm asking you,'' and Walter said, in a booming voice, ''Young man. Let me explain something to you. You can rephrase that question a hundred times and I'm going to answer you exactly the way I have before because I am too old and too rich to lie to you or anybody else.''

Talk about putting a guy under the table! The attorney looked bewildered as laughter broke out in the courtroom, and just dismissed Walter. As we were leaving the courthouse and I was helping Grandfather down the courthouse steps I smiled at him and chuckled, ''My God, Grandfather, what a terrific line. I couldn't believe it when you said, 'I'm too old and too rich to lie to you or anybody else.' '' Walter paused for a moment on the steps and, with a twinkle in his eye, said, ''Yeah, that was a great line. I loved it when Barbara Stanwyck used it in one of my RKO pictures in 1932.''

When I finished my contract with Summa I'm sorry to say that things began to fall apart and it became pretty unpleasant. It got down to ''push comes to shove,'' especially when they realized that I had bought the Aladdin Hotel and was now a hotel owner. Boy, it's amazing how executives can start dotting the *i*'s and crossing the *t*'s. How quickly they had forgotten that when I filled in for a performer who was ill I never charged. The hotel would pick up the band expenses and they would get paid extra, but as far as I was concerned, personally, I never charged. In fact, Summa owed me. So when it came to push and shove at the end of the contract, I didn't like their attitude.

There was no doubt that my love affair with the Summa hotels was over. There was no one in the corporate hierarchy whom I even knew. The new Summa hotshots found I was somebody they couldn't pull strings on. I refused to be the Howdy Doody of entertainers. Nor was I Clarabell the clown. I had basic principles and beliefs about the way entertainers, as well as the public and employees, should be treated. It's called respect.

In discussing the show-biz world with Grandfather, he said, "You've got to remember that a whole element of show business was fun and games and the stars were the beautiful people. And when you look at Elizabeth Taylor, Mickey Rooney, Jackie Cooper, and Judy Garland, you must remember that as child actors they were given drugs to stay awake. It seemed natural that they would develop problems. In those days, school was important, but work is what the studios really wanted out of them. So a lot of them became dependent upon drugs; not so much heroin or cocaine, but prescription drugs. Pills to wake you up and pills to put you to sleep. Drugs weren't drugs in the sense that we think of them today. By studio standards, they were just a means to get their stars to work." I think the same thing happened to Sammy Davis, Jr. I think his life-style became such that he was trying to do too much. In order to overcome his insecurity and prove his worth, drinking became a way of getting through, and so did drugs. You have to remember the social problems that Sammy faced and overcame in those days. While his name was on the marquee, he was not allowed through the front door or into the casino because he was black. Sammy was forced to enter the hotel through the kitchen, and was not even allowed to sleep on the Las Vegas Strip. He slept in the black section of North Las Vegas. Then his relationship with Kim Novak and marriage to Mae Britt literally made him the forerunner of the whole black movement, certainly in the entertainment industry. Sammy Davis, Jr., was the one who stood up and said, "No, I'm not going to be your patsy anymore. I'm a human being and I'm not going to take your crap."

When I started having problems with the Desert Inn Hotel and the Frontier over their dinner-show policy, I refused to let them use me as an excuse for putting four hundred people out of work. It was Richard Danner of the

Sands Hotel who told Walter Kane, "Give me Wayne Newton as many weeks as he'll work here at the Sands Hotel." Mr. Danner found himself at odds with the other general managers who said, "No, we want Wayne Newton to play the weeks he owes us at our hotels." Mr. Danner and I became really good friends. He realized that the length of my show had nothing to do with my ego; Mr. Danner knew I was doing the best that I knew how to make the customers satisfied.

If there's anything that the years in show business have taught me, it's that there is reason for supply and demand. I'm still doing the kinds of shows that I've become famous for and I thank God that I am. People who have come to see me may have walked out disliking Wayne Newton, but they've never walked out saying, "He didn't work hard for us or give us our money's worth." I know how tough it is to save up your money to go to see a star perform. As a youngster I remember collecting cans and milk bottles so that I could scrape up enough pennies to sit in the back row to watch a performer.

If there ever was a show business czar who sang my praises it was Walter Kane. In his office atop the Sands Hotel and Casino, Walter Kane loaded the walls with pictures of motion-picture producers, actors and actresses, and other celebrities he had known. Prominently displayed were pictures of billionaire boss Howard Hughes and at least six pictures of you-know-who. When I once asked him why he had more pictures of me than of any of the other stars, the eighty-year-old bulldog let the corner of his mouth twitch in a half-smile and responded, "You have meant nearly as much to the Summa Company and Howard Hughes as the invention of the slot machine."

CHAPTER 11

"The only interest I have in burying the hatchet is in your ass." Totie Fields was speechless.

I'VE ALWAYS BEEN far too sensitive and I've always considered it a basic character flaw. When I was younger, if someone hurt my feelings, I would immediately get tears in my eyes. I've always worn my heart on my sleeve. That kind of sensitivity was sometimes misunderstood as "sissy" and a sign of weakness. And if I became angry, I would have the same reaction. It took me a very, very long time to control my tears. It was one of the things I did not like about me. I hated it.

I decided I'd had it with being a sissy joke, and that's when I confronted Johnny Carson. Wherever I went, I used to hear that Carson was telling gay jokes about me. I sent him messages asking him to stop. Then, one night in 1973, I was watching his show and during his monologue he said, "I saw Wayne Newton and Liberace together in a pink bathtub. What do you think that meant?" I got so incensed that I decided to do something about it. With my anger burning inside me I went to see Carson the next day. I was in Los Angeles cutting a religious album that afternoon, and all during the recording session Carson's remark was still bugging me. I told my manager, Jay Stream, I was going over to Carson's office and he said he wanted to come along. So we hopped into my car and went over to the NBC Studios in Burbank. It was about three o'clock in the afternoon and I didn't call to see if Carson was there. I just went.

Driving over, I hardly spoke a word. When I get angry I tend to be like the calm before the storm. And this thing had been building for a long time. When I walked into Carson's outer office, his secretary said, "Can I help you?" I said, "No, thank you. I think he can." I walked right past her and into Carson's office. Freddy de Cordova, his producer, was with him, sitting on the couch. I'd known Freddy through Mr. Benny. I said to him, "Will you excuse us, please?" Freddy was so shocked that he left. Carson just sat there, even more shocked. I remember every word I told Carson. I said, "I am here because I'm going through a personal dilemma in my life. I want to know what child of yours I've killed. I want to know what food of yours I've taken out of your mouth. I want to know what I've done that's so devastating to you that you persist in shooting at me with those persistent gay jokes." Carson's face went white. He said, "But Wayne, I don't write these things." I told him I'd feel better if he did and he asked me why. I said, "Because at least it would mean that you're not a puppet, that you aren't just reading malicious lies written by some writer who crawled out from under a rock. It would be better if you did hate me. At least you'd have a reason for your lies. I'm telling you right now it had better stop or I'll knock you on your ass." Carson was shaken. He said, "I promise you nothing was ever intended in a malicious way. I've always been a big fan." And then he went through all this crap about how much he liked me. He just kept talking and it was obviously a nervous apology. But he never again told Wayne Newton jokes. In fact, I even did his show after that.

When I was on his show and talking to him, Carson would constantly look past me at Freddy de Cordova. We had no eye contact at all. This happened a couple of times. I felt so uncomfortable that I told my manager I wouldn't do *The Tonight Show* anymore unless there was a guest hosting it.

Since then, I've appeared on the show when Carson was gone, and I've even hosted it myself a couple of times.

As I said, the day I went for my reckoning with Johnny Carson I was cutting a religious album. What's funny is that I think what bothered me more than anything else was that he wouldn't put me in a position to forgive him and keep my own dignity. I don't like hating people. It takes too much energy. Therefore, I turn indifferent, which is worse than hatred because these people don't exist to me. But if the truth were known, I would like Johnny Carson to give me a way out, to this very day.

I wouldn't be in the same room with Carson; I wouldn't sit on a dais with him; and if the Nielsen ratings called and asked if I was watching *The Tonight Show,* I'd lie. There's no doubt that Carson has caused me a lot of pain in my life.

The stories he told got so bizarre, all the way from my being neutered to my being given hormone shots to keep my voice high. What was strange was that these things were never said to me, because if they were I would have taken them head-on. But I was never, at any time, aware of the gossip that was going on.

When my daughter came home from school and said about Michael Jackson almost verbatim the things that had been said about me, I sat her down. I said, "Erin, sweetheart, I don't know of anybody that Michael Jackson's ever hurt. He's done nothing but give, give, give. I think it's unfair that anybody would start those kind of vicious rumors that have no proof or accuracy and will follow him the rest of his life when he's done nothing but good." Holding her by the hands, I looked her in the eyes. "Baby, you can't stop the rumors, but if you don't repeat them then at least you won't help spread them."

Totie Fields also told some bad jokes about me. I met Totie long before she became a star, and I thought we had a real affection and respect for each other. I so liked her that I used her as my opening act, and she went everywhere I played. I was the first one to bring her to Las Vegas at the Flamingo. She toured with me for three years, and I wanted the Vegas crowd to fall in love with her. Totie Fields had been booked into Mr. Kelly's, a nightclub in Chicago, during a period when I needed her to work with me in Vegas. When she went to the owner of Mr. Kelly's and told her she needed the time off, the woman refused. Totie called me. She was crying and upset. She begged, "Maybe if you call her she'll have a change of heart." So I said, "Okay," and after I hung up with Totie, I telephoned the owner. After introducing myself, I explained that I was really going through a very important Vegas opening and I would consider it a personal favor if Totie could be let out of her engagement in Chicago to appear in Vegas. I told her that I would do anything to repay the favor, even work at Mr. Kelly's myself, and I would consider it an IOU. The lady calmly said, "Mr. Newton, I don't know you, but what I know of you I really like. It is very difficult for me to refuse a request from such a gentleman and it's equally as difficult for me to say no to such a fine entertainer. But I must decline your request. I'm declining because I know that the only way I can hurt Totie Fields is by not allowing her to play Vegas. And one day, Mr. Newton, you will find out that this woman is not your friend."

My mouth was wide open. I was in shock. She finally asked, "Are you still there?" I said, "Yes, and I appreciate your candor. I don't know what has transpired between the two of you and I don't care to know. I just want you to know that my relationship with Totie is a good one. And it's a friendship that I value. I hope that sometime, somewhere, we get a chance to talk. Thank you."

When I telephoned Totie, she didn't seem surprised that I was unable to get her out of her gig at Mr. Kelly's. Two months later, when she was playing that engagement in Chicago, a good friend of mine, Mona Montoba, telephoned from the windy city. At the time, Mona owned the finest Japanese restaurant in Chicago. It was late at night and she was in hysterics. "Mona, calm down. What's wrong?" She said, sobbing, "I don't know how to tell you this." And I said, "Tell me what? Did something happen to your mother?" "No, something happened at the restaurant." She then began to explain how Totie Fields and her husband had come to the restaurant and Mona had picked up the tab out of respect to me. Although Totie had only met Mona once or twice, she insisted that Mona join them. Mona, through her tears, explained, "Wayne, I have been agonizing over telling you. The first words out of Totie Field's mouth were, 'Mona, you have known Wayne Newton for a long time. Is he gay? Is it true he's a queer?' " I was deeply hurt. I had known Totie Fields for three years, not only as a friend but as someone I had helped by getting her work. Now the conversation with the owner of Mr. Kelly's made sense. So I called in Tommy Amato, who was my manager at that time, and I asked, "How many dates has Totie with us in the future?" "Why?" Tommy asked. And I said, "Just answer my question." Tommy looked in his book. "I think a total of about six months." I said, "Cancel them." I told him the story and he was appalled. My brother was going to kill her, but I said, "Leave it alone."

Then there was another story that came back to me from a couple who worked as domestics at the star's residence at Harrah's, in Tahoe. They were wonderful people and a great husband-and-wife team. Three weeks before they were to leave their employment at Harrah's, they were serving Totie Fields. And somehow the conversation got around to me. Smiley, who was the gentleman of the team, was serving the table. He was half Italian and half Irish, and he would fight you at the drop of a hat. When Totie said, "Newton is a fag and his old lady is a dyke," Smiley put the bowl he was holding down on the table and said, in front of Totie's dinner guests, "You're a lying bitch!" Now, here is the guy working as a butler insulting the star. Totie sat up. "No servant speaks to me that way." And Smiley growled back, "If I hear you say one more thing about Wayne Newton, I'm going to dump whatever I have in my hands right on that ugly face of yours."

Needless to say, he left Harrah's a little prematurely, a day and a half after that.

Well, now her star really began to climb. Totie Fields had become a headliner. And we hadn't spoken in years, although she had tried on several occasions. One of them was at the Jerry Lewis Muscular Dystrophy Telethon. She walked up to me backstage and said, "Wayne, I know that there have been some misunderstandings between us." Totie had even gone as far as telling everyone that there was a feud between us because we were both headliners on the Las Vegas Strip. And now there was Totie in front of me trying to be sweet. "I know we have had disagreements," she said. I smiled. "When did we have a disagreement?" She tried to talk her way out of it. "Well, I didn't mean 'disagreement,' necessarily. I guess it's sort of a misunderstanding. I think we ought to bury the hatchet." I looked at her and very calmly said, "The only interest I have in burying the hatchet is in your ass." Totie Fields was speechless. The only time in her life. I ended our conversation: "Totie, I don't like you. You're not a nice person and sooner or later the world's going to find it out. But until it does, have fun."

As I found out later, Totie Fields wasn't the only comic who was trying to get a laugh at my expense. People would stop by my dressing room and tell me about Jackie Gayle. They'd say, "Jesus, I saw Jackie Gayle the other night. Boy, does he do a number on you." And I would ask, "In what way?" Just by the looks on their faces and the fact that they wouldn't respond, I knew he was doing fag jokes. Jackie would never do them when I was present. So one day I came face-to-face with him. We were both appearing on *The Mike Douglas Show* at the Las Vegas Hilton. I had been sending him messages to stop the crap and to just forget my name, but he continued. All of a sudden we were in the hallway together. I grabbed him, shoved him up against the wall, and said, "What's your problem?" Before he could answer, his wife started to scream, "He's going to kill him! He's going to kill him!" For a moment,

I thought she was saying that he was going to kill me. That's the last time I ever had a problem with him.

McLean Stevenson was doing the same thing. He was a gem. His weren't necessarily gay jokes, just dumb ones. Stevenson would get onstage and say, "Wouldn't it be interesting to be a straw in Wayne Newton's ear and blow up his head to match the size of his body?" I sent word to him over and over and over through his agent to stop it. Every time I tuned in *The Tonight Show* and he was on, he was always doing his "thing," putting Wayne Newton down. He had been doing it for a year and a half and he refused to quit.

One time I was asked to do *The Jonathan Winters Show*. I walked into the studio and the show was already in progress. Jonathan was in the middle of an impromptu skit with McLean Stevenson. I was standing behind the camera when Stevenson looked over and saw me and about died. He lost all train of thought. So would I have in his place. Whatever he was going for, comedy-wise, died on the spot. I looked over and said to a friend who was with me, "I want you to go to the back door of the studio." He asked why. I said, "Because I want Stevenson, and the first thing he's going to do when he finishes this skit is make a beeline for the back door." Sure enough, that's exactly what happened. I'm told I got there just about the time he did, and I grabbed him under the arm and lifted him off the floor. He's no small man; he's about six feet one. But my anger was about to explode. I literally carried him upstairs to the dressing rooms, where I started to call him every four-letter word and every name, hoping that he would fight back. But instead of throwing a punch, he sat down in the corner and started to cry. "I didn't mean it. I shouldn't have done it. I'm sorry, Wayne. I'm sorry. Those were cheap shots." What we both didn't realize was that we still had on our body mikes, and the entire argument in the dressing room was being broadcast out into the studio for all the audience to hear. Within moments, there was pounding on the door. The producer came running up the stairs. They were sure I was going to kill him. While Stevenson pleaded forgiveness, I left him by saying, "No man has the right to do this kind of humor about anyone, much less someone he doesn't know. So the one thing I'm going to insist upon, Stevenson, is that you come and see my show. And after you've seen it, then you can make whatever jokes you deem necessary. Or, if you want, I can kick your ass here."

He promised he would come to the show and he did. After the show, he sent a lengthy letter of apology, and that ended McLean Stevenson's Wayne Newton jokes.

During the lounge days, Tommy Amato once went to see Jack Entratter, who was entertainment director of the Sands Hotel. Tommy took my brother and me along, and when we walked over to Entratter in the Sands coffee shop, Tommy said, "You know, I'm managing Wayne Newton and his brother, and I would like you to come downtown to the Fremont and watch us work." Entratter just looked up and said, "Get that fag out of here." I disliked Jack Entratter until the day he died. If he were still alive, I'd still dislike him.

When the jokes first began, my brother would say, "Don't worry. As long as they spell your name right." But for me, it depended on how the attack came. If a writer was attacking my show or if a performer was attacking what I did onstage, I didn't react. When they attacked me personally, then they had to deal with a raging bull. It's that line between a professional and a personal attack; when someone goes over it I go crazy. Then they have trouble on their hands.

I have never been approached in my life by a homosexual, nor have I ever been invited to a homosexual gathering. And I have never been approached at any time about dope. No one has ever tried to sell me the stuff. Perhaps my naïveté about all that contributed even more to those kinds of rumors.

One New Year's Eve, Paul Anka asked me to come over and walk onstage at Caesars because he was doing a second show and I wasn't. At the time, I was appearing at the Sands, and I always did only one show on New Year's because I threw my annual New Year's party. So when Anka called, I told him I couldn't. But Paul insisted. "Please, please, it's important to me. Please come over. I've written a special lyric to 'My Way.' " Before I could answer, he said, "I'm sending you over a copy and all you'll have to do is walk onstage and sing it. It'll be the closing number and the audience will love it." I'm a sucker for a friend. I gave in. "Well, if it's that important to you, I'll do it, and," I added, "if the audience thinks I'm surprising you, I wouldn't have known that you've written this special lyric. So just have it out onstage and you can hand it to me when I walk out and it will be a lot more fun." So I left my party, which was jam-packed with guests, and I took my wife and my manager and his wife and we rushed over to Caesars. When I walked onstage the entire audience in the Caesars showroom stood up. Anka looked at me and said, "Well, I guess you didn't get enough applause in your own show, so you've got to come over here and screw up mine." I glared at him as everybody screamed and laughed. I said, "Why, you son of a bitch." He knew I wasn't kidding. The audience may have thought we were taking polite jabs at each other, but we weren't. We continued through the special lyric of "My Way" and Anka took one short bow to the audience and walked offstage and left me standing there alone. He ran into his dressing room, closed the door, and locked it. By this time I was wondering what the hell was going on. So I walked offstage, and I was so sure that he was going to come back out and say, "Hey, I didn't mean to say that," that I waited around for a few minutes backstage. But there was nothing. He just stayed in his dressing room behind locked doors. So I went back to my party, wondering what the hell was wrong with him, and three days later he called me up and said, "Hey, I really apologize about the whole thing. I had a rough night." All I said was, "That's all right, Paul."

Shortly on the heels of the New Year's Eve incident, Anka made some unflattering remarks about me to some people who worked for me. They told me about them. At the time I dismissed the rumors. Then came the Cerebral Palsy Telethon incident. Anka was hosting the show from New York, and the director and producer decided to do a segment from Las Vegas and asked me if I would host it. Of course, I said, "Yes, and I'd be honored and happy to." They came to Las Vegas and we had four days of meetings and rehearsals at the Frontier. The day before we were to tape the Vegas segment for the telethon, Paul evidently found out that I was hosting the Vegas segment. Anka became furious and told the Cerebral Palsy Telethon producers that unless he hosted both the Vegas and the New York portions of the telethon, he was going to take a walk. Marty Pasetta, producer and director, along with the Cerebral Palsy people, tried to explain to Anka that it just wouldn't look right on television. After all, the telethon is supposed to give the impression that it's live; how could it be that Paul Anka would be in two places at the same time? Anka wouldn't listen to reason and stuck to his guns. At the last minute the telethon people decided to cancel the Vegas segment. I begged them not to. I said, "Look, I'll step out of it. You can get someone to host it. But you have all these stars who've rehearsed for four days, let alone the expense of the band and all the technical costs. If Paul Anka wants to do it, let him do it. It doesn't matter to me. It's more important that you raise the money." But Marty Pasetta said, "No way. That would just be giving in to Anka. We're just simply going to cancel the Vegas portion."

So I sent Anka a telegram. It read: "Dear Paul. Being short was God's choice. Being small is something you've worked at. Forget you know me. Wayne Newton."

I don't hate Paul Anka. I think he's a lot bigger talent than he gives himself credit for being. I wrote a line some time ago and it sums up Paul Anka: "What God takes away in height, he makes up for in arrogance." Anka may be low in sincerity, but he has a tremendous talent.

I do, however, believe in turning the other cheek, although I only have four. Jokey jokey.

* * *

Two of my closest friends in the world are physicians—
Ted Jacobs and his beautiful wife, Dr. Parvin Modaber
Jacobs. If ever sainthood would be given to a Jewish doctor, Ted would surely be the one. Ted, who has a tremendous practice, had both myself and Totie Fields as patients.
He tried desperately to patch up the feud between us. He
knew my side of the story but he'd always say, "Let bygones be bygones." I would always respond, "Ted, I'm
not that kind of guy. The day will come when that woman
will hurt you."

Shortly after that, Drs. Ted and Parvin Jacobs had their
names in the newspapers. They were being sued for mal-
practice by their good friend Totie.

The transcripts of the lawsuit stated that Totie had diabetes and decided she was going to have a facelift. Ted
repeatedly warned her not to do it and Parvin had an argument with Totie about how a facelift would be hazard-
ous to her health. But Totie wouldn't listen. She was
determined to have her face lifted, and because of com-
plications concerning her diabetes, she ended up having
her leg amputated. When that happened I thought, "You
cannot give off that kind of karma and not have it come
back to you." And boy, it was coming back to Totie in
spades. However, I felt sorry for her. So I called and got
her husband, Georgie, on the phone. He said, "Wayne,
Totie is going to be so thrilled." I said, "I'm calling to
tell you that I'm sorry for what she's going through. I
know there is nothing I can do, but I feel that if Totie had
any unhappy thoughts over us not speaking, this call might
put them to rest. So just tell her I send my regards." I
hung up. When Dr. Jacobs found out what I had done, he
called me and said, "That was really nice and she was
thrilled. Both Totie and Georgie were so happy." Before
Ted could continue his praises, I cut him right off. "Well,
Ted, it might be tough for you to understand, but that's
something I would have done for a total stranger. I have
not changed my attitude about her."

Not long after that she returned to Las Vegas and opened at the Sahara Hotel at a big celebrity gala. However, the happiness quickly turned to sadness as Totie was hospitalized, only this time she was dying. So Dr. Jacobs was on the phone urging me, "Will you go over there?" I said, "Go where?" He said, "Go to the hospital to see Totie Fields?" Without even a pause to make a decision, my answer was emphatic. "No, I won't!" Ted responded, "But you called her." And I said, "That has nothing to do with it, Ted. I called her because I considered that to be the humane thing to do. But I am not going over to the hospital and walk in the room and pretend I like her because I don't. I'm sorry for what's happened to her from a human standpoint." Dr. Jacobs realized that the conversation wasn't going anywhere. So he said, "Well, I'm not going to belabor the subject. I love you as my brother; I respect your feelings even though I don't agree with them." That's when I said, "Then we are in the same boat, Ted. I don't understand how you cannot see the viciousness in this world."

Before Totie Fields's funeral, which became a media event in Las Vegas, people were shocked by my answer when they asked, "Are you going to Totie's funeral?" I responded, "I'm not. I didn't like her when she was alive." Now, I know that sounds cruel and un-Christian, but I can't play that game. Life is too short.

In a way I can understand why Johnny Carson, Jackie Gayle, and Totie Fields started telling the gay jokes. I didn't hang out with any of them. My life has always been to go to work and come home. I never went to any of their parties. I have never been one of the "in" group. Therefore, they couldn't understand why people came to see me; couldn't understand why I was still around; couldn't understand the kind of music I performed, or the way I dressed, looked, and sounded. They didn't believe their gay jokes. They knew better. But they didn't know me, and that made them mean.

CHAPTER 12

☆

By the time somebody's become a sex symbol, it's usually the time they would really like to have just one woman ...

IN 1974, WHEN I was thirty-two I had reached a time in my life when I didn't like me anymore. I didn't like looking in the mirror and seeing myself heavy. I also realized that unless something changed, my career was at a standstill. My manager, Jay Stream, and I were having dinner one evening. He looked at me and said, "Well what do you want to be when you grow up?" I looked at my wife, Elaine, and she looked at me, and I said, "What?" Jay repeated, "What do you want to be when you grow up?" I was puzzled. "I don't understand the question." He said, "Look, you're in an industry that demands that you look the best you can. If you want to fulfill your destiny in show business, you have to come to terms with a certain fact, and that is, you're fat. If you want to be a bartender or a bouncer or star as a sumo wrestler, then stay fat. But if you want to be something else, then I think it's about time you thought about it."

Now, I'm the kind of person who will be affected a lot more by subtleties than by a direct two-by-four to the head, but this time it hit home. It got my attention. I had been singing in the same keys since the early Fremont days, even after my voice had changed, and it was a strain to reach the notes. My brother and Tommy Amato were reluctant to lower the music. They were afraid that the reason why the crowds came to see Wayne Newton was because of the sound of my voice. Any kind of change was out of the question. So when Jay suggested change, I was open. I said, "Besides the weight, how do you feel about the color of my hair?" Jay laughed, "What color is your hair?" To me it was no laughing matter. "It's dark brown," I snapped. It wasn't like I was bleaching it because I wasn't. I had deliberately let the sun bleach it because I wanted to get away from the half-breed look. Jay noted, "Well, let's put it this way. I don't know anybody, as the old saying goes, who's tall, blond, and handsome." It was at that very moment I decided to color my hair back to the original color. By the end of the conversation I knew the time had come for Wayne Newton to grow up.

Within three and a half months I had lost sixty pounds. I started lowering the keys in the music one at a time. Movie actor and bodybuilder and friend Steve Reeves designed my gym and worked out a plan with me. He was my inspiration. When I was a kid I had wanted to look like him. Don't we all? It was no easy thing to do. I refused to take amphetamines. I had taken some years before. Only once, when I was 270 pounds and was mistaken for the Goodyear blimp, did I turn to amphetamines. Over the years I had played with diets on and off. Everyone knows the story. It wasn't easy, but I was determined. I would eat Caesar salad six days a week, and on the seventh I would have protein. The fat just melted off. But I believe, in retrospect, a great deal of it was mental commitment.

Despite what everyone thinks, I was not a chubby teenager. It wasn't until early manhood that I started to put on weight. I really didn't start to grow in height until I was seventeen, when I grew four and half inches in four months. The weight was a direct result of my being so very unhappy.

Musically, we went through five different sets of arrangements over a period of about two years. Thank God we lowered the keys gradually, because my voice couldn't have taken it much longer.

It would be a great story to say that my moustache came about because of my admiration for Clark Gable or Errol Flynn. But in all good conscience I must tell you the absolute truth. I was in the hospital with pneumonia and pleurisy, one of two times I have ever missed work. The doctors couldn't diagnose what I was suffering from. I had been working night and day and was totally exhausted. Besides performing my own nightclub act and giving two shows a night seven nights a week, I had been writing an act for Buck Owens, who had been signed by the Summa hotels. Walter Kane always thought I could fix anybody's act. So if someone had a problem, he'd always say, "Call the Indian." So here I was, in the hospital, and the doctors were unable to diagnose my condition for seven days. They had me on morphine to kill the pain from the pleurisy, which masked the pneumonia. They believed I had spinal meningitis. Howard Hughes flew in a specialist from UCLA, Bill Harrah flew in a doctor from the Mayo Clinic, and they consulted with my own personal physician, Dr. Ted Jacobs. When it came to making the final decision, I insisted that Ted make it. But I was suffering with a temperature of 105 degrees for six days. It had the doctors confused. It would go down at night and peak at noon. That's the exact opposite of the way it's supposed to be. It was Dr. Jacobs who figured it correctly. Ted said, "Wait a minute. His noon is the middle of the night. He has lived an upside-down life-style so long that his metabolism has changed." They had a nurse with me twenty-four hours a day. I'm told I was delirious. I would shout, "Get my boots! It's time to go onstage! What suit am I going to wear tonight?" One night, when the nurse went to get some coffee, I took out all the IVs and lay down on the floor because I was burning up with fever and desperate to get cool. All during that illness I didn't shave. Nor did anyone come in and shave me. By the end of the ordeal I looked pretty haggard.

At the end of my two and a half weeks in the hospital, Dr. Jacobs said, "You have to go somewhere now and rest." He added, "I can either keep you in the hospital or you can go to your ranch in Logandale." I decided to go to the ranch to regain my strength since I was to be back at work ten days later. I started to shave, and for the first time I had a moustache. So I left the moustache because I've always loved the swashbucklers Errol Flynn and Clark Gable. When I went for the rehearsal for my Sands opening, Jay Stream saw the moustache. He was livid. He screamed across the showroom, "Get it off! It looks absolutely ridiculous!" Needless to say, that encouraged me to keep it on. I became stubborn and arrogant. The moustache even irritated Walter, not to mention my wife, which was reason enough to keep it on. It became a real showdown as to whether the moustache would stay or go. My girl singers, who had never seen me with one before, were screaming, "Keep it, keep it, keep it!" while my manager was shouting, "Cut it, cut it, cut it!"

Seated in the empty showroom watching the rehearsal were game-show host Wink Martindale and his wife, Sandy, who had been longtime friends of mine. I looked at Sandy and said, "Well, you've got the tie-breaking vote. Two girls like it and two don't. So you decide whether the moustache stays or goes." Jokingly, Sandy said, "Well you're so ugly that it couldn't hurt or help either way." Everybody laughed. That's when I announced, "I accept that. So I'll keep it." That's how the moustache came about.

One of the strangest stories I ever heard about myself was that I wore a frogman's suit underneath my costumes to push in the fat. Some people claimed that's the reason why I perspired so much onstage. That's ridiculous. You couldn't live very long doing that because you would suffocate. After two hours of the way I work onstage, I'd be dead or passed out somewhere. At one time I did buy a girdle because I couldn't fit into my clothes. And I even bought a wet suit. But I didn't wear it onstage. I would sit in the sun with it on to lose weight. But I could only take it for twenty minutes. That's probably where the story came from in the first place.

To be totally honest, I have never been self-conscious about my weight onstage because to this day I could not tell you what I look like. If someone gave me a pad and pencil and said, "To the best of your ability, draw your features," I couldn't do it. I don't *know* what I look like. I know that my legs are long and that I have slender fingers and a moustache, hair, two eyes, a nose, and good teeth. But the rest of it, I just don't see. I don't even see it when I'm putting on makeup before a show. When I watch myself on television, it's somebody else. Some of it I like, some of it I don't. I was appalled by the Nashville Network's special of me on my USO Persian Gulf tour. Although that was good for me because I realized I had put on some pounds that had to come off.

I can never understand when I'm referred to as a sex symbol. One time I was being interviewed and the guy said, "How do you feel about finally becoming a sex symbol?" I laughed. And although I said something off the top of my head in reply, I realized I meant it. "Where were the admirers when I needed them? By the time somebody's become a sex symbol, it's usually the time they would really like to have just one woman that they could count on and care about and know that she understood him."

I don't see myself as a sex symbol. I laugh about it onstage. I've even made jokes about it. I think the one thing that I've realized in my life is that I could never fulfill the fantasies of all those women. While I'm flattered, obviously, being a "sex symbol" just doesn't cross my mind.

Somebody made up a Wayne Newton T-shirt and gave it to me one night onstage. It was white and had an outline of my black hair, two black eyes, a line for the nose, and a moustache. Now, you would think, *How could anyone know that was Wayne Newton with just that outline?* There wasn't any definition to the face. But people said it was amazing how much it looked like me.

This is my right hand to God. I couldn't tell you what I look like. I could not tell you whether I have sharp features. I do, however, think I have pretty teeth; better to bite you with, my dear.

Speaking of teeth, I have always had a fetish about them. Elaine and I were married a week when I took her to the dentist to have her teeth straightened. Teeth are a real thing with me. It might have something to do with my training horses, because that's how you tell a horse's age. I don't know. But I have seen beautiful girls who, when they smile, I want to tell, "Go to the dentist. I'll pay for it." Teeth are so very important. It's part of one's physical being. If anyone said to me, "What do you look like?" all I could tell them is I've got pretty teeth.

CHAPTER 13

☆

I'd like to say that it was a Romeo and Juliet story, or that it was love at first sight, but that wasn't the case.

MICKEY ROONEY DID it three times in Las Vegas. He might just hold the record. Rita Hayworth did it once, but not to Mickey Rooney. Zsa Zsa Gabor, always looking for something different, did it. Even Elvis and Priscilla Presley did it. Paul Newman did it; Joan Collins did it; and yours truly did it with an airline stewardess on June 1, 1968, at the Flamingo Hotel.

Her name was Elaine Okamura and we met in 1966 on a trip back from Vietnam. When I had finished my first tour of entertaining the troops, I was boarding the plane in military uniform (to be protected under the Geneva War Act, anyone traveling with the military had to be in uniform) when an airline stewardess snapped, "Move to the back of the plane." When I tried to get her to look at my ticket, she refused and brushed me off. All she could see was my uniform and she had no desire to be on this troop plane. The more I tried to convince her that my ticket was for the front of the plane, the more she became belligerent. Finally my temper snapped. "Listen, you bitch, all of these soldiers should be in the front of this plane and us civilians in the back, and if you don't find my correct seat I'm going to throw you out of this plane." Well, the commotion caused quite a stir and the purser of the plane came running. He was very apologetic. "Please, Mr. Newton, accept our apologies." And he assigned another

flight attendant to come to the rescue. That was Elaine
Okamura and that's when we first met.

During the flight we chatted, but because she was working it was difficult for me to spend more than a few minutes with her at a time. I'd like to say that it was a Romeo
and Juliet story, or that it was love at first sight, but that
wasn't the case. When we both disembarked the plane, I
knew I wanted to see her again, so I telephoned her in the
airport. I got on a phone and had her paged, but all the
other phones were taken except for the one next to me.
Elaine came over, picked up that phone, and started to
laugh. And so our short-distance telephone call was to turn
into a long-distance romance.

For the next two years we would try to rendezvous
wherever her flights would take her. Elaine was very special. She was very naïve, a quality that drew me to her.
After dating lots of girls, Elaine was a blessing. Once she
flew down to meet me in Florida where I was appearing.
After the show I had champagne sent up to my suite, and
as we sat down for dinner, I thought she was acting a little
strange. She couldn't have looked lovelier except for the
long, theatrical cigarette holder. I had no idea she even
smoked. As I poured her first glass of champagne, she
drank it all down without stopping. I couldn't believe it.
Champagne, and she was downing it like water. I thought,
This is a side of Elaine I've never seen. Each time she'd
take a long puff on her cigarette holder she'd start cough-
ing.

After consuming a number of glasses of the bubbling
firewater, she stopped talking and a look of horror came
over her face. She stood up and softly stated, with tears
running her mascara down her face, "Wayne, I'm going
to be sick!" I helped her into the bathroom, as she could
hardly walk. That's when the fun began. To this day I
think of it as a situation that I had seen in an old Cary
Grant movie. Poor Elaine couldn't stand up. As I was
trying to lift the toilet seat, she was sliding down the wall.
I was trying to hold her up with one hand, and with the

other hand I was trying to reach the toilet seat. The stretch was too long. I would let go of her and she would slide down the back of the door as I was trying to kick the toilet seat up with my foot. Later I found out that her girlfriends had told her that if she was going to go with a guy in show business, she had to be worldly. To her that meant drinking and smoking cigarettes!

The first time she came to visit me in Las Vegas, I wanted to impress her. I had my Rolls-Royce waxed and polished, and I was so excited when I picked her up at the airport. As we were driving down the street, she asked, "Is this a Dodge?"

While it wasn't love at first sight, it was certainly romantic. I was intrigued by her sweetness and her naïveté. She always managed to fill my heart with love and lots of laughter.

One night when she had come to visit me in Vegas, I walked her back to her room at the Flamingo Hotel. She told me that I could come in while she telephoned her sister. Then I would have to leave. There I sat. And Elaine started to tell her sister in Hawaii how exciting Las Vegas was and how she was so "horny." Repeatedly, she kept saying, "When I get back to Hawaii, you won't be able to live with me 'cause I'm so horny." I couldn't believe my ears. Was I finally going to get lucky with this girl? At the end of her conversation, I asked, "Do you know what the word *horny* means?" "Yes," she said, "it means conceited." "Well," I laughed, "it may mean conceited in Hawaii, but in Vegas I wouldn't use that word in public."

Elaine and I had eyes only for each other. We were two young people who thought we could lick the world as long as we had each other. Because that's all we had. Her parents hated me because I wasn't Japanese and mine hated her because she was. She came from a successful Japanese-American family and I'm from Southern poor but proud.

Once again I found myself competing with my brother, Jerry. Without saying it, my parents were always implying that I should find a girl like the one Jerry married. Jerry's wife shared my mother's birth date; she also had the same background and the same basic family ties. My parents couldn't have gone out and handpicked a better daughter-in-law than Jerry did for them. So when I announced that I wanted to marry a Japanese girl, my father was outraged. He yelled, "After I killed them in the war you're going to bring one of them into our family? Over my dead body!" The sparks flew constantly at the mention of her name. But it was fireworks when they offered me an ultimatum.

One night after performing I came home at three in the morning and found my mom and dad seated at the breakfast table. We were all living together then. As I came walking through the door my father said in a stern voice, "I think it's time we talked." I smiled. "Okay, about what?" I could tell he had had a few drinks, and when he said, "About that," and started to use some unkind words about Elaine, I became angry. "Dad, I don't really think you'd better go on like that because you're talking about the woman I'm going to marry." He stood up from the table. "I would hope, Wayne, that you would have enough respect for your family that we would come first. It's either us or her." I stood there devastated. I looked at them both for a long beat, and then said, "Well, I guess you'd better start packing." There was a quiet moment because I think that was the last thing in the world they expected me to say. Before my father could say anything I stopped him. "I would hope that you would have enough consideration, enough love and devotion for me, never, ever to put me in a position of having to choose. But since you have, let me explain my choice. You see, either way I lose. If I choose Elaine, you'll leave. If I choose you, I lose Elaine. So, let me lose the one that's forcing me to make that choice because, in my mind, they love me the least. Elaine has never put me in that position."

I was determined to make it work. I told Elaine that I really thought we ought to work out the differences between our families before we decided on a permanent future together. Quite frankly, I was afraid neither of us could last and I was sure we would succumb to the pressures of our families. In retrospect, I realize that that was probably the most important thing, besides being in love, that forced us together. We were all we had. Years later, when everybody got off our backs, our relationship started to fall apart.

It was in London, England, that I proposed to Elaine. She flew into London to see me and was on a twenty-four-hour layover. We did a lot of talking. But none of it was very positive. We both told each other how miserable things were at home with our families. It was a very sad moment, as I realized that her life was being destroyed and mine wasn't in such good shape either.

She left and flew back to Hawaii. When I called to talk with her, her sister told me that Elaine had been hospitalized, suffering from bleeding ulcers. When I finally reached her at the hospital she was in hysterics because she was scared about not knowing exactly what she had. I told her long-distance, "We'll straighten this mess out," but she didn't believe me. I can't say I blame her. "I don't think it can ever be straightened out." It was then that I proposed. I said, "They'll simply have to do without us." Elaine said, "You mean they're going to have to do without us, not you or me?" I said, "Yes, sweetheart, us."

There was no doubt that I reacted to the condition and the circumstances she was going through. It was an emotional decision rather than an intellectual one. I felt great guilt about her illness. I felt responsible. I knew that I was a total enigma to her family and their way of thinking. I blamed myself for causing Elaine's great pain. The fact that she would endure that kind of pain and never use it as a weapon proved that she loved me. It encouraged me to make a decision. I decided to get married because I felt I was ruining this girl's life.

Maybe I should have listened to my friend Elvis's advice. Halfway through our courtship I bumped into Elvis on a flight from Los Angeles to Vegas. Elvis had just gotten married. We were sitting across the aisle from each other and because we were good buddies I leaned over and asked, "How do you like married life?" Presley shook his head. "Wayne, don't do it. Don't do it!"

Right after that Elaine and I were married and my parents moved out of the house and into a trailer. They said it was because of space. Even though I wanted to believe it was because of space, I knew it wasn't. We had three bedrooms. My brother and his wife shared one, and having one more person in my bedroom certainly didn't take up a whole lot of room.

Though they were trying years, they were wonderful years for Elaine and me. Although, looking back, I can see it became increasingly difficult for Elaine to deal with the tension between my brother and me. Of course, she took the brunt of a lot of it; if they were looking for someone to hate, they didn't have to look very far. So many nights we'd walk up and down the driveway between the house and the barn. She'd be crying because somebody had been unkind to her or had said something unkind. Or she had heard something nasty said about me. In those years she would take that very personally. It was as if they were talking about her, which is also something I loved about her. We were two people in love. Regardless of all the star ambiance and my name on the marquee, she was a wife living in a small house with her in-laws.

Every morning Elaine would put on the same white cotton dress. Every night she would wash it herself to make sure it was clean for the next morning. This seemed to go on for weeks. I'm sure it just seemed that way. And I jokingly said to her one night when she climbed into bed, "If you put that dress on one more time I'm going to tear it off you and burn it." She laughed.

I awakened the next day and, standing at the foot of my bed with her hands on her hips, wearing that same dress was Elaine. I blinked once or twice, climbed out of bed, put on my pajamas, and grabbed to catch her. While she made it to the door, I caught her, throwing her over my arm like a potato sack. I threw her on the bed and tore the dress off her. As I came out of the bedroom, she was still screaming and laughing. My parents and brother thought I was killing her. It was all in fun. I said to my dad, who was sitting at the breakfast table, "Do you have any lighter fluid?" He said, "Yeah, it's over there under the sink." Taking the lighter fluid and a book of matches, I went out in front of the house. I threw the dress on the ground, poured lighter fluid over it, and ignited it. By that time the ranch foreman came running up the driveway. Everybody was sure I'd gone nuts. It was call-the-paddy-wagon time. Of course, that always remained one of our favorite memories.

The first big fight Elaine and I had was in New York City. We had gone shopping at Saks. There was a Geoffrey Beene velvet print dress on sale for seven hundred dollars. When I announced to the salesgirl, "I'll buy it," Elaine started to shake and the tears rolled down her cheeks. When the salesgirl went away to wrap it, Elaine, through her tears, said, "There's no dress in the world worth seven hundred dollars. When would I ever wear a dress that cost that much?"

In those early, hungry years, my brother handled all the money. He put restrictions on Elaine's ability to spend. It was his way of getting back at her. She bought every dress off the rack, and to her, at that period of time, a hundred dollars was a lot of money to spend.

So many pressures on our marriage made its survival uncertain. Elaine and I started to grow apart. After four years of marriage, she just looked at me one day and said, "I can't and I don't want to go on the road anymore." Looking back, I think that was the beginning of the falling apart. She couldn't cope with the tension between me and my brother.

The environment was not a good one. It seemed that everywhere I turned there was turmoil. My brother and I were fighting and a new manager was coming into the picture. Elaine was throwing up her hands when she said, "I can't take it anymore." I understand that. In all fairness, a lot of the hostility was directed at her and the rest directed at me, which was the same as being directed at her.

No matter where I asked her to go with me, the answer was always "No." "Do you want to come see the show at the hotel?" "No," she'd say. "I'm going to do a television show. Do you want to come?" "No," was her reply. When you get turned down enough, you begin to feel rejected. I had learned to recognize the feeling. Love, for me, was the only bright spot I had. From a moral standpoint, I don't at all justify what I did then. I became unfaithful.

The first time I broke the vow was in Omaha, Nebraska. I remember it just like it was yesterday. Of course, the lady shall remain nameless because it doesn't matter. But the guilt trip was very difficult to live with. I told Elaine as everything heated up in one of our many fights, "Look, I will make you a promise. I will never leave you for another woman. I will only leave you when I can no longer live with you."

In the couple of relationships I had, I told the women straight out that I was very married and would not leave my wife. In those situations, each of those ladies gave me something important. I will always be grateful to them, for they fulfilled a need in my life then—they are my friends to this day.

Elaine and I split up after we had been married seven years. I think it was a general kind of unhappiness. Elaine had started to fulfill her own life insofar as she became very social. The more social she became, the more distant we grew from each other.

I was constantly in the papers for something. I remember one Christmas I was sound asleep on the couch when she came in and started belting me with the *National Enquirer*. It should have been a baseball bat. One of the columnists had written that I was seeing a particular redhead. Well, Elaine went berserk. There, on Christmas Day,

I was being accused of everything in the world. The fact was, I didn't even know any redheads.

Ironically enough, the ladies with whom I was really having a relationship were never the ones they accused me of. Not that there is any virtue in this, but at least it gave me the opportunity to look my accusers straight in the face and honestly say, "I don't know what you're talking about," which was a marked edge, I can tell you. The *National Enquirer* had gotten it all wrong. They had used the wrong Wayne. It wasn't Wayne Newton, it was Wayne Cochran who was running around with that redhead. I demanded the *National Enquirer* print a retraction. When they did, Elaine felt better.

But once the seed is planted, you're a suspect forever. In all fairness to Elaine, I don't know why I'm alive today. I mean, some of the stories that hit the tabloids were very untimely, not that they would have ever been timely. But they always seemed to come when our marriage was at its weakest point.

After the first time you break the vow and the bond, it becomes easier. It becomes easier to justify; it becomes easier to function. The worst part about it is, it arouses one's competitive spirit.

The time we split up for six months was a decision we made in Hawaii. We stayed at the Royal Hawaiian and talked and talked. Together, we agreed to call it quits. I set up a bank account for her, leased her a condominium, and sent her car over. I didn't want a divorce because I still loved her. However, we just couldn't live together at that point. We were at each other's throats constantly. We were at the breaking point. The day I left her in that hotel room was one of the toughest days of my life. You want to talk about guilt! Even though neither of us were the same two people who had gotten married seven years earlier, we still had a great deal of love for each other. If I could have turned the clock back and fixed everything, I would have given anything in the world to do it. But I knew it was impossible. Elaine pulled the sheet up over her nose because she didn't want to watch me leave the room. The tears were running down her face and the sheet was literally wet. I felt like the ass of all time. But I also knew that I wasn't doing her any favors by letting our marriage continue the way it was going, because if it continued we would end up hating each other. We could no longer use our family differences as an excuse. Her family absolutely adored me and are still friends of mine to this day, and my family grew to appreciate and love Elaine.

We were apart six months and it was the first time in a long time that I didn't mind coming home. Yes, the house was empty, but it also meant that I didn't have to fight. I learned some things about myself in those six months. I needed my space; and I needed a place where there were no wars.

I had the opportunity to go to Lebanon on vacation. When I came back from the trip, Elaine was home from Hawaii. There was no notice; no "let's talk about it." She simply said, "I've decided in all that time that I love you, and know you love me, and we should go on. We can make it." It lasted another seven years. I don't think it should have.

If the absolute truth were told, I've always been drawn by the clean, naïve, unaffected girl. It's not that I don't appreciate a more worldly-wise woman, and I have a great affection for them; it's just that they're not the type I ever wanted to marry. Maybe it's a character flaw, but I want to be a protector. I don't really believe there is anything wrong with that. In my eyes a lady is a lady and has to be treated a certain way. That's the way I've been raised.

Now, there are many who might consider me a womanizer, but I'm the kind of person who needs to be in love. It's a feeling you can't buy and I am the most unhappy when I'm not in love. It's not necessary that love last past twenty-four hours. I've been in love a lot of times.

Lola Falana was a lady friend of mine. She's beautiful, she's talented, and she's sexy. Lola and I have been on the fringes. We have had a mental love affair ever since I've known her, but nothing physical. She came into my life when she was appearing at Caesars Palace as a dancer with Sammy Davis, Jr.

One night she came over to the Sands Hotel and visited me backstage. She said, "I want to meet this bad guy that I've been hearing about." Dionne Warwick was there and we all sat around on the floor in the dressing room and played guitar and sang until ten the next morning. Lola began to drop by more often and it was then that the rumor mill began working overtime. It affected my home life. There was never a seed of doubt in Elaine's mind: There was a full-blown conviction. She was sure that Lola and I were having an affair. But she wasn't the only one. A lot of people were convinced that something was going on between the two of us, especially since she was married when we first met, and then shortly after got a divorce.

During that time she met Mark Moreno, an attorney and a close friend of mine, in my dressing room, and he later became her manager. Thanks to the help of Norman Brokaw, an influential agent at the William Morris Agency, she landed four TV specials for ABC. They were terribly good shows and she was contracted to headline at the MGM Grand.

When Mark came to me and told me, "We've got big dollars and we're building an elaborate show around Lola," he didn't like what I had to say. Straight out I said, "I'm only going to say this once, Mark, because I honestly believe it. In my opinion, you are going to kill this girl's career if you do that." Nobody listened and Lola Falana's headlining debut in Las Vegas at the MGM Grand turned out to be a bad move. The opening show was a smash, but from then on it went downhill. Nobody in town would touch her. We had all been there one time or another. She was hurting. Moreno became her manager and came to see me. "You're the only guy who can help me," Mark said. "What shall I do?" Once again I found myself being the bearer of bad news. "You're not going to like what I'm going to say again, but the fact is you've got to pull her out of the headlining spot. She is not ready yet."

Moreno was in shock. He said, "Oh, God, how am I going to tell her?" And I said, "It's not my problem, Mark. That's what managers are for."

When Lola was told the truth of my opinion, she went through the ceiling. She believed all that crap she was being fed. They were feeding her ego while my concern was for Lola. When she telephoned me, she was in a rage. I let her go on for five minutes and then I'd had it. And I told her exactly how I felt. "Hold it!" I said. "I don't know who you think you're talking to, but I want to tell you something, Lola. I didn't need you last week, I didn't need you yesterday, I didn't need you today, and I'm sure in hell not going to need you tomorrow. You've got nothing I want, or need. Now, let's start with that premise. Number two. If you have anything to say to me ever again, you do it like a lady. Because if you do it the way you are trying to do it now, I'm going to talk to you the way you deserve to be talked to. Now f____ off!"

Lola went on to become a co-headliner with Bob Newhart at the Riviera Hotel. Within a year she was a headliner. Thanks to her talents and Mark Moreno's, she became the "First Lady of Las Vegas Entertainment."

Meanwhile, at home, Lola's name kept coming up in my battles with Elaine. And it was a losing battle. Over and over Elaine would shout, "If it's not true, why is everybody saying it?" Well, I couldn't deal with what everybody was saying. I never could. When I was the brunt of gay jokes, I couldn't deal with it. Over the years I went from being the boy next door to being a womanizer to being gay, back to being the boy next door, and then linked to the Mafia. I wish I was capable of doing half the stuff I had been accused of. My life would have been a hell of a lot more interesting. Of course it *has* been very interesting, thanks in part to the ladies who have shared a part of my life with me.

One of those ladies who filled a void was Vanna White.

She is the consummate lady, regardless of all the crap that
you read. I sent her a note when her star was rising. I
said, ''Welcome to the loneliest fun in town.'' I adore her
and we are very good friends.

The thing that was gone from my marriage, and the true
reason for its demise, was passion. Pure and simple. I
liked Elaine, but at the end of it I didn't love her that way.
I think she liked me; I think the like sustained the marriage. If we had gotten through the St. Louis situation
I believe that our marriage would have gone on, and I also
believe that we probably would have made it last after that.
Maybe the passion might have returned.

I had been accused of having a relationship with Terri
Utley, who is a former Miss U.S.A. In fact, we did have
an affair, and to this day I think the world of her.

The St. Louis incident is a total, complete example of
being at the right place at the wrong time. When Elaine
and I arrived at the hotel, we discovered that all the con-
testants of the Miss U.S.A. pageant were there. Terri was
the co-host for the pageant. Of course, Elaine had a great
dislike for Terri, having heard from her girlfriends little
bits and pieces of gossip.

I went down to the pool one day and who was five
chaise lounges over? Terri. Now, I've got my daughter
with me and I've got my wife with me. Regardless of how
rocky our marriage situation was or what a chauvinistic
pig one thinks that I might be, I would never do anything
to make my wife look less in anybody's eyes. All Elaine
needed to see was that those people were there and one
particular girl was there.

We were appearing in St. Louis for a week and the
pageant was there the entire time. Elaine had been waiting
for me to do something that proved to her that Terri and I
were seeing each other. Elaine, who hated the sun, came
to the pool every day, even when I wasn't there.

It was closing night. Terri and I were no longer seeing
each other and hadn't in months. And we certainly weren't
seeing each other in St. Louis. The guys in my group

knew that I was not in the best of moods, especially with the kind of pressure I was under. Every time the phone rang, it was, ''Who was that?'' The minute I walked in the door; ''Where did you go? Who did you see?'' So after we had done our two final shows, some of the guys, without my knowledge, decided to get two ladies of the evening. Unfortunately, they ended up in a room that was next to my daughter's closet.

When I walked in, the scene was like a stag party. It was all rather embarrassing and I was thinking, *No, no, no. No way.* But the drinks were more in control of me than I was. In fact, I was too bombed to get out of my chair—and also tired because I'd just come offstage. The girls began to laugh and giggle and play around.

Now, little did I know that my baby's sitter had a glass up to the wall, and by now she had gone and gotten Elaine. They were both listening. I'm sure it sounded like what Elaine thought it was. I stayed no longer than five minutes and when I came out the door Elaine opened *her* door, three doors down, at exactly the same time. She had been waiting. When I walked into the suite, she was furious. From all indications and on the circumstantial proof, she had great reason to be upset. Elaine screamed, ''How dare you do something like that right next to our daughter's room! And with that Terri Utley!'' So I said, ''What does it look like I'm doing? I'm doing nothing!''

Elaine was convinced that Terri was in the room. Each time I tried to calm her down, Elaine screamed louder and louder. I said, ''Elaine, sit down. I'm going to tell you what was going on in there.'' I then told her what happened and asked, ''Now look at me. Do I look like I've been rolling around in the bed with two girls?'' Not a hair was out of place. I added, ''Do I have any kind of makeup on me?'' I rested my case. ''That's what went down. Nothing!'' But in Elaine's mind I was guilty. ''It's her, I know it's her. There was only one voice.'' Hoping to reason with her I just shook my head and said, ''Elaine, be serious.'' That's when she announced to me, ''I'm going down there." There was no stopping her, so I said, "Go ahead."

She knocked on the door but there was no answer. She called the hotel manager and insisted that he come right up and let her into that room. Now the three of us—Elaine, me, and the manager—were in the hallway, and the hotel manager looked at me when he got to the door. I told him, "Open the door." Well, in the interim, one of the girls had left and the other girl was asleep. Elaine went rushing over to the bed and pulled the covers down. She was shocked because, instead of seeing Terri Utley's face, it was a girl she didn't recognize. The girl said, "Can I help you?" It was like a dime-store novel, all the screaming and shouting. Elaine was embarrassed, but so mad that the embarrassment just egged on the anger. And that was the straw that broke the marriage; I guess if you're treating the symptom instead of the cause, it was as good a reason at any.

She wanted a separation. I asked that certain conditions be observed during that separation. One of them was that if she wanted to date or spend time with someone, she should do Erin a great favor, and ultimately me, I guess, by doing it out of town. Las Vegas was just too small a place. It was sad, but I realized that I no longer wanted to be in our marriage as it was. It took approximately two years to get the divorce.

I didn't really decide on the divorce, or even realize that's where we were heading until it became apparent to me that situations of such a nature that I knew I could never forget were mounting. I could forgive, but I couldn't forget. Other than myself and Elaine, and in that order, I really blame some of the people that Elaine surrounded herself with. They gave her infinitely poor advice. I don't mean advice about me; I'm talking about a make-believe world they created for Elaine.

After it was all over, I explained to the husband of one of the ladies who were confidantes of Elaine's at the time that they had hurt Elaine. He said that his wife had advised Elaine out of a sense of loyalty. I told him, "I accept that and I have no ill feelings toward any of them. But I just wish their sense of loyalty had transformed itself into friendship, because it's Elaine who's going to pick up the tab." I believe that our lives, Elaine's and mine together, became a real thorn in some of those women's sides. Elaine and I had survived some very rocky parts of our marriage. I think her "friends" were jealous of that.

It didn't bother me when the banner headline in the *National Enquirer* told of my divorce. I believe people are somewhat suspect of supermarket tabloids, and they take them with a certain grain of salt. The thing that bothered me the most was to turn on the television and see Elaine on the *Oprah Winfrey* show. There she was, along with Jerry Lewis's, Steve Garvey's, and Clint Eastwood's ex-wives. I couldn't believe the things that I heard; what these women were saying troubled me tremendously. The show itself troubled me. The premise of the show was more of the same nonsense I had been through for nine years, between NBC and the rest of the media. NBC spawned the whole arena of celebrity-attack because they told lies they thought they weren't going to have to answer for. I couldn't believe Elaine would do that—go on television and expose our private life to public view. That wasn't like the Elaine I had loved.

One thing in life that I have learned, a bit of truth I never wanted to accept: No matter what your relationship, no matter what you mean to each other, no matter what hard times and good times, when a parting comes, it's always a matter of money. The breakup is always reduced to its lowest denominator. It happened with my brother; it has happened with most past managers; it happened with my wife.

It's incredible what the legal industry has been allowed to do with people's lives. I'm not naïve and I understand the necessity for wives to be taken care of properly. It need not have been that painful for either of us. If we had had the ability to keep attorneys out of it, it could have been friendlier and easier on both of us. The attorney's job was to keep the situation stirred up, to keep everybody hating each other, not talking to each other. The longer they drag it on, the more money they make.

When a wife says, "It'll never be a matter of money," it's all crap. The attorneys get you so furious that you actually feel capable of doing bodily harm. So much anger built up between Elaine and me when actually we should have been angry with the lawyers, not each other. Just to prove a point, I was paying Elaine on a monthly basis in the beginning and it was a substantial amount of money. I was once twelve hours late with a payment. I received a bill from her attorney the next day for $895 for interest on that twelve hours.

I think both Elaine and I grew up during the time we were together, and continued to grow when we separated and ultimately divorced. I deeply regret the conditions that allowed that to happen and I take full responsibility and most of the blame. It's probably the one thing in my life that I would do differently if I had a chance to do it over again. I'm not talking about the end result of it, sad as it was. I'm talking about my own inability to communicate with Elaine when I saw a breach being created between us. I'm sorry for a lot of that. But I have never regretted our marriage, for out of it came the joy of my life, my daughter, Erin, my greatest love in the world.

CHAPTER 14

The minute I held Erin something special happened to my life ... the good man upstairs just earmarked this little girl for me.

I NEVER REALLY wanted children. I was afraid that I wouldn't have the time and energy to show a child the kind of attention that is needed. I was also aware that my marriage was headed for trouble. I didn't want to drag a child through that. It's ironic that I could have recorded a song like "Daddy Don't You Walk So Fast" just three years before my beautiful Erin came along. That song was prophetic.

Elaine may have been convinced, however, that our marriage and our relationship would once again be a happy one if we had a child. And it was Elaine who kept wanting a baby. I think I finally said yes just to placate Elaine because I knew that the adoption agency we were going through would take a long time to find us a baby. It wasn't as if you were going to apply today and pick up your child tomorrow. It took almost a year and a half, at a time when our marriage looked shipwrecked.

In fact, I had moved out of the house and was living alone in a hotel the day Erin came home. Elaine called me at the hotel and said, "You'd better come home." I snapped, "For what?" And she said, "They're delivering our baby today." Elaine called my parents, who lived in a house on the property, and told them that the baby was on its way. When they asked Elaine if she had diapers and baby formula, Elaine confessed that she had not had time to purchase them. My dad and my mom went running to the mall and bought the baby diapers and milk bottles.

In two hours I was standing at the front door as a nun walked up the steps carrying the most gorgeous little girl I had ever seen in my life. She looked so much like me it was incredible, which didn't help matters any. I remember the nun saying to Elaine, "Mrs. Newton, we want you to know we are aware that this baby looks very much like your husband. But we can assure you that your husband never knew the mother of this child." My heart stopped. I looked at Elaine's expression and said, "Oh, God!"

The minute I held Erin something special happened to my life. I sincerely believe that the good man upstairs just earmarked this little girl for me. There is no question in my mind about that. It seemed ironic that Aramis, my favorite horse, passed away in January 1976 and Erin was born in July 1976. Throughout my life, every time God has taken something special away from me and I've gotten to the point where I think I can't take it anymore, he sends a blessing to me. It gives me the energy and the courage to face another day.

As I looked at my daughter's little face looking up at mine, there was an immediate bonding. That baby and I literally became one. If I put her down, she started to cry. If I left the house, she started to cry. Once I went to Los Angeles and was gone for ten hours. She cried from the time I walked out of the house until the time I walked back—nonstop for ten hours she cried. Of course, it drove Elaine nuts.

With Erin, everything was "My daddy, my daddy." But then, Daddy seemed to have to deal with everything, from potty training to discipline; it all seemed to fall on my shoulders. Every parent remembers potty training. Erin was going through a rebellion period. She had been potty-trained for a year when all of a sudden she started wetting her pants. She wouldn't wet the bed, nor would she wet her pants at night, but only during the daytime. All her mother could do was scream and yell at her because she had a difficult time dealing with it. So Elaine insisted that I do something about it. Erin was playing when I said, "Erin, did you wet your pants again?" She smiled. "Yeah, Daddy, but I made a mistake and it won't happen again." As I picked her up I said, "If it happens again, I'm going to paddle your bottom." She again assured me that it was just an accident. I was hoping against hope.

I was having breakfast and it couldn't have been thirty minutes since our little talk when I saw Erin's governess coming through the house holding a pair of panties. Elaine started nagging right away. "You see, I told you so. This is what I've been telling you about. I just can't deal with it anymore."

Just to shut her up and end the nagging, I jumped up from the table, threw my napkin down, and said in disgust, "I'll handle it, I'll handle it." Of course, I didn't have the slightest idea of what I was going to do because I had never before been faced with a situation like this. But I thought my act looked good.

As I marched out of the dining room in a huff, I caught a glimpse of Erin sitting on the bottom of the stairs playing with a doll. When she saw me her eyes immediately started to fill up with tears. I said to her, "You wet your pants again." She began to sob. "Daddy, it was a mistake. It won't happen again. It was just a mistake. Everybody is entitled to a mistake." Before she could finish I shouted, "Go up to your room, I'll be up there in just a minute." Quite frankly, I needed the minute because I didn't have the slightest idea how to deal with it and I didn't want to deal with it. I knew that the world wasn't coming to an end and the Russians weren't in the living room. But Elaine was hot. She said, "She'll get away with it and we'll be going through this forever."

As I headed up the long winding staircase, I looked back at Elaine, shaking my head. "You're making me look like the bad guy, but I'll handle it." There was Erin, sitting in the middle of her bed playing with her toys, looking as happy as a little shitbird. The minute she saw me the smile turned to a frown and the tears started as if on cue. She was a real Sarah Bernhardt. So I pulled up two chairs so that they were face-to-face. And I said to Erin, "Come over here and sit. I think it's time, little lady, that we have a heart-to-heart talk."

Before I could even begin to say anything, my little actress had put her hands together and began pleading, "Daddy, it was a mistake." It was as if I were sending her to the guillotine. At first she pretended to be frightened to sit in the chair. In her mind, it was the electric chair. When I told her that I was going to have to punish her, she sobbed quietly. "The punishment is that you're not allowed to have any of your friends over for a week." Erin sighed, "Okay, Daddy." Then I dished out more punishment. "You're also not allowed to go into the swimming pool for a week." She once again accepted it with, "Okay, Daddy." Then I announced, "You're not allowed to watch television for a week." A little smile came over her face. "Okay, Daddy." With that I realized that with all the quick "okays" I hadn't accomplished a thing.

Then came the shocker. I moved my face as close to hers as I could get. Our noses touched as I said, "I always keep my promises to you, don't I?"

She stared back. "Yes, you do."

"And what did I promise you that I was going to do if you wet your pants again?"

She bit her lower lip. "You said you were going to kick my butt."

Eyeball-to-eyeball, I challenged her. "What do you think I ought to do about that promise?"

Without missing a beat, she looked at me with those big beautiful eyes and said, "I think you ought to think of something else."

Every father will tell you that his child is special. And I'm no exception to the rule. But in all honesty, there's something about Erin that makes her stand apart from other youngsters. She has always been one of the most giving, thoughtful little girls. Even before she started school and we would have guests over for dinner, she would go into the kitchen and take sheets of paper towel and wrap pieces of silverware up in them. After she tied a bow around each, she would come into the dining room and give all the guests this gift. And at the end of the evening, I would have to collect them all, making me feel a little embarrassed but proud. But she always had a way of upstaging me. And still does.

I know this sounds like a dad talking, and it is. Let me share a few more stories with you. When she first started to walk, I had to be very careful, especially when I took a shower. I always had to look around before I stepped out of the tub because she would sometimes be curled up on the bathmat asleep. Wherever I went, she went.

When she was about four she was a fanatic about watching the Disney character Baloo the Bear. The whole world could come to an end but she wouldn't miss that show for anything. She was in preschool and the only thing she talked about was Baloo the Bear. Phil Harris did the voice for the character and we happened to be appearing together at a charity show in Oklahoma. In my briefcase I always carry a little tape recorder to remind me to do certain things. Now, I had known Phil Harris since my days with Jack Benny, and I said, "Do me a favor. I've got my little tape recorder. Would you be kind enough to record a message as Baloo, 'cause my daughter, Erin, is a big fan of the cartoon?"

Mr. Harris got right into character.

When I arrived home to Vegas it was very late, but I always awakened her to let her know that Daddy was home and he loved her. This night I was overly excited because of the present I had for her. I said, "Baby, I've got something for you."

"What, Daddy?"

Then I pushed the button on the recorder. Erin's eyes got about the size of saucers listening to Baloo talk to her. In the message Baloo said some really nice things about me. After we listened to the tape several times, I said to her, "Why don't you take this tape recorder to school and during show-and-tell you can play it for your classmates." She became very shy and said, "Oh, no." When I asked her why, Erin's eyes filled with tears. "They'll know who I am and they won't like me."

I was taken aback that she could be so aware of that fact at only four years old. But it gives you some idea of her sensitivity. She didn't want to stand out from her classmates.

Once in kindergarten the teacher was asking each child to stand and answer the question, "What do you want to do when you grow up?" When she got to Erin, she stood up and announced very proudly, "I want to be a doctor or a Mexican." The next question the teacher asked each of the students to answer was, "What does your father do for a living?" When it became Erin's turn, she once again announced proudly, "My daddy sings and sleeps."

Life with Erin hasn't always been cute stories. We've had our problems too. We went through some real problems in the second grade because that's when the marriage was about to blow. I went on the road in fear of my temper. Erin almost flunked the second grade. One of the reasons why her grades were poor—and I know it sounds self-serving—was because I was gone. I've always been her stabilizer. So when I came home, I was informed that Erin was taking some school supplies from the other kids in her class.

Erin and I have always had an understanding, and that is, if I promise something, I will honor it. And it's never necessary for Erin to lie because whatever the problem is, we'll work through it as long as I know the truth. All parents like to think that they have such a rapport with their children.

When I confronted her with, "Erin, are you taking other kids' things?" I was hurt when she said, "No, Daddy, I'm not."

The next day, after I drove to school to pick her up, I was standing out in front of the schoolhouse. A little kid from the second grade walked up and said, "Mr. Newton, would you make Erin give me back my pencils?" So I looked at Erin and asked her politely, "Do you have his pencils?" Erin shook her head. "Oh, I don't think so." So I told her to look in her bag. The minute she reached in, she pulled out his pencils and gave them back to him. On the way home I asked the question, "Why did you take his pencils?" Erin shrugged her shoulders. "I don't know, Dad." When she looked at me she knew I was upset. I can do more with a look than paddling her behind because she doesn't want to look bad in my eyes.

As we were driving home, I began to realize that her taking these things was simply a manifestation of what was going on at home. She was reacting to the home problems. She was determined to get attention regardless, even if it was negative attention. That afternoon I held a meeting with some of the guys on the ranch and worked out a plan. I didn't say anything to Erin and didn't mention anything more about her stealing. I just left it alone and didn't belabor the point.

So the next day when I picked Erin up from school, a little girl walked up to me and said, "Mr. Newton, will you make Erin give me back my erasers?" I looked at Erin and she said, "Oh, I don't have them." And I quickly responded, "Why don't you just check?" Well, again she reached right into her bag and took them out and handed them to the little girl. Then she was watching me because she knew she was going to get it. The minute we got into the car, I looked at Erin and said, "Erin, why are you taking these things? You certainly don't need them." She confessed, "I'm taking them because I want them."

Now I was ready to explode, but I realized that I was dealing with a second-grader, not an adult. As I looked at her, the tears were right on the brims of her eyes. She was certain that I was going to blow because of her stealing. But calmly I asked, "Now, wait a minute. You mean to tell me that when you want something, you just take it?" Erin answered, "Yes." I yelled, "That's wonderful. That really is wonderful, honey. Do you know how much happier my life would have been and will be from this moment on? Tell me, how does it work?''

Well, now Erin was torn with confusion. She knew it was wrong, yet Daddy was saying, "It's wonderful." As she started to beam from ear to ear, she told me, "Well, if I want something, I just go and take it." When I asked her, "Don't the people that you take it from object?" She just waved her hand. "Yeah, but I take it anyway." Once again I announced, "Erin, this is wonderful." She sat up. "Really, Daddy?" I kissed her on the top of the forehead. "Honey, I could have had the time of my life if I had just thought about it 'cause you're one hundred percent right. Can you imagine what a wonderful world this would be if everyone did what you did?" Erin happily said, "Yeah, Daddy. I did good, huh?" I squeezed her hand. "You sure did, sweetheart."

I left it at that and we made our usual pit stop at McDonald's for French fries. By the time we got home, she couldn't be happier. There we were, the two of us, eating our French fries, sitting in the middle of the living-room floor, plotting and planning how easy it is to steal. One more time I asked her how it worked.

Erin explained, "Well, Daddy, if you want something, you just take it and you don't worry about anybody getting upset because they'll get over it."

She was laughing and giggling when I asked her to help me move two chairs into the foyer. Then we sat in the chairs, facing the front door, and she thought we were going to play a game. She giggled, "What are we doing?"

"Watch," I said with a smile. There was a knock on the door, and when I opened it there was a little girl standing there. When I asked her, "Can I help you?" she politely said, "Yes, Mr. Newton. I saw some of Erin's clothes when I was helping the housekeepers. Can I have them?" Without blinking an eye I said, "Absolutely!" pointing upstairs. So the little girl went upstairs and came back down with a whole armful of Erin's clothes. Erin had a puzzled look on her face like, *What is going on?* I squeezed her. "Isn't this fun?" Well, it still didn't register for Erin. The girl went out and moments later there was another knock on the door. "Yes, can I help you?" Another little girl smiled. "Mr. Newton, I saw Erin's doll collection upstairs. Can I have one?" Once again I pointed to the stairs. "Take as many as you want."

Now the tears were in Erin's eyes. The girl came running downstairs with Erin's dolls. After she left, the tears started pouring down Erin's face. My heart was breaking, but I said to Erin, "Isn't this fun? Isn't this a wonderful world?" Before she could answer, there was another knock on the door. This time came the ultimate request. "Mr. Newton, I saw Erin's horse in the barn. Can I have it?" I said, "You take it. It's yours." By now, Erin was in hysterics. As I closed the front door, I turned to her, "Now you see how it feels. Isn't this fun?" She didn't say a word. As she sobbed, and the tears rolled down her cheeks, I was dying of heartbreak inside. I said, "Now go upstairs and wash your face."

When she came back, we walked down the driveway hand-in-hand, but Erin didn't say a single word. Finally she stopped in her tracks and said, "Daddy, I know why you gave my stuff away." I said, "Why?" Her big brown eyes looked at me. "Because they are poor people and they needed it. Right?" "Wrong, Erin. That's not true. They wanted it."

To prove my point, I wouldn't let them bring any of the clothes, dolls, and even the horse back for a month. Needless to say, we never had to discuss stealing after that.

I'm sure most children find it difficult when there's a strain on the family, especially when two people who had been in love decide to go their separate ways. Although I can only speak for myself, there was never a point when Elaine and I sat down and talked about the fact that our marriage was tearing Erin apart and that we should stay together for Erin's sake. The discussion we did have was when Elaine accused me of staying simply because of Erin.

I tried to explain to Elaine that I felt we were doing Erin a greater injustice by staying together because it was not a happy home. We were fighting a lot and it was not the kind of environment that our child should grow up in.

While it deeply disturbed me and concerned me to think of what it would be like for Erin to go through our divorce, I thought she would be better off in a stressless broken-home situation than the one she was growing up in. At least she would be able to see that when the two of us were apart, and when she was with either one of us, it was a much more peaceful existence.

One night when Elaine and I were having one of our "think we should split?" sessions, I remember saying to Elaine, "The worst thing in the world would be for Erin to grow up and, when she's twenty-one, look at the two of us and say, 'You two are idiots to have stuck it out because of me because I'm going to have my own life and you would have done me a greater service by getting the hostility out of the house, even if it meant one or the other going with it.' "

But in Erin's mind there was never any question of where she was going. It wasn't something that I promoted or that Elaine tried to influence. Erin just looked at her mother and said, "I'm going with Dad." I was as surprised as anyone. Everyone assumed, including myself, that she would stay with Elaine. But that was not the case.

I even expected that as she got older she would say, "Now I want to spend time with my mother." That has not happened.

Regardless of what anyone tells you, there is something about "Daddy's little girl" and the bond between a father and his daughter. There's something that I have never confessed before: I never wanted a son simply because of the men I've observed in my life. A daughter seldom truly feels competitive with her father. Show business is an aggressive business and I have seen how it has affected the lives of the sons of famous men. You can go down the list of entertainers. They either try to walk in their father's shoes, which is impossible to do, or they become lackeys. Some even end up hating everything their father stands for. That's not the case in a father-daughter relationship.

I have great hopes that Erin will live as normal a life as is humanly possible. By that I mean I want her to fall in love. I want her to get married and I want her to live happily ever after. I don't want her to judge her boyfriend or future husband by me, because if she sees the best in me, it's because she brings out the best in me. I would love to be able to help her find the perfect boyfriend, and yet I would recognize a young man she brought home who might be the same kind of kid that I was. I don't want her to go through that if I can help it. It may be impossible, but I want to be able to help her.

My dentist has a little sign on the ceiling, so that as you're lying there having your wisdom teeth pulled, you can ponder words of wisdom. It says, THE MOST YOU CAN EVER GIVE A CHILD IS DREAMS AND WINGS. I truly believe that.

Having my daughter quickly caused me to become Mr. Mom. I never know what to expect and I never know how I'm going to handle any given situation.

One night backstage, I received a telephone call from Elaine. It was between shows and Elaine was being difficult. It was right before I had to go onstage. She was announcing to me that my daughter was a bigot. Erin was in the first grade at the time and was the last person in the world to be a bigot of any kind. Bigotry is taught, not inherited. Now, Elaine knew I had to go onstage, but that didn't stop her. She started to tell me about our housekeeper, Addie. "Do you know what your daughter said to Addie?" I said, "No, what did my daughter say to Addie?"

"She told her that she hated her because she was black." I said, "Leave it alone! Let me handle it." It didn't seem to satisfy her. "Well, okay, but you better do it quick."

There were only a few more days left to my engagement, so I figured I would wait till I was able to spend some time with Erin. I came home about six in the evening after a business meeting, and decided that it was time to tackle the problem. It was just Erin, myself, and the baby-sitter. Everybody else was gone. So I excused the sitter and then it was just Erin and me in the kitchen. When I asked her how things were going, she nonchalantly said, "Everything is fine." I looked at her and pulled her next to me and said, "I think we need to have a talk." Well, the minute I said that, she looked as if the world were coming to an end. I asked her, "Did you say something to Addie that might have hurt her feelings?" Erin looked at the floor and shook her head no. "Now think. Did you tell her that you didn't like her?" Erin put her finger up to her mouth and mumbled, "I guess I did."

"And what reason did you give her?"

She hesitated. "I told her that I didn't like her because"—you could hardly hear her voice—"she was black."

I just shook my head. "That causes me a problem, Erin." She looked up and asked, "Why?" I said, "Do you really feel that way?" Erin nodded her head and said, "Yes, I do." I leaned back in my chair. "What color do you think I am?" She said, "You're white." I looked at her and asked her to give me her hand. Of course, at that age her little hand was beautiful, milk-white skin. When I put her hand alongside mine, I said, "I'm black. I'm just a little lighter shade of black than Addie."

Erin looked shocked as she asked, "You're black?"

"You bet. What color do you think your mother is?"

Erin said, "White, of course."

I crossed my arms. "No, she isn't, Erin. She's black. She's just a little lighter shade of black than Addie and I am, but she's definitely black."

Well, now there was silence. She had a shocked, surprised look on her face. And I said to her, "How about Grandma and Grandpa?" Erin asked, "Black?" And I nodded. "Yes. The next time you're around them, Erin, don't say anything. Just put your hand alongside of Grandma's and alongside of Grandpa's and you'll see what I'm talking about. They're still a different shade of black than Addie and your mother and I, but they're black." Then I asked her, "Don't you think Mona's black?" And Erin nodded her head yes. "How about Bear?" Bear is my bodyguard. Erin just looked down at the floor and said, "Bear's dark black." That was the last time she ever reacted in a negative way to the color of someone's skin.

So I've become "Mr. Mom" and Erin is my reason for waking up in the morning. There isn't anything I wouldn't do for her. I've been through things with her that—forget being a single father—has made being a father quite an experience. But being a single father is really doing something—a full-time job.

I generally get home around three or four in the morning. I'm up at seven. I take my daughter to school and make the phone calls I have to make, and deal with any emergency of the day. Then, at two-thirty, I drive to school to pick up Erin. We usually have an hour and a half alone together, whether it's spent riding a horse or watching television. At five o'clock I shower and shave and have dinner at five-thirty with Erin, Sister Barbara, my dad, and Marla. We're usually finished at six-thirty, and then I quickly change and I'm backstage in my dressing room at seven and onstage at eight.

Erin has brought me the most joy of my entire life. I can't think of anybody else who can touch me with just a look. When I was going through the court battles with NBC for two and a half months, Erin always managed to lift my spirits. Obviously, I didn't let her come to the courthouse during the trial, but I did let her come the last two days, during the summations. She sat there and wrote me a note and passed it to the bailiff, and I still carry it with me in my wallet every day. It was a simple note on a yellow sheet of paper. It just said, "Daddy I love you and I always will." The night the verdict came in, she said grace, which she does before every meal. But that night she added a special prayer she wrote herself. While she's a little girl, and a child in every sense of the word, she is terribly wise. I can't remember what it was like when she wasn't around.

CHAPTER 15

If that show turned out to be a bomb, I would be the laughingstock of the whole country.

MENTION MY NAME to most people in Washington, D.C., and they still bring up the July 4, 1983, concert and how former Secretary of Interior James Watt hired me instead of the Beach Boys because rock music "attracts the wrong element." But the fact is, in February of that year, the Washington Parks Commission, not James Watt, asked me to do the July 4 concert and I accepted. Sometime after that, they told Mr. Watt, "Look, we know you wanted a change of policy from rock groups, so here's who we've picked to do this year's concert on the mall."

Well, around April 7, Mr. Watt made his statement about rock groups attracting the wrong element, and all of a sudden there was hell to pay. Overnight it was me versus the Beach Boys and rock 'n' roll. Now, I don't really think of the Beach Boys as a rock group, and besides, the Beach Boys happen to be friends of mine.

There's no question in my mind that Mr. Watt made an offensive statement and he shouldn't have said it. Incidentally, Watt never mentioned the Beach Boys by name. Quite honestly, there was no need to pit me against rock music. Hell, I've been singing rock ever since the first time I heard Elvis Presley.

A couple of days after Watts's statement, I was on my airplane going to San Francisco and the phone rang on the plane. Nobody knows the phone number. I picked it up and a voice said, "This is the White House calling. Mrs. Reagan would like to speak to you." However, we had a terrible connection and the operator said, "Because of our poor connection, will you please use the ground phone upon arriving?"

When I arrived at my hotel there was a message which I have framed in my library. It read, "Mrs. Reagan White House please call back."

When I got the First Lady on the phone, she said, "Ron and I are so embarrassed by all this. And I want you to know that we had nothing to do with it." Before she could say more I interrupted her. "I know that. Please, if that's all that is on your mind, put it aside and give the president my love." But Nancy continued. "We want you to know we would never put you in a position like this. We just feel so bad about it. Wayne, I really apologize for this whole Beach Boys thing. I'm embarrassed, the president's embarrassed, and we don't want you to feel we did this to you intentionally."

I told her not to worry about me and she laughed and said, "Well, other than that, Mrs. Lincoln, how did you like the play?"

The concert was the last thing on my mind and I really wasn't concerned in the slightest until three weeks later, when Frank Fahrenkopf, my attorney, called from Washington. Frank said, "You've got a real problem with the July Fourth show. A radio station here has been running a campaign to get people to boycott your concert, and some people in Washington are actually making effigies of you and then burning them. People who hate James Watt now hate you. I'm not kidding, Wayne, you'd better do something about this."

When it first happened, I took it all tongue-in-cheek. As a matter of fact, I thought it was pretty funny. After all, I knew the Beach Boys. We were with Capitol Records together. Deep down inside I knew Mike Love and the guys would never say anything unkind about me. And I certainly wouldn't say anything unkind about them. It was a political football game and I didn't want to play. I refused to comment on it. But when I appeared at the Circle Star Theater near San Francisco, I called Mike Love up onstage with me. Nobody knew who he was, so I said, "This is Mike Love of the Beach Boys and we both want you to know that we're friends."

Mike was saying, "I want you to know we had nothing to do with that."

Likewise, I assured him that I had nothing to do with it. Love surprised me when he announced, "Maybe we ought to try to do the concert together." Now I was in a catch-22 situation. It was my concert, but it wasn't my concert. It wasn't up to me to decide who appeared and who didn't. I tried to explain that to Love.

Other than that, I just assumed that all of the talk would die down. Boy, was I wrong. The Beach Boys didn't want to put an end to it. That absolutely resurrected their career. They did every interview they could about it. They appeared everywhere—in *People* magazine, on TV newscasts. If there was a microphone or a reporter, you were sure to find the Beach Boys. I still didn't get upset about them until they were invited to appear at the White House. I thought, *Here I am being quiet and taking the brunt of all this crap and the Beach Boys are playing the White House. I thought the president and the First Lady were my friends.*

Then I discovered that all the Reagans had done was to offer use of the White House to the Kennedys for a celebration honoring the Special Olympics kids. Teddy Kennedy had decided to invite the Beach Boys as a slap at the Reagans. The Reagans didn't know the Beach Boys would be entertaining until four days before the event. They'd simply said, "Here's the White House. Use it for the day and we'll be in attendance," which was a nice thing for them to do. We were all embroiled in this crap. That's what it was, pure and simple.

Just after the announcement about the Beach Boys was made, the president called and asked me to come see him.

(Left to right)
Gary Morton,
Lucy's husband;
Wayne Newton;
and Lucille Ball.

Wayne Newton as a
teenager.

George Burns with Wayne Newton on the Hollywood Palace stage.

(Above, left to right) George Burns, Jack Benny, Wayne's mom, Wayne, Wayne's dad, and Dinah Shore.

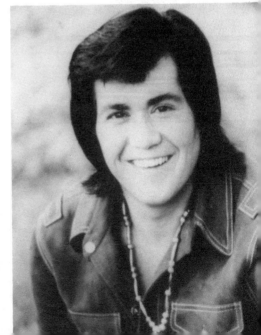

Wayne Newton in 1977 when appearing for Howard Hughes in Las Vegas.

Elaine and Wayne on their wedding day, June 1, 1968, at the Flamingo Hotel in Las Vegas.

Below,
Wayne Newton meets the first president he ever voted for, Richard Nixon.

Show-biz lineup: *(left to right)* Walter Kane, Summa entertainment director; Nipsey Russell, comedian; Doc Severinsen, *Tonight Show* orchestra conductor; Shecky Greene, comedian; Robert Goulet, singer; Glen Campbell, singer; Wayne Newton; and Dick Maurice, co-author.

Wayne and Bobby Darin. The message on the photo reads, "Wayne, I only wish you what I wish myself."

Photograph by Jim Laurie

Jerry Newton, Wayne's brother.

Nancy Reagan gets a kiss from Wayne Newton as smiling president looks on.

Walter Kane, Howard Hughes's right-hand man and entertainment director for the Summa Corporation.

Above,
Wayne Newton with
his father and mother.

Frank Sinatra paid
an unexpected visit to
Wayne Newton on
Wayne's opening
night at the Aladdin
Hotel when Wayne
bought the hotel.

Pallbearers carry the casket of Walter Kane. Wayne Newton *(in background at left)* was Kane's close friend and considered him his honorary grandfather. *(Photograph by Don Ploke)*

Wayne Newton discusses a few equipment purchases for the ranch with his father, Patrick, who oversees it.

Wayne Newton points to his star on the admiral's cabin when he performed for the troops in the Persian Gulf.

Below,
Wayne Newton performs in the Persian Gulf on a 1987 USO tour.
(Photograph by Dick Maurice)

Wayne Newton in his "red room" filled with show-biz memorabilia.

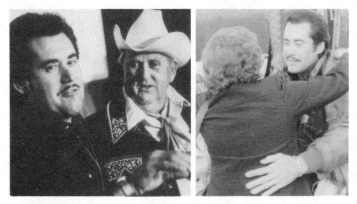

"The King of the Las Vegas Strip," Wayne Newton, with
Elvis Presley's former manager, Colonel Tom Parker; *Right,*
Wayne Newton gets a hug from his mother at the Hughes Executive
Terminal of McCarran International Airport as he arrives in
Las Vegas after a week's goodwill tour for U.S. sailors and marines
in the Mediterranean Sea and in Beirut. *(Photograph by David Brown)*

The Oval Office was crowded when Wayne Newton, accepting an
award on behalf of the USO, brought some friends to visit with
President Reagan. *(Left to Right)* USO representative; Mona
Montoba, Wayne Newton's secretary; Bear, Wayne's bodyguard;
John Fitzgerald, president of the Las Vegas Hilton; Dick Maurice,
co-author; President Ronald Reagan; Wayne Newton; daughter,
Erin; fiancée, Marla Heasley; Patrick Newton, Wayne's father;
Sister Barbara, Erin's governess; and Mark Moreno,
Wayne Newton's attorney. *(Official White House photograph)*

Wayne Newton arrives on board the deck of the USS *Kennedy* to perform for the troops. *(Photograph by Peter Kredenser)*

(Photograph by Peter Kredenser)

Left, An accomplished airline pilot, Wayne Newton often flies his own airplane and his own helicopter.

Wayne, shocked at
what NBC was doing
to him.

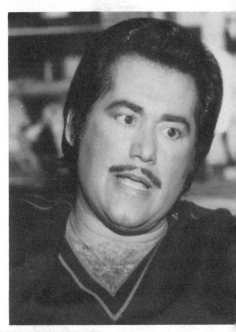

Wayne Newton, his
dad, and his fiancée,
Marla, on the way to
the courthouse to
hear the jury's verdict
against NBC in
Newton's case.

Erin, backstage with Daddy.

Below, Wayne Newton relaxes after a hard night's work in Cannes, France. *(Photograph by Peter Kredenser)*

Wayne Newton discusses his ESP experiences with *Las Vegas Sun* entertainment editor Dick Maurice.

Photograph by Jim Laurie

Wayne Newton addresses a crowd of well-wishers as Wayne Newton Boulevard, the main thoroughfare into and out of McCarran International Airport, is formally named after him. At left is county commission chairman Manny Cortez. At right is Dr. Elias Ghanem, a longtime friend of Newton's.

Wayne Newton *(above)*
was inducted into
President Reagan's
Council on Physical
Fitness and Sports
during ceremonies
at UNLV. Next to
Newton are Elaine,
his wife, and
George Allen, council
chairman and formal
football coach.

Wayne and his
daughter, Erin, "the
love of his life."

I was doing a concert in St. Louis. So after I finished the show, I flew into Washington and met with him in the Oval Office. The president was not his usual smiling self. He seemed very distressed. "Wayne, I don't know the Beach Boys and I'm sure they're wonderful guys."

I was in shock because there was a guy filming and another one holding a microphone. I said to the president, "I hope they're friendly." Reagan, playing to the camera and microphone, said, "Yeah, they're mine," obviously meaning the White House. As the cameras rolled, the president said, "I want you to know how badly the First Lady and I feel that we're not going to be here for the show, and we don't want you to think that because we're going to the ranch July Fourth, we're running for the woods. We always go there for the Fourth."

The president told me the story. He said, "I don't know how your concert's turned into this, Wayne. You've been middled, and we've been middled—and poor Jim Watt, he can take his own lumps, but he certainly doesn't deserve this. I want you to know you have my backing, and if there's anything I can do, name it."

I told him the visit was enough, then I went out and hired a public-relations person, Mary Jacoby. The day I met with the president, I did eight interviews. I met with reporters from UPI, AP, and a few newspapers. All of them were just clawing at me to put Watt down. But I wouldn't do it. I said, "As long as we're being fair, I don't need to be a spokesman for James Watt or for the Beach Boys. The Beach Boys had done two July Fourth concerts in Washington, and if the Parks Commission wanted them to appear again, I figure somebody would have called them." Well, the press took off on me, and I started feeling there was nowhere for me to turn. I got back to Washington three days before the concert, and everywhere I went people came up to me and asked, "Aren't you worried about appearing here?"

In one interview on television I said, "Look, it's very difficult for me to come here to do this interview or this television show because I don't need it and I didn't want it. I am here for the right reasons. I'm not being paid. The government is not having to pick up any portion of this concert. But there is one thing I want to say." I looked straight into the camera, totally ignoring the host, and spoke from the heart. "If the American public is dumb enough to believe all this, then they have to do one thing . . . to show their support and unhappiness of me being here. All they have to do is not show up. The press was right, the Beach Boys were right, Wayne Newton was wrong, the president was wrong, James Watt was wrong. You can wrap us all up because I guess we were kind of all wrapped up together by now. But if the American public is truly sick of drugs and truly sick of overdoses and truly sick of fights and truly sick of not being able to go out of their houses on the Fourth of July and celebrate the nation's birthday, they have to do one thing—they have to show up for that concert." Right there on television, I put my butt on the line. The risk was already taken. All I was doing was verbalizing it. It didn't take a rocket scientist to figure out that if they didn't show up it was over.

Every time my wife and daughter turned on the television or the radio, they kept hearing, "Well, the big fiasco is almost here. It has been predicted by all those in the know that this will be the biggest flop in the history of the Fourth of July festivities in Washington, D.C." The press was predicting the worst. They were forecasting doomsday. They even went so far as to announce that there would be riots at the concert. And then, on the day of the show, it hit me like a ton of bricks: The president and the First Lady were in California. It was called "You're on your own." I suddenly realized that my entire career could be on the line, because if that show turned out to be a bomb, I would be the laughingstock of the whole country.

In the morning I rode in the parade. As we began the parade route there was one sign on the side saying, WE WANT THE BEACH BOYS. Right behind the sign were three people chanting, "We want Wayne Newton." That's the first time I got a glimmer of hope that maybe this wasn't going to be the end of my career. By the end of the parade there might have been a few hundred chanting, "Where are the Beach Boys?" But there were thousands that were applauding and yelling, "We want Wayne Newton." When the parade ended about noon, it was 95 degrees and 100 percent humidity. The leather outfit I was wearing was soaked. I returned to my hotel to take a shower and lie down because I was both mentally and physically exhausted. I couldn't sleep because I realized the countdown had begun. The negative ramifications of that show were overwhelming. The concern and worry plus weariness on the faces of everybody connected with me began to show.

During the parade it was not a clear day. It was cloudy and humid, and as I lay on the bed at the Madison Hotel I heard the thunder start. At about three o'clock in the afternoon a thunderstorm hit Washington, and I mean it was a downpour that lasted for more than three hours. Now I was thinking, *My God. Would you ease up? What did I do that was so terrible in my life to deserve this position?* Here I was, in a situation that I didn't want to be in and didn't deserve to be in, and it was going to rain on top of it. So if anyone had any doubts about coming out to that show, the rain was a good enough reason to stay home.

Just when I couldn't stand it anymore I said to my wife, "I'm going over to the Monument to see if everything is coming along all right." As I started to leave, my security guard, Bear, grabbed me and said, "Where are you going?" "I'm going to walk over and take a look." He said, shaking his head, "No, you're not. There are protesters out there." So now I was thinking that if I lived in Washington, I wouldn't want to forge the rain and the protesters.

I hadn't slept in two days, and at about six o'clock I turned on the TV. With the concert starting at seven-thirty, there was an announcer on the TV station: "Ladies and gentlemen, we are standing in front of the Washington

Monument and, historically, when the Beach Boys and other rock acts have played here on July Fourth, we probably would be looking at one hundred twenty-five thousand people by now. But as our cameras scan, you can see that there are scarcely two thousand people here. This should send a message back to the White House and back to James Watt in terms of their opinion of what America wants in entertainment.''

I looked at Elaine and tears started to come down her face. I turned the TV set off and she said, "What are you going to do?" I shrugged my shoulders. "I'm going to get ready to go over there." With the sound of protesters in the background I asked her, "What are you going to do?" She said, "I'd better get ready, too." We both said a silent prayer and got dressed.

When we went down to the lobby, our public-relations person, Mary Jacoby, was waiting for us. Her face was very long. She had seen the same news broadcast.

As we drove over to the mall, there were a lot of prayers along the way. During that drive I prayed, *God, you must know what you're doing and take me wherever you want me to be.* In those moments, the only thing you can do is to have faith. When I got there, it was about 6:45, and between the time I'd seen the TV newscaster and then, two thousand people turned into two hundred thousand people. I had a lump in my throat. You can't imagine the relief I felt.

Standing backstage with Elaine, Erin, and Mary Jacoby, we watched the crowd with great relief. We were thrilled and in the most festive mood. Then there was a loud crash of thunder and lightning and the skies opened up again. We ran to the mobile trailers that were behind the stage. Elaine and Erin got in the limousine and Mary Jacoby and I went into the dressing room. As we were sitting there listening to the rain pounding on the trailer, we heard screams. "We have major electrical problems. Shut down all the sound and video equipment. Shut down the power now!" I didn't know what was happening to the crowd, but I could only assume. There I was, sitting in a mobile home, no furniture, literally, just a folding chair, and the rain began to leak through the ceiling. Mary Jacoby, sitting across from me, started to cry. She sobbed, feeling that she had let me down and that this whole thing couldn't have been more of a disaster.

All of a sudden I had a feeling within me that started to tingle my body. I actually got goose bumps on my arm. There was a light for a moment, and then it seemed like there wasn't any world around me. My whole body got the feeling that you have when your leg falls asleep. In one way, it was a good feeling, and in another way it felt so strange. My arm went numb. I thought I was having a heart attack. I became lightheaded and almost passed out. I looked up at Mary and I said, "Why are you crying?" She looked at me. " 'Cause I'm sorry for you." I said, "Mary, don't be sorry for me. It's going to be all right."

I had no idea what I was talking about; just that I had a sense of well-being for the first time that day. Within moments, a rainbow appeared over the Washington Monument and the crowd had grown to 350,000. But just as I was about to go on at seven-thirty, another rainstorm started, and it lasted for more than an hour.

All during the downpour we had a huge television screen on top of the stage. And as the rains came down, the screen kept flashing, "If you stay, I stay. Wayne Newton." Each time it flashed you could hear the roars of people standing in the rain. The crowd hid in the trees, under plastic. Some even held the tops of garbage cans over their heads. The harder it rained, the louder they chanted, "We want Wayne Newton. We want Wayne Newton." The stage was a mess; three quarters of our sound system wouldn't work and we were desperate. We telephoned the Madison Hotel and they sent over a truckload of towels to mop up the stage. Nobody left. And I finally went on at 8:45.

When I walked onstage, there was only one detractor in the crowd, and he was holding up a sign that said, WE ARE

THE WRONG ELEMENT. That was the only demonstration of any kind, and the sign went down after the first song. I ended the show with the American trilogy "Dixie," "Battle Hymn of the Republic," and "America." When I began to sing "America," the crowd, without being asked to, started to sing along. Just then it began to rain again, and the harder it rained, the louder they sang. I had to quit singing; I got too choked up. All I can tell you is that it was a moment in my life I'll never forget.

James Watt, who was standing on top of the Department of Interior building six blocks away, heard the crowd singing "America." When I came offstage, there was a Secret Service man waiting. He said, "Mr. Newton, I'm from the White House and I was ordered by the president of the United States to pick you and your family up and take you to the south porch of the White House." Now, you realize that there are regulations that allow no one at the White House when the president is not there. The Secret Service man told us that the president had insisted that we watch the fireworks from the White House. We were driven to the White House and the three of us sat on the porch and watched the most spectacular thing I have ever seen.

That night will remain in my mind as at once the most devastating and the most exhilarating experience of my professional life.

The next day the press did a complete about-face. *The Washington Post,* which really had been laying into me, ran an editorial that said, in effect, "Wayne Newton came here facing a great deal of adversity, caused mainly by the media, and he broke all records for the mall, and handled the adversity like the gentleman that he is."

The two things that I have never done in my life is lose faith in God or the American public. As corny as all that sounds, it's true. They have always been the two things that pull me through.

CHAPTER 16

*Richard Nixon didn't do anything
that the rest of them haven't done.*

I'M PROUD OF the fact that the first president I ever voted for was Richard Nixon in 1968. Nixon was a victim, to a certain extent, of the press being allowed to take over the White House. But, of course, his failings were brought to light. John Kennedy, supposedly, had done much worse things, certainly regarding the Bay of Pigs. Kennedy came out smelling like roses by using his good looks, charm, and sense of humor. In his inimitable style, he said, "I made a mistake," and the American people, along with the press, forgave him. I don't think Nixon at the time of Watergate could have come out and said, "I made a mistake."

At that time and place in this country, the press truly showed its manipulative powers. President Reagan was able to get through trouble with the press only because of his personal charisma. Senator Hart couldn't get through it and Senator Joseph Biden couldn't deal with it.

The press has become giant killers. They are hero killers. They tear people down and do their hiding behind the First Amendment. The press represents itself as the keepers of truth when, in fact, it is a big business. Until we can take that big business and ratings out of the news, they're going to continue to do whatever is sensational, and whatever it takes to sell newspapers. Watergate could have been the worst thing that ever happened to journalism, because from that point on almost every reporter I've come in contact with believes he is going to uncover the next big political scandal.

Basically, I'm a conservative. I might even be more of a conservative than Ronald Reagan. I don't think I ever really intended to get as immersed in politics as I have become. It happened by accident. When I came to Nevada, I was contacted by various politicians and asked to perform at fund-raisers. As time went on I discovered that I leaned more and more to a particular kind of person. I say person rather than partisan or politician. I have done fund-raisers for both Republicans and Democrats. I have gone on record supporting Democratic candidates. I'm a registered Republican, but it's "Give me the right man for the job," Republican or Democrat.

I have some very definite feelings about this country. They are really of a nonpolitical nature and more of a patriotic feeling. In February 1981, the Nevada Republicans held a posh Lincoln's Birthday dinner, and guess who was the guest of honor? My fellow Republicans, including Governor Robert List and Senator Paul Laxalt, said some nice things. But what they discovered that night was that I could out-conservative the most conservative. You could have heard a pin drop in the Aladdin Hotel ballroom when, at this dinner honoring the memory of Lincoln, I took on the issue of busing. Some were in shock when I started my speech: "You that know busing may neither be just nor wise, but it is the law and perhaps an altogether fitting law; because what does it do? It quickly initiates the youngest among us into a regulated society that we are passing on to them. It prepares them for the day when they come of age and find, well, like the bus rides of today, they will continue to be bused throughout life. They will be told by strangers what to do. When graduation comes and they have the dream of higher education, or little things like owning their own property or their own business, a whole fleet of buses will be ready to take them with their motors running, that is, if we have enough fuel."

I emphasized the fact that our country had become one gigantic bureaucracy. "Between the IRS, the EPA, and others, the code of federal regulations that govern almost every phase of our life now exceeds seventy-eight thousand pages. And last year we added five thousand pages."

The truth can sometimes be painful, but it has to be told. And that's exactly what I did that night. "Ladies and gentlemen, we've become a nation of minorities. We've become a nation of catering to and patronizing minority groups. Maybe that's not to the best interest of America and Americans as a nation and a people. We need leaders; we need heroes; we don't need egomaniacal robots; not popularity-poll winners. We need responsibility in politics. We need dignity in politics and we need pride in politics."

Then, in my speech with the Vegas media watching, I launched into my views: "As long as we are talking about responsibility, we also need responsibility in the press, dignity in the press, and pride. I think it's time that the press does some self-searching about what is really news, what is responsible news, what is a fact, and what is opinion stated as fact. What is yellow journalism? What is responsible reporting and what is sensationalism presented only to sell papers?"

The crowd applauded and so I continued: "But let's not leave out the news commentators on television. Watch any news broadcast and you see violence. Networks constantly cry about cleaning up violence on television. But if we take violence off television, the first thing that would have to go would be the news. Isn't this really just another bus ride? Let's not even begin to talk about what the news and television and the news media have done to the image of this state and city as a 'mob-affiliated' place."

Trying to inject some light moments into the heavy speech, I laughingly told the Republicans that I had seen the movies *The Godfather* and *The Godfather II*. "Show me one Indian in the Mafia," I said.

You could tell by the looks on their faces that I had

painted a pretty bleak picture, which I'm sure they hadn't expected from me. We live in the best country in the world. We individually and collectively have let our great country down. We've let it slide, and, trust me, nothing slides uphill. America became great not by accident, nor can we depend upon accident to keep us great. So where's the trouble? The trouble, my friend, is complacency, permissiveness, and indifference. Don't you think it's time we move back to the basics? Dignity, honor, and responsibility?

I'm not sure that the government of the greatest country in the world has been doing anything more than treating the symptoms and not the cause. The cause is anytime you make people wards of the government on a social level, on a farm level, on a welfare level. Their independent life is over. It's done. They no longer have anywhere to go. They have nothing to strive for. Their future is dismal. All you have to do is look at the American Indian.

Don't misunderstand—I understand why the social programs are necessary. And why they were initially instituted. But people have become too dependent on them. Anytime you pay a man not to grow a crop and then you announce, "Well, we don't need to pay you anymore for not growing that crop," the farmer reacts by saying, "Now, wait a minute. I've got loans." The farmers are not to blame; the government is to blame. From that standpoint I feel that our country is in a catch-22 situation at the present time. We can't win unless we get people thinking progress again.

We've got to get people off welfare, and it's going to hurt some innocent people to do that. But if it's not done, we will continue to experience the decline of our nation.

You see why I'm not running for political office. Even though the things I believe are correct, they're not popular. I believe that every politician in the country shares those views if they are realists. But they just can't articulate them, or, for that matter, won't, because they wouldn't get elected.

That's one of the reasons why I respect Harry Truman. I think it took some real guts to do what he did in very rough times. I agree with his give-'em-hell philosophy and his buck-stops-here principles. I believe that the enemy's head has to be cut off. I'm terribly sorry for the innocent people who were maimed and injured in those bombings in Hiroshima, Nagasaki, and Pearl Harbor. The Japanese people are very near and dear to my heart. But if it saved any lives, which it obviously did on both sides, then maybe some good came from it.

Harry Truman was the first president I ever performed for, although we never met. I was seven years old, and my brother and I were invited to perform at a USO celebration in Washington, D.C. In fact, we were the only performers on the show. What I remember most about the day is when they wheeled out a cake and the way the president reacted. The marines walked up in their full-dress uniforms, cut the cake, and gave the first piece to the First Lady, Bess Truman. The president got up and spoke his opening line. He was dead serious when he said, "This is the first time in my political life that a cake has ever been cut that I didn't get the first piece of." He didn't crack a smile and it was a moment before everybody roared.

The first president I ever met was Richard Nixon. I met him at the Western White House in San Clemente. I found him to be reserved and aloof. He was far from outgoing and gregarious, but he was brilliant.

Governor Reagan was there and we rekindled our friendship. I had done some fund-raisers for him a few years back. Even before meeting Reagan, I knew of him as a result of Tom Chauncey. And he knew of me as a result of this mutual friendship. I instantly liked Reagan and knew that he was going to be president. Years before he announced he was going to run for the office, Senator Paul Laxalt and Ronald Reagan came to see my show when I played at the Desert Inn Hotel. That night I introduced

Reagan to the audience. I said, "This man will someday be president of the United States."

Ronald Reagan is a man's man. He is the most loyal friend that anyone could have. If he believes in you, he'll stick by you.

After NBC had aired its slanderous news broadcast about me, I went to Detroit to the Republican National Convention. Senator Paul Laxalt was very supportive, knowing that what NBC imputed was not true. The president won the nomination and was coming off the podium. He looked at me, smiled, and said, "Takin' some heat, kid?" And I said, "Yes, sir." Mr. Reagan reached out his hand and said, "We're with you."

When Ronald Reagan was scheduled for a visit to Nevada, he chose my home for his appearance. I was told by very reliable sources that his aides didn't want him to come to my home because of the broadcast stigma. But the president said it was going to be at Wayne's place.

If there's one thing that can be said for Ronald Reagan's presidency, it is that he gave Americans back their pride; the pride that was lost as a result of the Watergate scandal under President Nixon followed by the apathy of President Carter was restored.

There's no doubt that my political appearances bother some of my fans. In fact, I was saying some years ago that performers should stay out of politics. Let the politicians handle that, and we performers should simply sing and dance and do whatever it is we do. But I've changed my mind. A time came when my country had more meaning for me than my career did. It was because of what I felt about America and where it was going. I went to Vietnam twice; I went to Beirut and the Persian Gulf. At one time I felt that if I went onstage as a performer and suddenly became political, I'd be wrong. And I've never changed my mind about that. People weren't paying to hear me do that. Yes, I've lost fans. But I think there comes a time when being an American has to mean more to you than any personal gain or loss.

In March 1988, I was invited to the Oval Office by President Reagan. The president had asked me to come to Washington to accept an award from the USO. While I was standing in the Cabinet Room waiting to enter the president's office, a very attractive lady handed me a note. I flipped the envelope over and noticed that it said on the back, "Office of the Vice-president." The note was from Vice-president George Bush, who apologized for not being in Washington to greet me personally, for he was busy campaigning for the Republican presidential nomination.

At the time, everyone predicted that Bush not only didn't stand a chance of winning the Republican nomination, but certainly wouldn't be the next president of the United States. I remember showing the note to Erin and telling her, "This is from the man who's going to be the next president of the United States." I believed it wasn't just a prediction. I was stating a fact. It was something that I knew and felt both in my mind and in my heart.

I always knew that George Bush had what it took to be president. He is busy, hard at work negotiating a strong arms deal with the Soviet Union, improving our economy, and building a greater America.

President Bush will make a great president.

CHAPTER 17

No award has ever meant as much to me as the acceptance by the troops in Vietnam.

OVER THE YEARS I've been lucky enough to have had my fair share of honors. I've been awarded the Freedom Lantern Award by the Commonwealth of Massachusetts, an honor I share with people like the late Winston Churchill, John F. Kennedy, and Queen Elizabeth. Other honors range from being named one of the Ten Outstanding Young Men of America, to being listed on the roster of the National Jaycees, to being put in the Hollywood Walk of Fame, to having a boulevard in Las Vegas named after me and being voted Entertainer of the Year by the Academy of Variety and Cabaret Artists. I'll never forget the feeling of being presented an Honorary Doctorate of Humane Letters from the University of Nevada. It was an honor to be named Most Distinguished Citizen of the Year by the National Conference of Christians and Jews. I've even been presented with the prestigious Founders Award of Saint Jude Children's Hospital and the AMC Cancer Research Center's Humanitarian Award. But no award has ever meant as much to me as the acceptance by the troops in Vietnam.

When the Vietnam War broke out, I had determined that I wanted to entertain our troops. My brother and my manager weren't too thrilled about the idea. When we contacted the USO they were more than willing to send us over. We went for the first time in 1966. We went back in

1968. We hit Vietnam the first time during a monsoon, so when I got back from Vietnam, I was in the hospital for three days with pneumonia just from the rain and the wetness of it all.

People confused the idea that I was pro-Vietnam with the fact that I was simply pro our guys in Vietnam. Prior to my second visit, I was in Australia, which had a lot of their own forces in Vietnam. The war was just as controversial there as it was here at home. I was doing a concert at the Sydney Stadium, and the anti-Vietnam protesters started to demonstrate against me at the concert. I went out to see it because I was shocked. I'm pretty tunnel-visioned when it comes to patriotism. When one protester tried to put an anti-Vietnam sign in my hands, I shoved him. As I did a photographer was taking a picture. The next day the headline in the Sydney paper was NIGHTINGALE TURNS NASTY. It's a small price to pay for entertaining the GIs, and if I had to do it all over again, I would do it the same way.

I think what I personally got out of Vietnam, and later the Persian Gulf, was the looks on the faces of the guys on the fields and on the carriers and to know I was doing my bit. I've been blessed, tremendously blessed, with being able to do something I enjoy, and that's perform. If I can be a morale builder to the guys who are away from home and their families, then I've been blessed again. It's important for these guys to know that America cares.

When I performed in Vietnam, I began by saying, "If you want me to call your families when I get home and tell them I saw you, I'll be happy to do that." So we ended up coming back from Vietnam the second time with about five thousand phone numbers. We set up a bank of phones where I was appearing in Boston at the time. Everyone in my group helped. They called on the telephones and got the families on the lines. Then I would come on and say, "Hello, this is Wayne Newton. I just returned from Vietnam and I saw your son [or daughter] over there and he's doing fine and he sends his love." Well, it was such a rewarding thing for me to be able to talk to those people; however, five thousand calls took up a lot of weeks. I was always worried that perhaps something would happen to one of the GIs between the time I left Vietnam and when I got the family on the phone. Out of all of those calls we made, there was only one family that had lost a loved one in the interim. She was a nurse, and when I got her mother on the phone I said, "I saw your daughter in Vietnam and she asked me to call and give you her love." The woman said, "Well, Mr. Newton, you know, my daughter was killed a week ago." My heart went to my feet, as you can imagine. And I said I was really sorry. She said, "No, no, I didn't tell you for that reason. My daughter had written to tell me you were going to call. And you are truly the last one I can talk to that saw her alive. The fact that you did call gives me a great belief in human nature."

There's nothing greater than serving your country. I'm sure that my patriotic beliefs have a lot to do with my mother and father. I remember my mother saying, when I was a little boy, "As much as I hate to see you called in the service for obvious reasons, should you not go if you are called, it would devastate me."

When I'm performing for the troops overseas, I think it's important to spend time with the guys. I enjoy shaking their hands, signing autographs, eating with them, and, along the way, answering thousands of questions. It goes all the way from "My mother's one of your greatest fans" to "I wanted the chance to talk to you about Elvis." It goes from "I haven't been able to get guitar strings" to "I need some valve oil for my trumpet." They want to discuss everything: their girlfriends, their wives, their children. You have to remember that unless they're on base or offshore, those boys haven't been in port, in some instances, for seven or eight months. They want to hear about home; they want to hear that the American people haven't forgotten them and that they're not going to be treated the same way the vets from Vietnam were treated. And you're their link. You're from home.

When you stand there on that stage and see those guys who are homesick and haven't seen their loved ones, and watch them wipe their eyes when you sing—well, it tears me up. I keep the shows on the ships very upbeat, with high energy and fun. And yet, toward the end of the show they always request those songs that touch their hearts and make them cry. It touches me just as much.

CHAPTER 18

☆

Elvis would walk out at the start of his show and say,
"Good evening, ladies and gentlemen. My name is
Wayne Newton."

ELVIS AND I became friends long before he played Las
Vegas. As a matter of fact, I was filming the television
series *Bonanza* on the Paramount lot and he was shooting
one of his films right next door. One day he sent one of
his guys over to tell me that Elvis was a longtime fan and
would I mind coming over and saying hello. When I did
it was an instantaneous friendship. We shared a lot of the
same background. We had similar tastes in music and both
of us had become proficient in karate. Yes, we also had a
similar taste in women. Unbeknownst to us, we dated the
same girl for about a year until we both found out and quit
dating her at the same time. She was later to marry game-
show host Wink Martindale.

Before he opened in Las Vegas, Elvis came to see my
show five times, and when he started to perform in Vegas
we hung out together. We'd go to his suite and have some
of the musicians up, take a few drinks and swap stories.
A lot of them were show-business stories. One of them I
remember in particular. Elvis hardly ever introduced anyone in the audience because he had difficulty pronouncing
names. On one particular night, I was in the audience and
sitting at another booth was Liza Minnelli. Liza had come
to see him, and Elvis, in his inimitable style, couldn't
pronounce her last name and introduced her as Liza Min-
ugi. As people started a quiet applause, Elvis immediately

cut to, "Also in our audience is a dear friend of mine, Wayne Newton," a name that was easy for him to pronounce. So it was those kind of stories that we used to laugh about.

Elvis had a great sense of humor and the ability to laugh at himself. One time Elvis was singing "How Great Thou Art," which is a beautiful Southern hymn. Some guy sitting in the balcony started yelling to Elvis onstage. Elvis stopped right in the middle of the hymn and said, "Shut up, goddamn it!" and went right back to singing the spiritual tune.

Elvis used to love to tell the story of how he got into a fight with his father, Vernon, and stormed out of Graceland and headed to the White House unannounced. It was the first time that he ever bought a ticket on a commercial airliner, and he flew from Memphis International Airport to Washington, D.C., all alone. He was like a kid when he told the story. But, then, you have to remember, at the age of thirty-five, he had never even been inside a bank. As a youngster he was too poor; and when he was older, he was so successful that other people took care of such matters.

When Elvis arrived at the American Airlines check-in counter, he was immediately taken into the VIP lounge. Elvis laughed, "They couldn't believe it. There I was, wearing a purple velvet jumpsuit, a cape, a gold belt buckle, and amber glasses, carrying a jeweled white cane and a forty-five-caliber pistol in a shoulder holster." Because he was the King of Rock 'n' Roll and American Airlines didn't insist he go through a security check for weapons, the forty-five pistol was never discovered. On his arrival in Washington he hopped into a cab and headed for the Washington Hotel. But on the way, Elvis spotted a ghetto doughnut joint and insisted on stopping. He paraded in with all the diamonds on his fingers. Needless to say, Elvis would joke, the customers found religion. "When they saw me they'd scream, 'Lord, have mercy.' "

Elvis loved to tell how, on the airplane, he wrote a letter

to President Nixon expressing his ideas on every issue from communism to Jane Fonda and the drug problem in America. In the letter he told Nixon, whom he admired, that he wanted to do something positive. He told the president he was staying at the Washington Hotel under the name John Burroughs and gave his room number.

Elvis was very patriotic. He loved his country and, since he served it in the armed forces in Germany, he felt a special camaraderie with servicemen. After writing the letter to President Nixon, Elvis started to talk across the aisle to Vietnam soldiers on leave. After a few minutes, the king pulled out a wad of money and gave them all the cash he had—approximately five hundred dollars. When he gave it to the soldiers, he wished them a merry Christmas. Before Elvis went to the Washington Hotel, he rode straight to the White House. He wrote on the envelope containing his letter: "Personal—For the President's Eyes Only." There Elvis stood, at the front gate of the White House. He stepped out of the car and handed the envelope to the guard, who instantly recognized him.

Upon arriving at the Washington Hotel, Elvis received word that the president had cleared twenty minutes in his schedule and wanted to see him right away. By now Elvis had called two of his friends, Jerry Shilling and another bodyguard, Sonny West. Elvis went to the White House, where the three of them were told that they would have to leave their pistols in the car, except for one. Elvis insisted that the gold-plated commemorative World War II Colt forty-five was a present that he had picked up in Los Angeles for President Nixon. Security wasn't about to take any chances. Later Elvis said, "They checked to see that it was empty and spent a lot of time whispering in the corner. After a while, however, I was finally told that I was going to be allowed in the Oval Office." But bodyguards Jerry and Sonny were given disappointing news: They were told that it was impossible for them to enter the Oval Office with Presley because more security was required if more than one person went in. But knowing

Elvis, this was his one great moment and he wasn't about to let security stand in his way. Within minutes the inter-office telephone buzzed. It was President Nixon asking that Jerry and Sonny be allowed in. At the same time, Elvis appeared and opened the Oval Office door. "Come on in, guys. I want you to meet President Nixon."

Every time Elvis would tell the story he always grinned from ear to ear, as excited as a small boy. He still saw himself, in many ways, as the youngster who grew up in poverty and was now standing with the president of the United States in the White House.

Nixon, all smiles, came forward as he shook their hands. There was even a White House photographer who snapped pictures every few minutes. Elvis went into a deep con-versation with the president about his need for a federal badge and how he had offered to donate five thousand dollars to the government's narcotics bureau but was turned down. The president assured the king that he would take care of it. Then Elvis said, "Mr. President, you know that presidential button that you gave me?" Nixon smiled. "Oh, yes," and he pulled two lapel pins from his desk drawer and handed them to Elvis's bodyguards. Elvis shut-tered for a moment. "Sir, uh, they've got wives, sir." The president went running back to his desk to get two bro-chettes. Nixon put his arm around Elvis and they walked to the door. He also told security that he wanted the boys to be given a tour of the White House. The badge that Elvis couldn't buy for five thousand dollars arrived twenty minutes later.

Elvis was one of the guys. When you went to one of his parties, the girls usually stayed over to one side of the room and talked girl talk while Elvis surrounded himself with guys and sat around telling stories.

There has been this picture of Elvis as the King of Rock 'n' Roll, with girls hanging on each arm. It's just not so. It was always a bunch of guys standing together in a little group, with Elvis doing his thing. I can only think of one or two instances where the women mingled with the men.

I think most guys raised in the South are inundated with this respect for the female gender. You open their doors, you treat them with courtesy, you don't say dirty words in front of them. Elvis was very much like that. So when he wanted to have a good time with the boys, he insisted on being with "just the boys." He liked a woman to be a woman. It had nothing to do with being equal. It's just that he compared women to his mother.

Don't get me wrong. I believe that it's been blown out of proportion, this obsession Elvis Presley supposedly had for his mother. I mean, it's not uncommon for an only son who is also an only child to think about his mother in loving terms. I know a lot of people in the world who are a lot worse about their mothers than Elvis ever was. I don't think Elvis could have become the performer and man he was if that momma's-boy thing were true.

I think that when Elvis first came to Las Vegas he cared about his fans and about giving them the best performance he could, and it showed in everything that he did. But he started to care less and less as his personal life deteriorated, and anytime a guy is hurting, he does one of two things: He either opens up and talks about it, or he withdraws and puts up a façade because he doesn't want anybody to think he's vulnerable. Elvis withdrew.

In addition to being good friends, Elvis and I had professional respect for each other. We used to come to each other's shows at least once a year, and Elvis would walk out at the start of his show and say, "Good evening, ladies and gentlemen. My name is Wayne Newton." I was one of the few people he came to see perform. I loved Elvis and we stayed close, until he really started to have a drug problem.

The next-to-last time I ever saw him perform was three years before he died. Watching him that night I got so depressed that I sat there in the showroom and cried. I couldn't believe what had happened to the man I loved as a friend. I couldn't believe his deterioration. Elvis probably had been the most handsome man I'd ever seen, but that night he looked terribly out of shape and overweight. You could barely see his eyes; he must have weighed a good 280 pounds. He phoned in his act that night—he seemed completely indifferent to the audience and didn't care, or wasn't able to care about his work at that point. Then, when I went backstage, he spent more than two hours being concerned about me: What was I doing; was I healthy; was I working too hard? I understood about every third word. When we left, I told my wife I wasn't going to see Elvis perform ever again.

I broke that vow when I got a call from Elvis. The last time he sang in Las Vegas he telephoned and said, "You haven't been over, Chief," so I said okay and went to see his show. But I didn't want to go because I loved my friend and didn't want to see his decline. Once again as I watched him I found myself with tears in my eyes. It turned out to be the saddest thing I've ever seen onstage. It was obvious to me that this was Elvis's swan song because practically every song he sang was a way of saying good-bye: "My Way," "Lord, This Time You Gave Me a Mountain," "Just a Closer Walk with Thee." He must have done nine of these songs. He was saying good-bye to the world. Anyone who was tuned in had to realize he'd had it. I don't think Elvis saw anything in his future that would bring him happiness. And I believe the drugs were just a way out. Instead of putting a gun in his mouth he did it the slow way.

I think his mental attitude contributed to the weight problem. But his mental outlook was brought on because he thought people had betrayed him. Like myself, loyalty was everything to Elvis. When those guys wrote the book about him, the guys he had trusted and grown up with, it was as if they had knifed him in the back. They might as well have stabbed him to death, for Elvis realized that if you couldn't trust your friends, who could you trust?

When the show was over his Vegas doctor told me that Elvis wanted to see me. I went backstage. There were about sixty people in the outer room. Elvis opened the door and said, "I want to see Wayne." I went into the small back room, the size of a closet. Just the two of us. His eyes were blood-red. He mumbled through a whole dissertation about going home, about his daughter and how much he loved her. This went on for nearly three hours. I got up to leave three or four times, but he asked me to stay, saying he needed to talk to me. I couldn't leave, but it truly hurt to see him that way. I told him to get rest, to take care of himself, and to keep going on. Just then he suddenly looked up for a moment, clear-headed, really seeing me, and said, "Good-bye, Chief." Nothing more. Three months later he was dead.

I understood what Elvis was going through, that he had had it all. Elvis had felt all he had wanted to feel. He had gone everywhere he had wanted to go and now it was done. It frightened me that I understand that so well.

I remember August 16, 1977. I had gone to my ranch at Logandale to show some people some horses. We were walking around when a ranch hand came running over to me. He said there was an emergency telephone call. I went to the phone and when I picked it up an associate said, "It's Elvis." He didn't have to say anything more, for I knew what he meant. But he added, "I'd thought you'd want to know that Elvis just died." I was in shock the rest of the day. I went to work that night and the telephone rang in my dressing room. It was Elvis's father calling. He asked me if I would sing onstage "If I Can Dream," which was one of Elvis's favorite songs. He openly wept as he apologized for some of the things that had gone down in his mind; things that had kept Elvis and I from spending more time together as friends.

Vernon knew that the distance that had come between us was due to influences that surrounded Elvis. For example, for the last year and a half of his life, when I would telephone Elvis, I would almost repeatedly get the same response. One of the guys, whoever picked up the phone, would say, "Elvis is in the shower"; "Elvis is sleeping"; "Elvis is getting ready to go onstage." There was always an excuse why I couldn't talk with my friend. It got to the point where I believed that Elvis didn't want to talk to me. Now, I'm not one of those people—and Elvis and his dad knew it—who would ever call and ask a favor of Elvis. But I still couldn't get through. The last time I saw him, I said, "I tried to reach you." Elvis mumbled, "I know, I know."

Strangely enough, I know from my own standpoint how many people try to call me and never get through. They call not because they want something but just to say hello. And whoever picks up the telephone in the dressing room or at home decides who does or does not talk to me. It depends upon their mood whether or not I get the phone call or message that someone has been trying to reach me. So, in a way, I understood why I could not reach Elvis.

While bodyguards sheltered him, they probably thought they were protecting him. But all they were doing was forcing him to become more and more a recluse.

Elvis, as a performer and as a person, was not getting the feedback he needed from those who had nothing to gain from him but friendship. It was as if his people had cut him off from the world. Deep down inside Elvis was a lonely man who felt betrayed and abandoned. He found himself going from his dressing room to the showroom, coming alive onstage, only to return to the isolation of his hotel room. If anything drove Elvis to drugs, it was loneliness. I don't think there was any way around it. When you're that isolated it can be hell. Of the people in his crowd, Elvis Presley was the only loner. The others could go out and have fun. They had a separate life away from the stage. Elvis began to suffer the Howard Hughes syndrome. He became a prisoner of his own people.

I cannot cast any stones, for I am guilty of falling into the same trap. I think that I do not consciously allow that to happen, but anytime you've got people accepting phone calls and reading your mail, you're in danger. I have not gotten a letter from anybody in the last ten years that has not been previously opened.

I didn't go to Elvis's funeral, and I told Elvis's dad that I wouldn't go. I was afraid it would be a zoo. I didn't want to be party to any of that spectacle. I couldn't take a three-ring circus. I went to his grave a month later. When he died I lost not only a member of my family but also a hero, because he was the guy who opened the door for guys like me.

What I've learned from departed friends is what they might never have understood; it's the audience who gives you your image, and you can never really be what they think you are. If you try you end up distorting yourself, and then you start to need the booze and pills. You become afraid of change. Your audience might not understand that you have to change. So one day you wake up and discover you're forty years old and still doing the same old act you were doing at twenty, only it's no longer believable. We become caricatures of ourselves and we die.

If you have a very close friend, the last thing you ever think about is that one day they'll be gone. If you have a picture of that person, then that's fine. But I don't need Elvis's picture to feel his presence.

You have to understand that Elvis had hit it big when I was still in high school. One of the girls wrote me a note when I left school to begin my career performing in Vegas. She wrote, "One day you'll be on the same stage with Elvis Presley." I've often reflected on that statement.

Elvis Presley performed at the Las Vegas Hilton, where I perform, sharing the same stage, the same dressing room, and the same hotel suite. The Hilton could be a problem for me if I allowed it to be, not only because of my love for Elvis but because it was also the last place that Bobby Darin worked.

It's eerie. I have never been into the supernatural to any great extent, yet there are things that are unexplainable. I've never confessed this to anyone, but I actually saw the ghost of Elvis once. It happened during an engagement while I was singing "Are You Lonesome Tonight?" Just as I began I caught a flash in my eye like a camera bulb from the balcony and I saw an image of Elvis. Incredibly, the apparition was wearing the same outfit depicted on a statue of Elvis in the Hilton lobby. Talk about goose bumps, what do you say when that kind of thing happens?

I've often asked myself why Elvis is reaching out to me. I think the answer lies in our last conversation before he died. He told me, "I don't know how many songs I've got left to sing. Just remember it's yours now. It's all yours."

The Priscilla Presley whom Elvis introduced me to and the one we see on *Dallas* are not the same person. There's no resemblance between the two. I thought Elvis and Priscilla made a very handsome couple. She seemed to be everything he needed. She catered to him. I liked Priscilla a lot. But I don't like some of the things she has done.

Priscilla says that Elvis really didn't want to live beyond forty, that he had planted this seed in his mind. Well, if I had to live the way he was living, I probably wouldn't want to live past forty either. Everything is relative, isn't it? From the movies and books, one is given the impression that Elvis was stupid. They have attempted to portray Elvis as this "geek" running around with black sunglasses on, wearing capes. But you've got to remember that you're seeing him from the viewpoint of others. He's the only one who didn't write a book and do a movie about himself.

CHAPTER 19

That separation with my brother was no different than any divorce. . . . Blood is thicker than water, only if it doesn't run green.

THERE IS SOME truth that you are your brother's keeper. There is a bond between brothers that even is stronger than a marriage. But my brother Jerry's problem is with me. I don't have one with him. And it's something that I'm certain started in our childhood. There are things that I would like to say to Jerry that I will probably never get a chance to say any other way than in this book. I think Jerry views me as having been a success at his expense. Jerry blames the world for his personal failures and maybe he always did, but I was just too close to the trees to see the forest. He's always been like an acorn that's been unable to blossom into a tree.

Jerry got involved with a Tennessee bank and ended up owning a percentage of it. He borrowed money from a bank whose president happened to be one of his closest friends. There wasn't anything really illegal that went on, except that they got caught at a time when all the interest rates were up. They had money. For example, Jerry had a pipe-fitting place and a car dealership. He would take out a loan when he was already over his limit. So they'd say, "Well, bring in a friend who will co-sign."

But when interest rates went up, Jerry couldn't make his payments. So the bank was lending him money to make payments back to them. When all that happened, the Federal Home Loan Bank came in, and while they really didn't

174

want my brother, they wanted to go after the president of the bank. So they compromised. The district attorney got him to spill the beans on my brother. My brother wouldn't have gone to jail if he had told on the other two guys. And that's the way they won.

My mother couldn't cope with any of it. She didn't believe he did it. She wouldn't believe anything about it.

So-called friends would bring up the incident and ask me how embarrassed I was. I can't tell you how many people sent me the *National Enquirer* with Jerry's picture and the story. That didn't embarrass me as much as you might have thought. I was embarrassed for him because I was embarrassed for his family. I felt that anybody who knew me would know that I would not be involved with those kinds of problems.

I honestly believe that Jerry might not have been sent away to jail if he had not had the Newton name to bear on his shoulders. So I think from that standpoint, having me as a brother worked against him. They held Jerry up for ridicule because he was Wayne Newton's brother. They used him as an example out of viciousness. Their attitude became "Let's get him because he must be part of the rich and famous." I really believe that to that extent my brother was persecuted.

The truth of the matter is that if my brother could find any happiness, if he could take all that crap and put it behind him and be happy, it would have been worth it all. But he hasn't found happiness so far, and I don't think he will until he accomplishes something of a major significance on his own.

It's tough to walk in your brother's footsteps, particularly for an older brother. It probably would have been much easier for Jerry if he were younger than I.

When he was in prison he wrote me a couple of letters that were beautiful, and I'll always treasure them. But those feelings were things of the moment and are fleeting for my brother.

Even before he was sentenced I wrote a four-page letter

to the judge, the Honorable R. Allan Edgar of Tennessee. Jerry was indicted on ten counts of bank fraud. He pleaded guilty to two of those counts and the others were dropped when he agreed to testify against his alleged co-conspirator in the case, the bank's ex-president. In my letter I told the judge, "Jerry is not a bad guy, much less a criminal. . . . In school, Jerry was a good student and worked very hard to maintain his grades. Nothing seemed to come easy for him.

"Because of his intense pride, his homework would run early into the morning . . . and that left little or no time to play or just be a kid. Because between work and school, there was no time.

"Our dad started working sixteen to eighteen hours a day as an auto mechanic while Jerry worked two and three jobs a day, one of which was cleaning garbage cans for a local grocery chain mornings before school."

In my letter I tried to make it clear to the judge how important Jerry's influence had been on me when we started performing together as teenagers in Las Vegas. "I often reflect on those days, and now realize the possible negative influences and problems two teenage boys alone in the fast lane could have gotten into. It was always Jerry who made sure we stayed on the straight and narrow.

"As you can see, Jerry's pride and sense of responsibility was not only in our own family, but for this great country of America and all the people in it."

I went on to describe Jerry standing at the grave of our mother. "I was looking at the pain in his face, and hearing him say, 'Mom, if you only knew how much I miss you. Can you ever forgive me for the shame I've brought to our family?'

"Yes, Jerry made an error in judgment. He trusted the wrong people. But, my God, haven't we all at one time or another?

"Your Honor, if all the good Jerry has done for others his entire life is ever to count, let it count now, when he needs it most. To incarcerate him will serve no positive purpose for society, our government, or Jerry Newton.''

My plea fell on deaf ears. Judge Edgar sentenced my brother to six years in prison.

Fortunately, Jerry was paroled a lot sooner and didn't have to serve his entire sentence.

I found out that he was getting out a month before he even told his son. And Jerry knew it. He finally told his son about three days before he actually left prison. I was going to send my plane to pick him up, but his wife wanted to meet him and they decided they wanted to drive back. I rented a car for them. And then I waited to hear that he had arrived home safely. But Jerry never called. He got out in January and I didn't hear anything until my birthday, which is in April. He telephoned and said he'd come over to the house to wish me a happy birthday. While I was out working around the ranch, he left a message for me to call him. He could have called long before then to say he was okay, because he knows I care.

Believe me, it hurts. I don't know why he has this thing, but whatever it is, it's his; it's not mine. I have recently come to that conclusion, and it took years. I did everything in my power.

I've tried to look at it from every angle. I've tried to justify his feelings for me, and have probably spent more time thinking about Jerry than he's ever thought about me. To my mother, Jerry was always the apple of her eye, and I quickly realized that early on. Oh, it hurt me. Sure it hurt me! As a child I couldn't understand it. I tried so hard for her acceptance and love, but Jerry always came first. He could do no wrong. I think perhaps because of that I leaned so much to animals and spent so much time with them. Even today I love them for their loyalty and the love they give back. They ask for nothing and give a lot.

As I grew older I realized that the firstborn is really a hard position to fight. And I look at my own daughter, Erin, and when people ask, ''Don't you want more chil-

dren?'' my answer is always no. I don't think I could feel
the same way about another child, and while I could love
another child, or many, it's just not the same. The first
time you go through that is like no other first time in life.
There's nothing to compare to that feeling. And yes, in-
tellectually I understood my mother's feelings for Jerry,
but emotionally it hurt my feelings.

I remember saying to my mother once when we got into
some heated words over Jerry, "If I could, I would give
Jerry whatever I had in the way of talent in exchange for
the love and acceptance you gave him." I told her, "I
would be absolutely happy and content to have been Jerry
Newton's brother with none of the problems of being a
star, and none of the pressures one has to deal with. I
would have been thrilled if he had become the headliner.
I would do it in a flash, but you know I can't. And you
can't hate me because I can't."

My mother took it all wrong. To her, she never showed
any favoritism, though it was obvious to most everybody
else. It was never obvious to her.

I'm sure that Jerry was devastated when Bobby Darin
suggested and insisted the name of the act be changed
from the "Newton Brothers" to "Wayne Newton."

I contributed to many of the problems because I didn't
want to hurt Jerry's feelings. If I was going to do an acting
show, such as *The Lucy Show*, I always insisted that part
of the deal was they use my brother or I wouldn't do the
show. When the act became just Wayne Newton, I became
more sensitive to Jerry because I didn't want him to think
I was trying to take over the whole show. I didn't want
that, but Jerry, I think, thought I did.

Jerry went through a phase for about six years when he
hated show business. He'd tell people that he was only
doing it to make a living and when he made enough he
was going to quit. If he said it once he said it a thousand
times. His quitting show business, or at least threatening
to, could have been a defense mechanism, so that when
we did split, he could feel it was just what he always

wanted. His attitude was "I don't ever want to see another guitar. I never want to be around show business. I hate show people. They are phony bastards." He felt that anything to do with show business was distasteful. Perhaps what he really felt was "I'll leave it before it leaves me."

It became stressful. He was going to quit every other night because of anything I said or did that he didn't like. And then he'd quit. The next day we'd be right back to square one. I could have handled it if he had quit. At least that would have been something to deal with instead of the threats and uncertainty every day.

It got to the point in the late sixties where, no matter what I was doing onstage, he would either interrupt or make jokes about it. When my back was to him, he would do anything for no rhyme or reason. It just got to be ridiculous. I knew that I was going to end up with a nervous breakdown. Being the perfectionist that I am, it was driving me crazy; I realized that I could no longer be effective onstage because he was sitting behind me cutting up.

I think that's the most depressed I've ever been. I tried to eat myself out of the depression, which only made matters worse.

Here I was, almost thirty years old, and I was onstage playing the naïve, wide-eyed, innocent kid every time Jerry said something that was a double entendre. I'd give him one of those "what-do-you-mean-by-that?" looks and the audience would roar. While they were laughing, I was tormented inside. I couldn't play that role anymore. That wasn't me anymore. I was no longer a singer onstage; I was an actor who sang and the role was choking me. The very thing that I needed to survive was my own creativity, which was being eroded by Jerry's "I quit." Then, one night it was over. I simply went to him and said, "This isn't working for either of us. And so I suggest you either buy me out, or I'll buy you out."

Now, by the expression "buy out," I thought we were splitting everything right down the center. What I didn't realize was the way my brother had been managing "our" money. When we caught our business manager embezzling, Jerry offered to take over the reins of handling the finances, which he did for about two years.

The night that I told him we would split he didn't like it and yelled, "Well, I'll get my attorney and you get yours!" I said, "I don't need an attorney. For what? We're brothers."

Our splitting up caused some of the unhappiest moments in my life. I can tell you that when we split up we spent two days sitting in an attorney's office in Los Angeles trying to divide everything up, and at that early stage in my career, there wasn't anything that great to divide up.

I didn't have an attorney. I decided not to get one because I didn't want it to turn into a contest. And yet it took me two days sitting in the office of Jerry's lawyer to realize that that is exactly what it had turned into.

After being abused verbally about not being able to walk onstage without him, and hearing about how Jerry Newton was the reason for my success, I discovered something in that lawyer's office: My brother had resented me for a long, long time.

It still rings in my ears today: He said that everything he got he wanted tax-free and insisted that I pay all the taxes. Then I heard the worst nightmare of all. I heard him say he wasn't going to contribute anything to our parents' support. I heard his attorney say that my brother was the reason the show was a success and that if Jerry were gone there would be no show. Deep in my heart I think Jerry believed that because it had to have come from him to his attorney. The attorney didn't know me from Adam. He was just doing the best for his client, Jerry.

At that time I wasn't talking to Mom and Dad about our breakup. They didn't know the true story for about five years. In the lawyer's office my parting words to Jerry were, "I want to thank you. You've taken a situation that's been the most difficult thing in my life and you and your mouthpiece have made it easy for me. You've taken my willingness to get along and confused it as a sign of weakness. That was your first and last mistake with me. You can sell a horse, you can sell a house, you can sell a car, but you cannot sell your obligation to your parents. And let me tell you what it's going to be. You're going to get what I say you get and not one cent more. And not one cent less. And you're going to get it when I say you'll get it.'' I turned and walked out.

We went to Denver the next night, and were given adjoining suites. But evidently the bedrooms were back-to-back. He called my dad and they had a screaming contest. I remember overhearing the conversation because Jerry's voice was so loud. My dad apparently had said something to the extent of ''Well, if Wayne wants to give you all that, why don't you just take it and be happy?'' My dad concluded the conversation—because he was tired of Jerry's whining—with ''If you feel like working together, then go ahead and do that. And if you don't, then you have to do what you think is best for you.'' That's not what Jerry wanted to hear. Through the wall I could hear him yelling, telling my dad off. Then there was a loud door-slam.

When I got up the next morning one of the musicians came to me and said, ''I just thought you ought to know that Jerry's left.'' I said, ''Left? Where did he go?'' He said he didn't know but was certain he'd left town. Then I had to make a decision: Would we plan to go on and do the show as scheduled? After all, Jerry and I were like salt and pepper onstage. It wouldn't be the same act without him. Still, I knew it was coming, even though Jerry gave me no time to make a change. It was probably best for him and me.

Both panic and calm set in at the same time. It was kind of a mixed emotion, sort of like a relief. If you live in limbo long enough, even a negative becomes kind of a positive. I realized that I had to be strong, had to make quick and accurate decisions. I wish I would have had a little more time, because here we were, four hours away from rehearsal and six hours away from a show. So I called my group together and said, "You all know that there's been some stressful things going on and I also want you to know that Jerry has left." Not one of them said a word.

I really didn't know what to do about his comic part of the show. But I figured that by the time rehearsals came around I would come up with some conclusions. I looked at my musicians and announced, "Right now my instincts tell me I'll probably hire another guy to do what Jerry did." I'll never forget what happened next. My drummer turned to me with a puzzled look and asked, "Why?" He said, "Wayne, why would you do that?" I confessed that I didn't know any other thing to do and it was a habit. The drummer just smiled. "Don't you think Wayne Newton should break the habit?" I looked at him and said, "Your point is well taken."

We began our rehearsal one hour early and I went on-stage that night. It was really tough for about four songs, because I was, of course, expecting somebody to say, "Where's your brother?" Jerry had covered all the comedy in the show. I was the straight man. Well, nobody said, "Where's your brother?" In fact, nobody said it the next night and nobody said it the night after that. And by the time the tour was over, only three or four people had said to me—not from the audience, but after the show—"Where's your brother?" I always came up with the excuse that he had some family problems he had to take care of. I didn't give any explanations of any kind.

After the two-week tour ended I arrived back in Las Vegas for my opening at the Frontier Hotel. As I was walking through the lobby for my rehearsal on opening night, I got word from the secretary to the general manager that they really didn't think Wayne was going to be able to go on by himself. According to the general manager, "His brother was the act." The general manager took it upon himself to hold all the bar setup, such as the liquor and nuts, and anything else coming back to the dressing room—including flowers—until after the opening show. Luckily everything went off without a hitch and the show was a success. I'm glad I didn't know their expectations of me before the curtain went up, because, to be honest, that might have been one time that I wouldn't have been able to go on with the show.

After the Denver incident Jerry and I didn't speak for ten years. Jerry got everything except my home and my horses.

When I split up with my brother I gave him whatever we had—and then I discovered I was three million dollars in debt. I had business managers putting me into tax shelters that sounded romantic; I owned two oil wells in Oklahoma, and once when I was singing there, I actually went to visit them. One of them turned out to be about thirty feet deep, and the other was just a shallow hole. You see, performers are artists with blinders on; they'd rather sing and dance than worry about money, so they let somebody else take care of their finances. There are an awful lot of people willing to do that for them.

I honestly don't have a high opinion of entertainers' business managers. There are exceptions to every rule, but I happen to believe that most of them are the leeches of society. I'm not saying, "Woe is me," or, "How can all these bad people take advantage of us?" The truth of the matter is that performers tend to live in vacuums of their own making; we're sitting ducks because we don't know enough to realize when we're being helped and when we're being taken advantage of.

The only reason I didn't fight my brother was that it would have broken my mother's heart and I knew it. Friends had come to me and said that they thought I ought to talk to my brother. Each time they were surprised when I informed them that I thought they ought to mind their own business.

Jerry had to come to town for something and I think, in reality, he was starting to get involved in some areas that ended up causing him his problems. I'm not going to speculate on what his motivation was, but he wanted to talk to me again.

One night I went over to the Aladdin Hotel to meet with one of the former owners. The two of us and my manager, Jay Stream, were seated in the bar. I noticed an attractive young woman out of the corner of my eye who was sitting at a table with three guys. Within five minutes a guy came in and sat down facing me. He ordered a drink. My manager looked at me and said, "Are you all right?" And I said, "Why shouldn't I be all right?" He did a Marx Brothers double take and said, "Do you know who that guy is over there?" I looked again and said, "No." He said, "It's your brother, Jerry." I responded with one word—"Bullshit." For the guy who was seated across the lounge weighed a lot more than Jerry ever did. His face was so heavy I couldn't recognize him. Each time I looked over I still didn't believe it was Jerry. Finally someone paged him. I could hear his name being paged throughout the lobby. "Telephone call for Jerry Newton." Jerry got up and answered the phone and I got up and left. As I was parading to the front door, moving at a fast pace, a girl ran up and said, "Your brother wants to see you." But I just hit the front door and walked out into the night.

We finally did get together, but it was strained. I gave him a hug as I would any friend, although it was very difficult for me. We agreed to bury the hatchet and decided we'd surprise Mom at Christmas. She was so happy she cried. But you know how you get that old feeling that nothing changes? Everybody was trying to get along, but it was still uncomfortable. A year later I went to the place Jerry owned in Tennessee and did two performances.

It was difficult to be critical of my brother. I was sensitive to his problems onstage. So I would try never to say, "Why are you doing this?" or, "You're out of tune and you're behind the beat." But sometimes I'd lose my cool and there would be a fight.

Jerry Newton may very well have seen himself standing in the spotlight instead of Wayne Newton. Being up front wasn't something I consciously thought about. I don't believe that it was a conscious thing at all in the beginning.

But it manifested itself in some strange areas. Jerry's attitude was, "I'm the older brother and you do what I say to do when I say to do it and if you don't I'll kick the crap out of you." And he did on many occasions.

Once we got into a fight in Houston, Texas, on New Year's Eve. Our drummer quit that morning with no notice and so we had to scrounge. Can you imagine trying to find a drummer on New Year's Eve? If they can bang two drumsticks together and can play at all, they've got a job already. But we found a guy.

We were at the Shamrock Hilton. We were sitting in the suite after the show and a cockroach crawled up the portable bar. The ice had melted in one of the sinks, so Jerry took the cockroach and put it in the water and watched it try to swim. Just as it was about to die, he took a swizzle stick, picked it up, and put it on the counter to let it dry off. He did that three or four times. Finally, about the fourth time, I said, "Jerry, if you're going to kill it, kill it. If you're not, leave it alone." He shouted, "Mind your own goddamn business!" I jumped off the sofa and walked over to him. "I don't understand why you're making that bug suffer. If you're going to kill it, step on it. Otherwise, leave it alone." It turned into a knockdown fistfight for all time. We were punching away at each other and I knew I'd probably lose. I always got beat up.

Brothers will always fight. It was worse for us because not only were we together all day but we also worked together at night. That's pretty tough. I don't think Jerry ever meant to do me any harm. Jerry would fight for me, fight anybody who tried to harm me. He truly felt, "I'm the older brother, and Mom and Dad expect me to take care of you." Well, that's fine if you're nine or ten years old. But as you grow up you develop your own emotions and survival instincts.

While I may not admit it out loud, there's obviously love there. There's a bond. So often I've thought about calling him over to the house and saying, "Hey look, Jerry, this is BS."

We all have that one thing we wish we could say that we've been unable to say. I wish that Jerry would let me be the friend to him that I am, and accept it. I don't have any ill feelings toward him. I know that part of what I've become I owe to him. And, at the least, he taught me to stand on my own two feet.

If Jerry Newton had been a nice guy and easy to get along with, we might have been together forever. But I owe Jerry this: I met one of my closest friends in the world, Dr. Ted Jacobs, through him. Jerry wanted a guarantee that he would get everything I owed him. He wanted a life-insurance policy on my life so that if I died, he'd still get paid. The doctor I went to for the insurance physical was Ted Jacobs, a friend who's become like a brother to me.

But Jerry wasn't the only one. After all those years of marriage, Elaine, when we were divorced, insisted on the same things until she was paid off. That's when you wish you could open up your refrigerator door and see your wife's picture on the side of a milk carton (jokey jokey). That's when you realize that you're nothing more than a meat market.

That separation with my brother was no different than any divorce. The first thing they want to know is, if you get sick or die, "how am I going to get my money?" Blood is thicker than water, only if it doesn't run green.

It's easier now to look back on that period of my life and say I'm sorry it had to happen, but I believe that the fire I went through has had a great many more positive than negative effects. It hurt me at the time, though in the end it helped me, as a performer and as a person.

CHAPTER 20

☆

*The caller said, "We're going to kill you, tough guy,
and we're going to get the nigger too."*

A MILLION WORDS couldn't describe the feeling of driving
up to your own hotel. Owning a hotel has been a dream
of mine my entire life. Since I was fifteen years old I have
spent my life in casinos. I had reached the point where I
wanted to work for myself; and probably most important,
I wanted something working for me when I wasn't. Most
of my income was derived directly from my ability and
energy to work two shows a night seven days a week. I
thought it would be awfully nice to have something that
would give me some other income, where I didn't have to
walk onstage, or felt that I didn't want to, or couldn't
anymore. I do a very physical show and it's a hard show.
A great many performers in Las Vegas and Atlantic City
work less than an hour. Many spend only fifty or forty-
five minutes onstage. That's usually combined with a co-
headliner. By choice, I don't have an opening act. And I
try to give the audience the best I can give them. Usually
my shows run anywhere from an hour to two hours. So
my style of performing is difficult both physically and
emotionally. It seemed that owning a hotel was a logical
extension of what I do. Because when I finished work and
was tired, I could simply go upstairs to bed rather than
drive home. At least it *sounds* good.

I walked into the opening of the Aladdin Hotel not as
an entertainer but as a hotel owner. We opened the casino

first, and a few days later we opened the showroom. The reason why both were not opened simultaneously was because I had committed to Barbara Mandrell to do a fundraiser for her in Alabama for an orphanage. I wouldn't break my word. Since I had made Barbara Mandrell the promise a year before, I kept it.

Elaine and I walked into the Aladdin like excited kids. How far we had come! The casino was packed and I threw the first dice and played the first game on the roulette wheel. Grandfather Kane came and stood on one side of me and Elaine on the other. It was such a wonderful feeling.

As I walked through the casino a little old man handed me a dollar slot-machine token. And he said, "It'll bring you good luck." I broke it in half and gave half of it to my partner, Ed Torres. I kept the other half and I still have it framed. Little did I realize that four days later, after having one of the most incredible days of my life of all the years of dreaming, it would turn into a nightmare that would forever change my world.

Four days later, on October 6, 1980, NBC was on the air with its vicious attack on me entitled "Wayne Newton and the Law." NBC ran a weekend of promos announcing that they were airing it. I heard about the promos but I never saw them. It's the kind of thing that people don't want to talk to you about. They wouldn't come up and face you and say, "Did you hear what NBC is saying about you on the air?" My friends weren't going to embarrass themselves, or me, by discussing it.

The ink was scarcely dry on the Aladdin purchase contract when NBC broadcast a "special segment" on its *Nightly News* show anchored by John Chancellor. The report opened with footage of a car and narration by reporter Brian Ross about a "stakeout" of Guido Penosi by organized-crime investigators from the Los Angeles District Attorney's office.

Penosi, "a New York hoodlum from the Gambino Mafia family," was believed to be the family's West Coast representative in narcotics and in show business, the broadcast said. Penosi was a key figure in a federal grand jury probe of Gambino family activities in Las Vegas and of "the role of Guido Penosi and the mob in Newton's deal for the Aladdin," it noted.

The report said that Newton, just before he announced he would buy the Aladdin, called Penosi for help with a problem. "Investigators say whatever the problem was, it was important enough for Penosi to take up with leaders of the Gambino family in New York," the news broadcast said. "Police in New York say that mob boss Frank Piccolo told associates he had taken care of Newton's problem and had become a hidden partner in the Aladdin Hotel deal."

It went on to say that at a Nevada casino-licensing hearing on September 25, 1980, Newton said he had no hidden partners in the deal. He testified that he knew Penosi but said Penosi was just a fan and longtime family friend. Film from the hearings showed me being asked if I knew that Penosi was a purported member of the Gambino organized-crime family and replying, "No, sir, I did not."

"Federal authorities say Newton is not telling the whole story," Ross said on the broadcast, "and that Newton is expected to be one of the first witnesses in the grand jury investigation. Newton became angry when we tried to talk to him about his relationship with Guido Penosi."

Film then showed me saying, "I really don't care what you want." Ross's report concluded, "Guido Penosi told us he doesn't know anybody named Wayne Newton. Federal authorities say they know of at least eleven phone calls Penosi made to Newton's house in one two-month period, and authorities say those phone calls and Penosi's relationships with Newton and other entertainment figures are now part of a broad yearlong FBI investigation of the investment of East Coast money, of narcotics and racketeering in the entertainment business in Las Vegas and Hollywood."

If a million words couldn't describe the feeling of driving up to your own hotel, then a billion words couldn't describe the feeling when NBC ran the news story. I was sitting in my TV room with Elaine and Erin and my parents. At the end of that broadcast my mother broke down and cried. I got up and left the room and went for a long walk. I was incapable of talking with anybody. I don't remember being as devastated about anything as I was that night when I realized that everything I had worked for, dreamed about, sweated over, and achieved might come tumbling down. They tainted me with their lies, and did something to me I could never live down. I'm not sure I can ever put into words my feelings when I watched the broadcast. I couldn't believe it. I don't ever remember experiencing in all my life the feeling that came over me at that moment. It was just that everything I had worked for in my entire life, the reputation that I had built, was smashed in a moment. I never took a cent from anybody or hurt anybody. How could these people portray such a vicious lie? I switched channels to see if it was being broadcast on any of the other stations. It wasn't then, and it never has been. It has only appeared on NBC.

After I quit shaking and realized I had to go to work that night, I called Frank Fahrenkopf, who had been forewarned by the promos that he had seen. He flew in from Reno that night. I don't remember much about that night other than the broadcast. For that matter, I don't remember much about that week other than the broadcast.

In between shows it was decided that I should call a press conference and immediately explain that it was our intention to sue NBC and everyone else involved in that smear. The very next day we held our press conference in the boardroom of the Aladdin Hotel.

Within three days a letter was sent to the National Broadcasting Company from my attorneys. It read:

Gentlemen:
On October 6, 1980, the NBC Television Network broadcast a story about our client, Wayne Newton, en-

titled "Wayne Newton and the Law." Said story was and is untrue and slanderous in that the content of said broadcast, among other things: 1. Alleges and/or asserts that the financing of Mr. Newton's acquisition of his interest in the Aladdin Hotel and Casino, Las Vegas, Nevada, was obtained by and through "Mafia" and "Mob" sources and that Mr. Newton holds a "Hidden" ownership interest in said Aladdin Hotel and Casino for the benefit of said "Mafia" and "Mob" sources; 2. Alleges and/or asserts that Mr. Newton has not truthfully related to Nevada Gaming Authorities the facts of his relationship with Guido Penosi and that Wayne Newton is associated with Guido Penosi, who is involved in both the narcotics business and show business on the West Coast; 3. Visually depicts Wayne Newton testifying, under oath, before Nevada Gaming Authorities and in connection with said testimony states that "Federal Authorities say Newton is not telling the whole story." Demand is hereby made that you immediately broadcast a correction of said story in substantially as conspicuous a manner as was the above-stated story, on the same program, and that in said story of correction, you state: 1. That Mr. Newton's acquisition of his interest in the Aladdin Hotel and Casino is financed totally through a loan to him personally from Valley Bank of Nevada, Nevada's second largest bank; 2. That Nevada Gaming Authorities have investigated fully Mr. Newton's relationship with Guido Penosi and are satisfied that Mr. Newton has truthfully and fully testified regarding said relationship; 3. That Wayne Newton is not "associated with Guido Penosi" in either "the narcotics business" or "show business on the West Coast," or elsewhere. This notice and demand is being served upon you within 20 days of knowledge of said broadcast.

On October 27 NBC responded. Their letter read:

Gentlemen:

This is a response to the retraction demands you have made upon NBC and those of its affiliates to whom you have sent letters who carried the NBC Nightly News broadcast concerning Wayne Newton on Monday, October 6, 1980.

We believe that your letter inaccurately characterizes what Nightly News actually stated in the broadcast. Nightly News did not state that Mr. Newton had acquired his interest in the Aladdin Hotel and Casino through "Mafia" or "Mob" sources, that Mr. Newton had untruthfully related to Nevada gambling authorities the facts of his relationship with Guido Penosi, or that he is associated with Penosi in the narcotics or show business on the West Coast. What the report did state is:

"Federal authorities say Newton is not telling the whole story and that Newton is expected to be one of the first witnesses in the grand jury investigation."

We would like you to know that we have carefully reviewed the Nightly News script and have concluded that the report was accurate and newsworthy. For this reason, on behalf of NBC and its affiliates carrying the report, we decline to air the retraction as demanded in your letter.

I began to feel like Sherlock Holmes putting together the clues to figure out the reason for this brutal attack. I remember that around 1978 a writer for a local tabloid in Las Vegas called *Backstage* magazine had come to the dressing room at the Frontier Hotel and was very upset over the fact that he couldn't make his car and house payments. The writer, Ron Delpit, was afraid that both were going to be repossessed. He had given me many good reviews over the past years and had always been kind to me in print. So I called my manager at the time, Jay Stream, and explained that Delpit was having some financial problems and needed five thousand dollars so that he wouldn't lose his home and his car. My manager said to go ahead and lend it to him. My wife wrote the check. I didn't, and still don't, write checks. If I go anywhere, I deal in cash or credit cards. Because of the urgency to get the money, my manager felt it would be better if my wife wrote the check, which was from a local bank in Vegas, rather than have the office send it, which would take two days. So my wife wrote the check and the accountant reimbursed her account. I gave Delpit the five-thousand-dollar loan, and he took it to the bank.

Evidently my wife had signed the check with a different color ink than she had written it out with; the first pen had run out of ink, so she had picked up the next pen and signed it. When Delpit took it to the bank they wouldn't honor the check because of the two different colors of ink. He called the dressing room that night in a panic, saying that the people would be on his doorstep the next morning and please could he get another check.

Once again I called my manager and he instructed that it would be okay for Mrs. Newton to write another five-thousand-dollar check. So she did and I gave it to Delpit.

I found out a month later that he had, in fact, cashed both checks. Delpit came to the dressing room prior to my finding out about his cashing the first check and asked if I would be interested in a business partnership in his newspaper. He claimed he had been in touch with the *Los Angeles Times* and he was going to be a part of the centerfold of the Sunday newspaper and a Dallas newspaper was picking it up. He was planning to become syndicated throughout the country. I then put him in contact with my manger. Jay flew in to Las Vegas from San Luis Obispo, California, which is where he lived.

Delpit and Jay had a meeting and Jay came back and told me that he had set up a line of credit for Delpit at the Valley Bank in Las Vegas. It was at $125,000, which was going to be used for the magazine, cleaning up any old debts owned by the tabloid, and getting it in the proper position to become a syndicated paper throughout the country.

After a while, there came a time when my manager expressed concern about the business transaction. It was a year later and he said that Delpit had not been honest with us and in fact had drawn money out of the bank account under false pretenses. Jay canceled the line of credit and said, "There's no need to chase good money after bad."

Delpit discovered that the gravy train had stopped in early February 1980 while I was appearing at the Frontier. As always, I arrived an hour before I went onstage. I was in the dressing room when the first phone call came. Mr. Forch, commonly referred to as the Bear, who's been my associate, guard, and friend for years, answered the phone. It was Ron Delpit calling from upstairs in the casino. He said to Bear that he wanted to come down and have a meeting with me right away. Bear put him on hold and entered the back part of the dressing room, where I was preparing for the show. He said, "Ron Delpit is upstairs and he wants a meeting with you. About what I don't know."

So Bear went back to the phone and said, "Mr. Newton would like to know what the meeting is about." Delpit quickly responded, "I'll tell him that when I see him. But it's important that I see him and I will see him."

I assumed that, after Jay's conversation with me, it was probably a money matter concerning himself or the paper. So I informed Bear that I would not see him, that Delpit had done business with Stream for the past year, and that I would prefer that he continued that way because I had removed myself from those negotiations.

That was not what Delpit wanted to hear. He continued to say that he was going to see me, and Bear, in frustration, finally hung up.

Delpit was determined! The calls to the dressing room were nonstop for the next thirty or forty minutes. Each time Bear would simply say, "Mr. Newton is not accepting calls."

I went onstage and did my first show. And when I came offstage, Bear informed me that Delpit and some other guy with him had stayed in the casino and were causing something of a riot. As I walked through the dressing-room door, I looked at Bear and gave him one of those "Well, why don't they throw him out?" looks. Bear said, "Security was afraid to throw him out because he keeps telling everybody he's your partner and you've welched on a deal and he's going to see you."

I shook my head and laughed, "I'm not seeing him."

For the two hours between shows Delpit continued his outrageous behavior. It got so bad that the casino host even got out of bed and came to the Frontier to try to calm him down. The phone kept ringing every minute and we continued to decline to take calls.

After doing my second show, which was approximately two hours long, the phones were still ringing in the dressing room. No matter what we said, the phone calls continued. So after about an hour I finally said to Bear, "Go upstairs and explain to Delpit that I'm not going to see him. There's nothing I have to say to him. I've spent all the money I'm going to spend and he might as well go away."

Bear went upstairs to the casino and took Delpit, and whomever this other guy was with him, into the lounge. He explained to both of them that I was not going to see him.

Delpit yelled at Bear, maligning me and degrading me and calling me every filthy name. It was at that point that Bear called me from the casino and said, "You're either going to have to see him or I'm going to have to kill him. It's that's simple. He won't go away."

Well, this nonsense had been going on from seven o'clock that night until three in the morning. So I instructed Bear to take him to the suite. As part of my contract as an entertainer, I maintained a suite in each hotel I worked in. I went directly from my dressing room to the suite. It was now approximately three-thirty in the morning.

I walked through the parlor of the suite and into the open-doored bedroom area where Bear had taken Delpit. As I walked in, I saw two regular-size beds, not unlike a Holiday Inn setup. Seated at the end of one of those beds was a guy I had never seen before. Delpit was leaning up against a long table with a lamp and Bear was standing alongside him. I didn't enter the room alone. Walking next to me was Larry Wright, who was a part-time security guard, part-time bartender and schoolteacher.

I didn't even have a chance to say hello when this guy I had never seen before jumped off the bed, ran over to me, and hit his finger in my chest. He said, "Listen, Newton." Before he could say anything more I lost my temper and backhanded him, not with my fist but with an open hand. He flew over the bed. Bear and Larry put their arms around me, trying to contain me. I pushed them away, saying, "I'm fine. It's okay." I looked at Delpit and said, "Who is this?" at which point the guy said, "I'm your partner." I said, "Partner in what?" I didn't even look at him. My eyes were glued to Delpit. But the guy continued to speak. "I'm your partner in the newspaper." Delpit just laughed and said, "He's your partner."

Once again I lost my temper, only this time I reached for Delpit. But before I reached him, Delpit and his friend ran out of the room. I was furious, but I managed to calm down and assured Bear and Larry that I was not as angry as I was before and to try to bring them back in.

So Larry Wright went out in the hallway and, sure enough, the two were both standing there. They came back into the suite and I said to Delpit, "What is the meaning of all this?" Delpit explained that the guy owned 5 percent of the paper. I laughed at Delpit. "Five percent of nothing is nothing." Delpit snapped back at me, "Oh, you're going to pay," and I reached for him again. This time I managed to get hold of his coat. Delpit's body left the coat and the two of them ran out the doorway. It was like a grade-B movie.

When Bear tried to contain me, after having been harassed all night, I lost my temper and hit him in the chin with my elbow to simply get loose. I pushed Larry Wright over a table. Bear and Larry were pretty shaken up and understandably so. I finally calmed down when I realized that I had hurt two friends. I quickly apologized to both of them and sat around for thirty minutes asking for their understanding, which they quickly gave. Then I went home.

It seemed like a bad dream, but it was only the beginning of a nightmare. A nightmare that would quickly continue the next night. After the altercation, Bear and I started to get death threats. The very next night there were phone calls to the dressing room. The first couple of calls Bear took. It wasn't until the third night that I personally spoke to the caller. I didn't recognize the voice. It seemed to be disguised. There was a lot of profanity and it was kind of a low, gravelly voice. The caller said, "We're going to kill you, tough guy, and we're going to get the nigger too."

Before he could say more, I lashed back at him. "You don't have to look for me and you don't have to look for Bear. Tell us where you want us and we'll be there."

The next thing that happened was that Bear's tires were slashed and a window was broken in his car. I didn't even know it had been done until the night after it happened. Bear didn't call me at home, but when I arrived to do the show he informed me of what they had done. The phone calls continued and they were all pretty much the same kind of threats with the usual dose of profanity. While it upset me, it didn't really disturb me until the death threats started coming to my home. It was then that I realized I had better contact a representative of a law-enforcement authority.

Ironically enough, about the third night that this was going on, I received a call from Jay from his home in

California. He said, "What's going on?" Not wishing to alarm him, I responded, "About what?" Stream told me that an editor in Las Vegas had called him and said that he had received a multipage story that had been typewritten and shoved under his door at the newspaper. It was written by some guy by the name of Cross and in the story Cross supposedly overheard three or four hoodlums at the Marina Hotel discussing how they were going to kill the Indian and the nigger. And they had been called to Las Vegas and were planning on doing it.

After receiving the story, the editor had called a few of his friends around Las Vegas who owned newspapers and tabloids, and they told him that they too had received a similar story slipped under their doors. It had evidently been circulated to every person in town who had a news-media position.

Ralph Petillo, who owned a weekly newspaper, *The Las Vegas Mirror,* met with me in my dressing room at the Frontier Hotel. I wanted to keep all of this away from my wife and child, and so he was nice enough to hand me the article at the hotel. After reading it, I called the police. I asked for Sheriff McCarthy and was given one of his aides. Three officers from the Las Vegas Metropolitan Police Department came to the dressing room. I explained the conditions that had transpired in the last three nights, including the loss of my own temper and the death threats and how I had come in contact with publisher Ralph Petillo, and then I suggested that this article seemed to coincide with the death threats we were getting. It could only have been coming from one place.

They put extra guards on my ranch for a night or two. Then one night the police came back to the dressing room and explained that they had gone to see Delpit and found out that the guy with him was a man by the name of Bob Adams. The police warned them that this kind of nonsense, such as death threats and the article, was not going to be tolerated. Both Delpit and Adams denied having had anything to do with it. The police explained to me that until there were further problems, meaning until these people actually moved against us, they couldn't keep police at my home. There was nothing we could do until they actually tried to carry out their threat. The police pulled their guards off the grounds of my home and left.

It was quiet for a couple of days, and although my nerves were frazzled, things started to return to normal. Then, two days later, the death threats started again at my home. My wife received the first call while I was still asleep. When I woke up she told me, "I got a funny call." I said, "What was it?" Elaine's face lost all of its color as she said, "Some gravelly-voiced guy said that he was going to kill you on the way to work." She looked stunned. As I held her hand, I said, "What else did he say?" She said, "Well, I asked him why he'd want to do such a thing but he didn't answer. He just hung up." I assured her there was nothing to worry about.

I didn't call the police again. I simply told Bear what had happened.

The next day one of the housekeepers received a phone call. She spoke very little English, so she didn't understand very much of it. She told my wife that some guy was talking mean, and that's about all she knew.

The following day my wife was in the kitchen and a gravelly voice called again. He started to talk about my daughter. He knew that she was in preschool, what gate she left from on the ranch, what time she left, and who was with her. He even knew what classroom she was in at school. And then came the shocker. Elaine almost fainted when he proceeded to tell her what parts of Erin's body they were going to ship back in a box. I will never forget, till the day I die, the look on Elaine's face when she wakened me with this news. I called the police. They again said there was nothing they could do . Elaine was stunned. Who wouldn't be? She sat there almost in hysteria. I was yelling at the officer, "What do you mean there is nothing you can do?" The officer, trying to calm me down, spoke softly. "There's nothing we can do until they move against her."

Pacing back and forth, all I could think of was my daughter. I loved her more than life. The thought of harm coming to her was driving me crazy. I tried to think of people who might be able to help me. Names went through my mind like a Rolodex. Then I remembered that Guido Penosi had said that he was living in Los Angeles. He had been in prison. Probably he could find out who was doing this and either stop it or put me in contact with them. So I called Guido and I told him the story. He calmly asked, "Do you have a name?" I said, "Well, the only name I have is this Drapper." That name was in the story given to me by publisher Ralph Petillo. Guido said, "Is that all you have?" I said, "Yes, I'm afraid that's all I have." That's when I asked him if maybe he could check around to see if he could find out who was behind it all. He said, "I'll call you back." So I gave him my number. The next night he called me back and said something to the extent of, "Well, I don't have any leads, but I'm still checking. I'll get back to you. I'm just calling to let you know that I'm still checking and working on it."

Guido lived up to his promise. He called back the next night and said that he might know somebody who knew this guy. Guido said, "When I call you back, I'm going to give you a number. Call the number. A guy will answer and I will be on the extension. Simply tell him the story, nothing more, nothing less." I responded by saying, "Okay." The next day the phone rang. Guido did give me a number—no name; just a number—and told me what time to call. I did call at exactly the designated time. The guy did answer. Guido was on the extension. I said, "This is Wayne Newton," and I related the entire story. When I finished, the no-name voice said, "Is that all?" "Yes," I told him, "that's all." The voice once again asked, "Is that all you know?" And once again I assured him that that was all that I knew. He said, "Guido will get back to you."

I didn't hear back. Guido did not call me. But the death threats stopped.

If there are any regrets with regard to Ron Delpit, it's that I didn't kill him, because I couldn't have had any more problems if I had gone to jail for murder. I'd have been out by now. Jokey jokey. There's no doubt that Ron Delpit will get his someday. The only thing that really concerns me is that it will probably not be me who does it. When I say that Delpit will get his, I really mean that a guy cannot go through life hurting people the way he hurts people without having that karma destroy him in the end. It's plain and simple. Ron Delpit is slime. To call him a parasite is paying him a compliment.

In March 1980 I was involved in heavy negotiations for the Aladdin Hotel in Las Vegas. We were negotiating with the Pritzgers at the time. They are the family that owns the Hyatt chain of hotels. They arrived from Chicago and were in Las Vegas with their battery of attorneys when my attorney, Mark Moreno, came to the villa behind the Aladdin, where we were meeting. He seemed overly serious as he held me by the arm. He said, "Can I see you? I must see you outside." As we stood outdoors with the wind blowing, Moreno looked as if he had seen a ghost. "I've been getting death threats," confessed Moreno. I couldn't believe my ears. We had been through this before and I just couldn't imagine why they'd be going after my longtime friend and associate. Mark said, "I guess they thought if they couldn't get the money from you, they could get it from me." I said, "What money?" Moreno paused and said, "Thirty-five thousand dollars." In shock, I said, "Thirty-five thousand dollars for what?" Moreno then explained, "This is what the thugs figured that it cost them to come here and kill you and Bear." I laughed out loud thinking Mark was joking with me. But I could tell in his eyes that he was serious. "What did you tell them?" I asked. Mark leaned a little closer. "It was a woman calling long-distance who then put some guy on the phone." Moreno said it had been going on for a couple of days, but he had kept me unaware of it because he didn't want to upset me. Then Moreno said that the caller made it clear. "Don't get in your car; don't start your car; we'll blow it up."

Shaking my head, I just looked at Mark. "You're not serious about thirty-five thousand dollars?" Mark nodded his head. "That's what they want." We walked a slight distance as I told Mark that I had called Guido with this nonsense for me and that he should call Guido and tell him that they were starting in on him. Moreno nervously agreed to place the call.

The next thing I remember was that Mark told me he had called Guido and Guido had gone through somewhat the same scenario. He gave him a number and told him to call at such-and-such a time and tell them his story.

Guido told Mark that it was Guido's cousin and that his name was Frank. Mark made the call at the scheduled time. Frank said that Guido would get back to him. And then, just as before, the death threats stopped.

I'm sure you're wondering why I would call Guido or have Mark call this man. After all, he was associated with the Mafia. But I swear on my life I did not know that. To me, he was just a fan I had met in 1963 when I was working at the Copacabana. I had seen him during that six-month period, and when I appeared in Florida I had seen him a total of three or four times. Once he invited us to his home for dinner and another time he took us to an Italian restaurant. Those were the only two times I was in his company other than when he came to the place where I was working to see the show. To be honest with you, for many years I only knew him by his first name. After all, how may Guidos do you know in a lifetime? I know a lot of fans only by their first names, fans who have shaken hands with me, or whose autographs I've signed. You never remember their last names.

Guido had come to see the show when I was appearing in Miami seventeen years earlier. And he came backstage with his guests, whoever they were, and asked if all of us could come to his house for dinner. All of us included my parents, my brother, my drummer, Tommy Amato, and my conductor, Don Vincent. Guido said, "My wife's a wonderful cook and we'd love to have you over for dinner." He had driven into Miami and brought his daughter with him. My parents and my brother and I followed in one car and my drummer and conductor followed in another. It was a Sunday afternoon and we drove into a driveway and the house looked like an average house. There were no maids or butlers, and Guido's wife, Sarah, greeted us at the door. She was a very nice lady. That's when we met his daughter and son. I don't remember the daughter's name, but I do remember the son's name because he didn't stay for dinner. Anthony had a motorcycle outside and quickly hopped on it and rode off. They had a dog and seemed like a typical family. Sarah was constantly getting up from the table and going in and out of the kitchen, serving. We had a fabulous six- or seven-course mouth-watering Italian dinner.

The talk was just small talk; we never discussed business, his or ours. But it wasn't the first time I'd gone to a person's home and didn't know what they did for a living. If I'm on the road and we're living in hotels and eating hotel food, it's awfully nice when someone offers you an invitation to enjoy a home-cooked meal.

Throughout the years I've been fortunate to have fans who have opened their hearts and doors to me. We were in Valley Forge, Pennsylvania, one Thanksgiving, and a lady who had been a fan for a long time invited us to a restaurant which, when we got there, we found out she owned. It was a terrific Thanksgiving meal and I can't tell you her name either. Then there's a gentleman who has seen an awful lot of my shows, and every time he comes to a performance he always brings six or seven, sometimes eight, people. If he's in Las Vegas for a week, he catches two shows a night during his stay. He's been doing this for twenty years. His father started a tire business in Lethbridge, Canada. When the family was celebrating their fiftieth year in business, I decided, because this guy had been such a longtime fan, to surprise them. I flew up to Canada after my two shows in Vegas, attended their party, and got back on my airplane and came home in time to do a show at the Convention Center.

If fans who I know are ill, it's not uncommon for me to fly to Oregon or anyplace else to visit them in a hospital. I have flown fans to Las Vegas at my expense because they had some kind of physical problem. It's just something I enjoy doing. God has been good to me, and I think it's only fair that I give back a little. It's my way of sharing God's blessing.

To this day there is a nun in Las Vegas who has seen some 256 of my shows and I couldn't tell you her last name or what parish she's with. We literally have people coming in from all over the world, and I know some first names only because they'll hand me a note saying, "Do a song for Jackie," and if they do that enough, then I remember the name Jackie. You wouldn't necessarily know their last name. Guido's first name is the only name I ever knew Guido by. And he's the only Guido I have ever known.

I'll always remember that Sunday dinner at Guido's home and why I remembered Tony's name. When Tony didn't stay for dinner and hopped on his motorcycle and said good-bye to his dad, tears came to Guido's eyes. Like any father who loves his son, he admitted, "We've had some real problems with the boy. He has epileptic seizures, and we don't know if we're going to be able to keep it under control and for how long." Guido turned his head and brushed a tear away from his eye. It was sad; Tony was a handsome boy and you could tell that his father loved him dearly.

Sarah was special. She was so animated. With her apron on and her hands flying in the air when she talked, she is what you'd expect Mamma Leone to be like. At the end of the dinner, my drummer, who I think had eaten everything but the silverware and the plates, looked at Guido and said, "What are we having for dessert?" Guido chuckled and yelled at Sarah, "Hide the dog." That line has stuck with me all these years because it was so funny.

Guido came to Las Vegas sometime in the mid-sixties and stopped by the house on Eastern Avenue and said hello to my parents. My brother and I were not home. I think he came to my brother's wedding in 1966, although I'm not sure who invited him, whether it was my brother or my drummer, Tommy Amato. To the best of my knowledge, Guido has never done anything to hurt me and has never done anything but fit into the categories of friend and fan.

Years later, my manager Jay Stream called me and said he had gotten a call from Guido, who said that his son Tony was producing a country-music television special with a country singer whose name was Johnny Rodriguez, and would I consider flying down to California just to sing a song as a guest star. Before I answered, Guido and Tony's relationship flashed before my eyes. Without batting an eyelash I said, "Sure, I'll be there." So I took my conductor and my drummer and my guitar player and we flew to Los Angeles in the afternoon. We went directly to the site of the television production and Guido was there with a big hug and a hello. I went to talk to the director of the show; I did a song or two; we got back on the plane and came back to Las Vegas and did two shows that night. Although I felt tired, I also felt blessed because I knew that I had given Tony a shot at doing something, knowing his physical handicap. It wasn't costing me anything to do it, and the reward I felt was great.

The first time I heard anything about his background was when Guido called to tell me that his wife had died and he wanted to come to Las Vegas. I was appearing at the Desert Inn Hotel in June 1979 when I received the phone call. As usual, Bear took the call first and said to me, "There's a Guido on the line who wants to talk with you." Well, there was only one Guido I had ever known so I took the call. "Hello, Wayne." Small talk. "How are you?'' "Fine, Guido, how are you?'' His voice cracked when he said, "My wife died.'' I said, "I'm sorry to hear that.'' Guido admitted that he had been depressed and wanted to come to Las Vegas. I said, "Come on.'' That's when Guido stated, "You don't understand. I have a prison record.'' I said, "So what!'' Guido admitted, "I have to register with the police.'' (Nevada law requires that anybody ever convicted of a felony has to register with the police department when they come to Nevada.) It was then that I volunteered to call the police and tell them he was coming. He came to Las Vegas.

My contract, no matter what hotel I play, will hold a certain number of rooms for our use that are not billed to us; they're simply called comps. I put Guido in one of those rooms.

Upon registration, the assistant manager said, "What's his last name?'' I said, "I don't know.'' It was then that I realized I had never known his last name. When I called Sheriff McCarthy and got his aide, they asked me, "What is his last name?'' Once again I had to confess that I didn't know, but I told the sheriff's office that he was registered at the Desert Inn and I gave them the room number. They said fine, they'd come down to the hotel and register him.

So the police actually went to the front desk of the Desert Inn Hotel, looked up his last name on the registration, and went up and either took him downtown or registered him there; I don't remember.

After he had been registered by the police and came to the dressing room, he said he had brought my daughter a saddle. He had never met her and wanted to bring her a gift. He said that he would like to meet her and I said, "We'll arrange for you to bring it by the house.'' I had a car pick him up and he arrived at the house carrying the saddle. He set the saddle down and my daughter looked at it and, being around four at the time, thought it was nice and toddled off to do her thing. Elaine was also there and my parents were present. He didn't stay any longer than fifteen or twenty minutes. We just stood around and talked, and in a few minutes he said he had to go and he left. We didn't talk about anything important, just about the saddle, and he complimented me on how pretty the ranch was. And I thanked him. The saddle was a thoughtful and nice gift.

I remember one Christmas Guido came into the Copacabana as I was leaving the stage and said, "I have something for you guys," and he gave us wrapped little boxes, one to me, one to my brother, and one to Tommy Amato. We opened them and they were watches. All three were identical.

It's not unusual for an entertainer to receive gifts. Almost every night people give us things, either handing them to us onstage or sending them backstage. We get rings; ladies make us afghans; we've even received Indian pottery and basket weaving and paintings. I have a dozen paintings. They're a pretty normal gift. I think the most surprising gift I've ever gotten was brought to me by a gentleman from Saudi Arabia who had seen me on *The Tonight Show*. Don Rickles was hosting and, in his own inimitable style, was making fun of that part of the world. After Rickles was through clowning around, I told the audience that I had just been to Saudi Arabia and found the people to be wonderful, and had a fabulous time, and looked forward to going back. This young student, a member of the Saudi royal family, heard the program and came from San Diego, where he was in school, to give me a diamond watch, matching cuff links, a matching cigarette lighter, a matching pen, and a matching key chain. Guido's watches were more of a thoughtful gesture than a gift.

When Guido told me that he served time in prison, I didn't try to find out what he had been convicted of because I felt it was none of my business. He's served his time and paid his debt to society.

When the word *Mafia* was used on the NBC broadcast, the only thing that flashed into my mind were the *Godfa-*

ther movies. The Mafia is as foreign to me as the KGB or Communists. You know they exist, but that's all.

I'm from Virginia, and when you think of Mafia, you don't think of Virginia. I think one of my problems was my undying belief in America and what it stands for. You're innocent until proven guilty. During my suit against NBC, some of the lawyers may have been shocked by my responses. I remember NBC's attorney saying to me, "Well, after hearing all these things about Guido, what do you now think of him?" And I said, "I have a real problem and that is, if Guido Penosi is not in jail for something, what right do I have to say he's guilty of anything? If he's paid his debt by being in jail for whatever it was that he did, then hasn't he paid his debt to society?" The attorney looked me straight in the eye and asked, "Well, what do you think about the Mafia?" I said, "I don't think about the Mafia." He asked, "Did you see *The Godfather?*" I smiled. "Yes." He pointed his finger, "Did you see *The Godfather II?*" Once again I smiled with a yes. The attorney looked away for a second and then quickly asked, "What do you think about the Mafia?" I said, "I didn't see one Indian." Laughter broke out in the courtroom.

But I meant that. Mort, my attorney, said to me after all the facts had come out about Guido, "Knowing what you know now, would you still have called Guido to help your daughter?" And I said, "I would have called the devil himself." As funny as it sounds, whatever the Mafia is, it has been so far away from me, and yet maybe around me all my life. Even though I've been in show business all my life, my work and the Mafia are as different as daylight and dark.

CHAPTER 21

☆

A contract on my life had been ordered. . . .
Wayne Newton was now on a Mafia hit list.

I REMEMBER CALLING the FBI after NBC had said on their national broadcast, "Wayne Newton is under investigation for his ties with organized crime." When I phoned Joe Yablonski, who was then head of the FBI in Vegas, he took my call immediately. I don't even remember saying hello. I recall saying, "This is Wayne Newton. I'm confused about something. Am I under investigation for anything?" Yablonski responded, "You must be talking about the NBC thing." And then I couldn't believe my ears; the head of the FBI said, "You're not being investigated to my knowledge." I thought to myself, *What is that supposed to mean?* So I asked him, "What do you mean, not to your knowledge? Could something like this happen and you not know about it?" The FBI chief paused for a second. "I can't tell you anything on the phone, Mr. Newton," Yablonski said. "I can just tell you we have never had an investigation of you nor do we plan an investigation of you." Then he surprised me. He said, "I think you'll have to look other places."

Obviously the head of the FBI knew it was a "jacket." When someone is framed, the police call it a jacket job. They put a jacket on you. So when I was supposedly the star witness against the mob, I called him again and said, "What do you know about all this?" Yablonski answered, "Mr. Newton, there is nothing that I know about this."

We are all raised to think that if somebody is doing something wrong to you, you can go to the police. If the police can't help you they will put you in touch with the FBI. I cannot tell you what a rude awakening it was to me as an American who had been raised in this society, had gone to school and watched police shows such as *The Untouchables*, to have been so naïve. Here I was, a grown man who still believed all those wonderful things about how the law protects the innocent. All of a sudden my eyes were opened.

Maybe a great many of the laws today do not protect the innocent. They protect the guilty. As shocking as that statement may be, if I were truly a member of an organized-crime family and I needed protection, I'd get it. The police and the FBI would protect me from the other members of organized crime. But because I am not, I was told there was nothing they could do until the mob moved against me or made an attempt on my daughter's life. That's pretty frightening, isn't it? The fact that somebody would say to me "I'm going to kill you" or "I'm going to kill your daughter" is not a crime. Does that surprise you? It's only a crime if that person calls another person and says, "Let's you and I go kill Wayne Newton and this is how we're going to do it." Now they can arrest him for conspiracy. But the law today does not protect the victim or the innocent. Only the guilty.

When NBC aired the broadcast, I didn't make a video-cassette of it. And I'm glad I didn't because I couldn't have watched it that night. It pains me to watch it today. Nine years later I feel the same anger and I have the same anxiety.

When I held my press conference the next day, it was my mother's tears that made me say that I would fight all of them till the last drop of blood in me and the last penny I had. I meant it. When I said I'd see them all in hell, I meant that too.

They really thought that through depositions they could wear me down. It was twofold. In legal terms, they call it a paper war. What that means is, if they file enough motions and enough briefs, it slows things down. Every time they file one my attorney has to file one in answer to it. Then another date has to be picked. It sometimes takes as long as a year for those two attorneys to go and argue that point. So they felt that they would wear me down physically and, more important, financially.

You see, the real shame of what happened to me is that NBC, like every other network, and the press are all insured. I'm not insured that way. So every penny I spent on the case came from my pocket. There's nothing that NBC had to put out until the final determination was over. But in the event of punitive damages against them, their insurance firm does not cover them. Anytime it's punitive, they have to pay it. But they didn't put out one cent to defend their case. The insurance company spent a fortune. Over eight years, I'm the only one who continued to pay.

I'll say one thing for it all: I quickly found out who my true friends were. My situation became instant gossip. I would walk into a room and I was the person everyone was talking about. The whole thing tore the heart out of my marriage. Elaine's self-worth was threatened. In a large way, Elaine's self-image was determined by what parties she was invited to. Why was she excluded? That became very important to her. I don't know whether it became important to her then, or if it was always there right under the surface and I never noticed. Since she couldn't perform onstage at night with me, she had to occupy herself in other ways. And she became very close friends with the social butterflies of the town.

After the NBC broadcast, we were shunned in Las Vegas. Invitations stopped coming. There were very few people who still hung around us for any period of time. In the middle of the desert, we were set off on an island. You've got to remember that a great many people who make up the social circle of Las Vegas are also casino people. They don't want that kind of heat. Even though none of them believed the NBC report, they still couldn't afford to be seen with us or around us.

It seemed it wasn't just our friends who turned on us. Even the man who gave me my first break in Las Vegas when I was fifteen years old, and who was now my partner in the Aladdin Hotel, changed overnight. Eddie Torres and I had reached an agreement before the broadcast concerning the minimum number of weeks per year that I would appear in the Aladdin's main showroom. Torres wanted upward of twenty-six weeks of appearances. However, shortly after the NBC broadcast, he started to operate the hotel as if I didn't exist. Things that were in our agreement about entertainment, about expenditures, Torres just totally ignored.

Performers who were close friends of mine, whom I suggested would be good for business at the Aladdin, he ignored. When I asked him about it he said that he had contacted their agents, and I said, "Why would you do that when these people are friends of mine? It would just be a matter of a phone call." And he said, "That's the way I prefer to work."

To save money, he made the glasses smaller in the showroom so that people couldn't have more than a certain amount of booze in a drink. He began to complain constantly about the length of my show. Anything he could complain about he did. Guests who were my guests in the hotel were treated badly.

It wasn't something that was immediately evident. Gradually I became aware that, with my trouble, Torres figured he didn't have to worry about me anymore. I called him on it, but he denied it. But it continued and prevailed. As far as my appearances in the Aladdin's Bagdad Theatre, Torres said that the hotel really couldn't afford my services for that amount of weeks and that he was going to cut them back. He refused to sign the contracts for me to appear there. So I made a deal across the street at Caesars Palace. I was still half-owner of the Aladdin Hotel at the time.

One night I arrived at the Aladdin to find that Torres had fired my conductor. He had brought in a trombone player and made him the leader of the orchestra. I called him immediately, but he was nowhere to be found. The next morning Torres explained that he thought my conductor was padding the orchestra bill and so he just simply replaced him.

Then came Torres's ultimate entertainment decision: Not only had he cut back my weeks but he wanted to put in a production show. I immediately responded with, "No, I won't have it." I said no because, at that time, every hotel in Las Vegas with the exception of two had gone to a production-show policy because it was cheaper. They could amortize the price of the show over a four- or five-year period and write it off. I felt that that's not what made Las Vegas what it was, what people come to Las Vegas to see. People would come to see Elvis Presley or Tom Jones or Engelbert or Liberace, but they wouldn't come to Las Vegas for just a production show. Torres had washed his hands of me. It was as if I were considered soiled after the NBC broadcast.

Yes, many of my friends did shun me and my business partner turned his back. But a lot of people who I never expected surfaced. Right after the first NBC hatchet job, Billy Graham telephoned. I had never met the Reverend Graham and he said he was coming to town and wanted to meet with me. When I told Elaine, she said to me, "What does he want?" I laughed, "Who knows? He might want to stay at the ranch." Then I realized that that wasn't as farfetched as it might have sounded. He's a very respected religious man and it's conceivable he would not want to stay in a hotel that had gaming.

We set our meeting and he came over to visit with me in one of the little cottages behind the Aladdin Hotel. We sat down and Billy Graham said, "Wayne, I've always admired you and I know that what you're going through now you don't deserve. I wanted to come here and tell you that you have my support in this hour of crisis. Is there any way I can help?''

It blew me away. It seemed that in my darkest hour God had sent a messenger. Then Dr. Graham reached over and touched my hand. ''Can I say a prayer for you?''

I said that I would be most appreciative. Afterward, I mentioned I had a friend who was dying of cancer and it would mean a lot to him if he telephoned this gentleman. Dr. Graham smiled. ''Get him on the phone.''

So he talked to my friend for about twenty minutes, and at the end of the conversation he told my dying friend, ''I'm going to pray for you and Wayne at the same time.'' He said a prayer and in the calmness of the night he left. But before he did, Billy Graham pointed out his observation that it wasn't just Wayne Newton on trial, but Las Vegas as well.

Hasn't Vegas always been on trial for one thing or another? Now they had someone to pin the tail on the donkey. After all, I was the man whom *Newsweek* magazine called ''King of the Strip.'' NBC took elements they thought nobody could ever fight: One was the mob. I mean, who's going to come up and say, ''Okay. NBC, I'm taking you to court.''

Look at Geraldo Rivera and what he's gotten away with. I watched Rivera one night on television when he said, ''I can't believe that Wayne Newton got twenty million dollars' libel against NBC, when you realize that the astronauts that died only got one million dollars each.''

I would have loved to have had him by the throat at the time. My answer would have been simple: If NBC had killed me, that's probably all my heirs would have gotten or deserved. But they did something worse. They killed me and let me live. They let me live in order to try and live down what they had done to me. It would have been much kinder simply to put a gun to my head, because they took away the two things that I fought my whole life to keep—my dignity and my honor. They're not for sale. Not to them. Not to anybody. One time when I was a child my mother held me on her lap and said, "Your name, Wayne Newton, is what your father and I give you. And it has the dignity and the honor of our life. What you do with it, that's what you pass on to your daughter or your son."

NBC attacked the Mafia knowing that nobody was going to come forward and say, "You can't talk about the Mafia that way." They attacked Las Vegas. Who is going to step up from the city and say, "Hey, you can't talk about us that way." They just threw in Wayne Newton. NBC figured, "What's this Indian going to do about it?"

The one thing they didn't plan on was me stepping up and fighting back. When I went up to bat, it wasn't just for Wayne Newton. It was for Las Vegas as well. Some of my friends felt that the town where I had lived my life let me down when they ran banner headlines. But it didn't surprise me. I didn't take that as Vegas. I realized that the local press looked to NBC as the giant. Let's face it, they are! Wayne Newton was David fighting the mighty, powerful Goliath—the NBC network. Every writer and every commentator wanted a job with NBC. In all fairness to the local press, how could they be objective? While I was disappointed, I was not shocked by their behavior.

NBC met daily with the Las Vegas press during the trial. So when the newspapers and the television broadcasts delivered the news, there was never anything pro–Wayne Newton. No one would dream that there was a second side to the case. When I won, a news director of a local channel said to a friend of mine, "How can this be?" My friend, being naïve, didn't understand the question. The news director said that he was in shock because the media had done such an incredibly poor job covering the trial. He felt that everything that had been reported, on TV or in the papers, was surely not favorable to Wayne Newton, and it seemed unlikely that I would win. Quite frankly, I didn't read the newspapers or watch TV. That was survival. To this day I don't and I believe that's wise. If something concerns me, it'll reach me. If it's nothing I can do anything about, then "never cross a bridge before

you get to it because, invariably, you'll pay the toll twice."
I always believed that there is time enough to be sad when
you have to be sad. I don't anticipate sadness. I don't
anticipate bad news because once I'm faced with it, that's
time enough to react.

September 25, 1980, is when I should have smelled a
rat. Or at least a dirty peacock. It was on that date that,
while attending a hearing of the Nevada State Gaming
Control Board in Carson City, Nevada, I came in contact
with NBC reporter Brian Ross. After emerging from the
hearing room and talking to various reporters, I walked
out into the upstairs hallway of the Gaming Control Board
building. Ross was caustic. He was on the verge of bad-
gering me, not even giving me a chance to answer one
question before firing another one at me. We walked down
the stairs. First Frank Fahrenkopf, my attorney and national chairman of the Republican party, patted me on the
back and said, "Come on," realizing that these people
must have been there for something other than an interview. As we made our way down the stairs, so did Brian
Ross with his crew. There was a guy holding a boom microphone and another operating a video camera. Ross continued to badger me and I finally said, "This is not the
time or the place." Ross responded, "There is no better
time and no better place."

I put my hand on Ross's shoulder and said, "Look, do
me a favor." And Ross snapped, "I'm not doing you any
favors." At that point Fahrenkopf grabbed my arm and
we continued to walk out into the actual parking lot area.
But that didn't stop Ross. He kept shouting, "Tell me, tell
me, tell me. I want to know, I want to know, I want to
know." My attorney said to me, "No statement."

I finally had enough of Ross and said, "I don't care
what you want to know." Ross quickly responded, "I'm
sorry. I want to know about Guido Penosi." With that I
answered, "I don't want to talk to you about Guido Penosi." Ross, egging me on, said, "Go ahead and talk."

Ross's behavior went beyond just being a persistent reporter. From the moment we stepped into the hallway, which was no more than four feet wide, he seemed desperate. It was like Ross had something that he needed to get on tape and he was going to make damn sure he got it. It was instant hostility the moment I stepped out of the hearing room. Ross obviously had come to Carson City to get footage of me being riled and angry, and NBC edited that film in such a way that they could put me on the screen next to Frank Piccolo, Guido's cousin.

NBC wanted to interview me, but since I was too involved in negotiations for the Aladdin Hotel as well as doing two shows every night, I turned them down. Before my September encounter with Brian Ross, Mark Moreno called me and told me that there were NBC reporters who were going to interview Lola Falana with regard to the Aladdin and wanted to know if I would do an interview with them also. I explained to Moreno that not until after we were licensed, or had the hotel, would I be willing to sit down before TV cameras. Because if we didn't get the hotel, I didn't need the publicity.

On that Thursday, September 25, the day of the hearing, we had all gone to lunch—"we" being my partner, Ed Torres; Parry Thomas, president of Valley Bank; my attorney, Frank Fahrenkopf; and me. During lunch, Steve Schorr, a reporter and friend with the NBC affiliate in Las Vegas, approached me and asked, "Wayne, can I talk to you?" I said, "Sure." That's when Steve told me, "Do you know that there's a team from national television here filming the whole hearing?" I assured him that I didn't and asked him why. Schorr said he didn't know why they were here, but thought that I should know about it. That was the first time I was ever aware that NBC was filming the entire hearing.

Two hours later Brian Ross was to throw up the name Guido Penosi. Until that moment NBC wanted to interview me as to why I would be interested in purchasing the Aladdin and putting my name and reputation on the line. They said they wanted to talk about show-business kinds of things. They never once mentioned Guido Penosi. Had they mentioned his name, I perhaps wouldn't have refused them. But there was no doubt, after the incident in the corridor, that NBC was out to get me. You can't imagine how I felt having Brian Ross shouting questions at me. I was bewildered. I had gone through everything that the Gaming Control Board asked me, and all of a sudden the gestapo tactics were beginning.

Like the expression "when it rains, it pours," it seemed a monsoon. Even the newspapers jumped aboard the "Let's get Wayne Newton" bandwagon. The *Chicago Sun-Times,* on October 14, 1980, ran the headline NEWTON MAY BE SINGING A DIFFERENT TUNE. The newspaper wrote:

Wayne Newton, the slimy Las Vegas singer, is playing with fire when he implies that Johnny Carson may be trying to smear him with Mafia-oriented innuendo.

In a report last week by correspondent Brian Ross and producer Ira Silverman on NBC Nightly News, Newton was accused of having a cozy relationship with reputed mobster Guido Penosi. The Ross-Silverman story said that Newton sought Penosi's assistance in buying the scandal-scarred Aladdin Hotel in Vegas for $85 million. The sale went through, and according to NBC, the New York Mafia family of Carlo Gambino became a silent partner in the deal.

An angry Newton denies the charges, admitting only that he went to Penosi for help when Newton's four-year-old daughter had become the target of unspecified threats.

He's talking about suing NBC for slander, defamation of character and everything else, and he calls the Ross-Silverman report "the most blatant abuse of national press I have ever seen."

But Newton, whose voice finally changed about ten years ago, may have stubbed his toe by uttering Johnny Carson's name. According to Newton, Carson probably

had something to do with the NBC report. That's nonsense, of course. It's true that Carson once wanted to
buy the Aladdin and that he was muscled aside by Newton's investment group. It's also true that Johnny pokes
a lot of fun at Newton during his *Tonight Show* mono-
logues. However, to link Carson's professional and personal distaste for Newton with the straight news report
that's admittedly damaging to the singer's image is pretty
stupid.

Reliable sources say if Newton opens his trap once
more about this absurd Carson connection, he will wind
up on the receiving end of a lawsuit.

Although the article was syndicated around the country,
our demand for publication of a retraction went unnoticed.
The *Chicago Sun-Times* could have cared less. It was open
season on Wayne Newton and they were all out for blood.

I went from being Mr. Clean to being a hood. I've never
been involved with drugs or arrested for drunk driving,
and, to my knowledge, I'd never been around Mafia figures. I've worked very hard my entire life to maintain a
good reputation, and in three two-and-a-half-minute seg-
ments, NBC destroyed it to the point where it can never
be restored to its original condition. You think people who
saw those broadcasts are ever going to forget them? I don't.
Do you know what it feels like to have parents forbid their
kids to play with your daughter because you're a member
of the Mafia? Or to receive fan mail that says, "Jeez, we
thought you were okay, but now we realize you're successful because you're a member of the Mafia"?

It was a nightmare, and a month later it got even worse.
I got a subpoena to testify before a federal grand jury in
Connecticut. The reason I was there was because one of
the NBC broadcasts said I had lied under oath to the Nevada Gaming Control Board about my association with
Guido Penosi. NBC reported that I was going to be the
government's star witness against the mob. I was sitting
at home watching this with my wife and I said, "I'm a

dead man.'' She asked me why NBC would report such a
thing, and I told her I didn't know, but I was a dead man.

Approximately a month later I was in Los Angeles vis-
iting my then manager, Jerry Weintraub, and I received a
phone call from the Las Vegas Metro police. They asked
me when I was coming home. When I arrived at the airport three Metro policemen met me. I was escorted to the
Aladdin Hotel to my dressing room and found two FBI
agents waiting for me. I listened to what they had to tell
me. The FBI proceeded to reveal to me that some informant within the mob had found out that my name was on
a hit list. One of five people. Four of the people had already been killed. They told me that I shouldn't go home,
that it would be safer for my family if I stayed at the hotel.
I asked the FBI agents, ''Why would they want to kill me?
I don't know anything about them.'' One of the FBI agents
said, ''Well, from what NBC has reported, they don't
know that you don't know anything about them.'' In my
disbelief I asked, ''Where do we go from here?'' The FBI
agent shook his head. ''We don't know.''

As I took the bulletproof vest they gave me and proceeded upstairs to the hotel to stay in a suite for two weeks,
I couldn't believe that this could be happening. A contract
on my life had been ordered by the New York Gambino
mob family. Wayne Newton was now on a Mafia hit list.
The hit list was real. About a week before the FBI talked
to me, Frank Piccolo was blown away with a shotgun, and
he was one of the five guys on that list. The FBI told me
he'd been killed because he was trafficking in drugs, and
the particular Mafia family Piccolo belonged to didn't believe in selling drugs. They felt that what Piccolo was
doing by himself would get them in trouble. So they took
care of him.

The contract was ordered because of publicity sur-
rounding my involvement in a federal investigation in New
Haven, Connecticut, of the Gambino family's activities
within the entertainment industry.

When the FBI told me that they would check with me

daily, I was shocked. I asked them, "What do you mean you're going to check with me daily? Aren't you going to offer me any protection at all?"

Frank Fahrenkopf, chairman of the Republican National Committee, found out what was going on in Washington and called Governor Robert List. The governor called me in my dressing room at the Aladdin between shows and was just aghast. He said, "Wayne, I don't know what to tell you. Is there anything at all I can do within my power?" I said, "Governor, to my knowledge there isn't anything anybody can do. We just have to sit and wait." And he said, "Please know I'm there if you need me."

It was almost like déjà vu. I had heard it before. The FBI said, "Mr. Newton, there is nothing we can do until they move against you." So I moved into the hotel and my protection consisted of busboys who were friends, a schoolteacher, a couple of waiters, and a stagehand. I had twelve guys who slept on the floor and took turns around the clock protecting the hotel suite. Immediately after working every night, I went directly to my suite. My big fear was that some innocent person was going to get killed. Everybody became a suspect. Room-service waiters, maids, even people walking down the hallway carrying a bag.

One night I decided to hell with it. I was going to go home to see my wife and daughter. As we went out to get into my car, there was a guy walking down the alley carrying a sack. All of a sudden six weapons were pulled on him. He dropped the sack when he realized that his life was in danger. There wasn't anything in it but magazines. He could have lost his life because our nerves were frazzled. Every night as I walked onstage, it more than crossed my mind that it could be my last performance.

I'm very much a fatalist. However, in the back of my mind I realized that if anybody was going to shoot me they probably wouldn't do it when I was onstage because there would be too many witnesses. Every night before the show began, my bodyguards stood at the main door of the showroom and observed everybody who came in. They kept their eyes peeled for a weapon. Two bodyguards were stationed at the stage door and three in my dressing room.

I never expected it to hit the press with a banner headline, NEWTON MOB TARGET. My friend Senator Paul Laxalt was receiving an award at Caesars Palace and I was supposed to be the keynote speaker. Former Governor Mike O'Callahan was chairman for the affair. The FBI told me not to go. They said, "If you're going to be killed, that's the place they'll do it." O'Callahan and Laxalt are very dear friends of mine, and I felt I owed it to them to tell them the truth. When I called O'Callahan on the telephone, I told him, "Mike, I cannot give the keynote speech. I will however, come over for a moment, introduce Paul, and leave immediately. I'll explain to you later. I can't do it right now."

Governor O'Callahan was obviously irritated. So the next day I went to his house and told him the entire story.

About two weeks later the FBI said, "Well, our informant tells us that your name has been taken off the hit list. So you can go home." Right after that, I went to Mexico on behalf of the Las Vegas Convention Authority. Former Governor O'Callahan, associate editor for the *Las Vegas Sun*, broke the story about me being the target of the Mafia hit list.

People and *Esquire* magazines, among others, reported that Penosi might have gotten those death threats stopped, but then made threatening phone calls of his own in order to extort money from me. That was all BS. The press came out with that only after NBC said Penosi and his cousin, Frank Piccolo, were going to be arrested and tried for conspiracy to extort part of my ownership in the Aladdin Hotel. After they were arrested the federal attorneys asked me if I'd testify against Guido. I told them, "Look, if you put me on the stand, I can only hurt your case, because I've got to tell the truth. The man never tried to extort anything from me. He's never asked me for a cent or a comp or anything. To my knowledge, Guido's never been anything at all to me but a fan and a friend. I'm not going to stand up and say anything different in court."

Before our battle with NBC began, my attorney, Mort Galane, said to me, "You're going to lose your wife, you're going to lose your family. You are not going to walk away from this trial without scars regardless of how many scars you think you have now."

When he told me this I looked him squarely in the eyes and spoke from the heart: "I have a bigger faith in the American people than that. I have a bigger faith in our judicial system than that. I want to tell you, if there's a right and there is a wrong, we will win this because they're wrong."

There was never a moment, even when I became exhausted after a day in court, when I lost faith. It was difficult to hear the things that NBC accused me of; it was difficult to control my temper and anger. But through it all I kept my faith in God and the American people, and neither one of them let me down. Yes, I prayed during the trial. But, then, I say a prayer every night before I walk onstage. I didn't pray to win; I didn't say, "God, please help me win this." What I said was, "God, do what is right by me. Whatever you've sent me into this battle for, let your will prevail."

In my heart I believe God sent me into battle against NBC for a reason. I believe that what came out of my war with these people will benefit all Americans who have been unjustly accused and, for financial or other reasons, couldn't fight back.

When the jury was out and we were waiting for a verdict, I received calls from President Reagan and the First Lady and Senator Paul Laxalt. The day we won I received more calls at the courthouse from all three. They were most sympathetic and understanding. At that time, the president was going through the whole Iran thing where the press was claiming he had known everything that Oliver North and Admiral Poindexter were doing. Senator Paul Laxalt, who was battling the newspaper The Sacra-

mento Bee, realized, like every politician, the importance of this trial.

The jury was out for six days. President Reagan told me, "Keep your chin up. No matter which way this turns out, you've got a lot of friends. And I'm one of them." Nancy Reagan telephoned a number of times to say that she was just checking to see if I was all right and letting me know that they were saying a prayer for me.

I was at home, sitting in my living room, when the phone rang and the housekeeper said, "Mr. Newton, it's your attorney, Mr. Galane." My heart went to my feet. I didn't think I'd be able to walk from the living room to the phone. When I picked up the phone my attorney said, "The jury is in. You'd better get down here. How long will it take you?" I said, "It's going to take me fifteen minutes." Galane said, "Get here in ten."

My friend and associate Joe Schenck was with me, and he said, "Do you have any indication?" I looked at him and responded, "No." Then, all of a sudden, I started to shake because I realized at that moment that round one was really over. I put on a suit and I didn't even bother to shave. I jumped in the station wagon and drove out the front gate and saw my dad on a tractor clearing away some brush in the middle of the field. He was dirty and dusty. As I passed him I did a U-turn. My friend Marla was in the car with me and she frightfully asked, "Where are you going?" I answered, "I'm going back to get my dad."

I drove across the field, and as I pulled up I could see that he was filthy from all the dust and sand. I just looked at him and said, "Hop in. The jury's in." We didn't even exchange words.

Tears of joy streamed down my face as the verdict was read. I had won my multimillion-dollar defamation suit against NBC. It had taken more than five years of legal maneuvering, ten weeks of testimony, and nearly six days of federal jury deliberation. The jury awarded me $19.3 million in total damages. The date shall always be in my mind and in my heart—December 17, 1986. The jury made

it clear that NBC, Brian Ross, Ira Silverman, and executive producer Paul Greenberg knew—or should have
known—that the series of broadcasts in 1980 and 1981 gave
a false and defamatory impression.

The jury, seated in a makeshift court in the Cashman
Field Complex in Las Vegas, went through hours of deliberation before awarding me $5 million for damage to my
reputation, $225,000 for my physical and mental suffering,
$7.9 million for loss of income, and $1,467,500 for loss
of future income. It was one dime for each reported viewer
of the NBC broadcast.

The network was ordered to pay $5 million in exem-
plary or punitive damages because the jurors believed that
we had "proved by a preponderance of evidence that one
or more of the individual defendants harbored ill will or
hatred toward Wayne Newton and intended to injure him."

My attorneys, Morton Galane and Frank Fahrenkopf, had
urged the jury to send a message to the media, NBC, and
corporate stockholders by returning a guilty verdict.

In rebuttal, the chief lawyer for NBC, Floyd Abrams,
along with a battery of attorneys, said that I had created
my own problems by turning to organized-crime figures
for help in halting death threats against my family.

In the final argument to jurors on December 10, Galane
had blasted NBC for a "total absence of institutional conscience" and asked the panel to rule for me and thereby
set an example to top levels of network management. "You
don't have to go to college and professional school and
graduate school to say you're sorry. You have to have a
conscience," Galane stated. It was interesting to see the
way the jury broke it down: so much for malice, so much
for loss of business reputation, so much for health and
stress, as well as an amount for future earnings and an
amount for past earnings. The jury did an incredible job.

It incenses me that NBC, after losing, attacked the jury's
decision. They stated that this was just a case of a local
boy with a local jury. How could they say that when there

wasn't anyone on the jury who was born and raised in Las Vegas? Everybody was from somewhere else!

In late November 1987, U.S. District Judge Myron Crocker gave me until February 1 to accept a reduced award, or undergo a new trial on the issue of damages only. Since this was never a matter of money but a matter of vindicating my name, we accepted the $6-million libel award. My lawyer told reporters that the interest accrued on the reduced award of $5,275,000 brought the total to $6 million. According to Galane, "such an amount would be higher than any libel award ever affirmed by an appellate court in the history of this nation by five times."

During 1988, we conducted a survey to test public response to the reporting of a high libel award in favor of me. This survey confirmed that the public believed the award was fair, and the fact that I won such a large amount has helped to restore my positive image. That means more to me than all the money in the world.

CHAPTER 22

My brother was always the apple of her eye, right up to the last words she ever spoke.

MY MOTHER HAD always said that when she died she wanted to be buried within twelve hours. She was only in the hospital a total of five days and had never been sick a day in her life. I had gone to Virginia to surprise them and buy them a home. I had made a tentative deal on a big plantation of twelve hundred acres to the tune of $2.5 million dollars. They were living in Las Vegas at the time and deep down inside they always wanted to go back to Virginia. I thought it would be neat if they could have a plantation they could enjoy in the spring and in the fall. The home was built in the early 1700s and was just like the one in *Gone With the Wind.*

The plan was that I was to pick up my parents under the pretense that we were all going to Ted Jacobs's daughter's graduation. After the graduation in Chicago I would surprise them by flying them to Virginia and giving them the keys to their very own plantation.

The day before we were going to do all this I received a call with the news: "Your mother's in the hospital." I called my dad and he gave me the bad news. She was in intensive care and he said, "They think she's got pneumonia and maybe you ought to come home." At that moment I felt selfish. I felt I had been cheated because I had dreamed of buying them a plantation ever since the early days of poverty. Here I was, within one day of fulfilling that dream.

As I flew home I said to myself, "The dream is only going to be postponed. I've had pneumonia four times. So in a few weeks I'll be showing them their new paradise."

She died three days later.

My dad doesn't like to talk about it, and tears always come to his eyes when he tells the story of how she died: "She was stubborn. If she had her mind set on something, she'd do it. I couldn't get her to go to the doctor. The two of us were out trimming roses and I was running a gasoline engine pumping insecticide when she came up to me and touched me on the shoulder. She said, 'I just fell and hurt myself.' I said, 'Where did you hurt yourself?' You could tell she was in a lot of pain. She just held on to her spine and said that it pained her terribly. She was as white as a sheet. I cut the motor and had her lie down on the grass for a moment. She kept saying over and over, 'I'll be all right.' Well, she lay down for a while and then sat back up. I got her in the golf cart and started driving for home. All the way she kept throwing up.

"The minute we reached the front door I said, 'Let me take you to the doctor.' She just looked at me and shook her head no. She came in and lay down on the couch and asked me to fix her a little bourbon and hot coffee. After she drank it, it seemed to ease the pain for a little while. Unfortunately it didn't last.

"Within a couple of days she was all bent over and every movement was extremely painful. Finally I got mad at her. I walked into the bedroom and didn't ask but told her, 'You've got to get dressed. Now, get your dress and shoes on 'cause, lady, I'm gonna take you to the hospital.'

"As bullheaded as she was, she said, 'You ain't takin' me nowhere. If I leave, I know I'll never come back.' I just looked at her and said, 'That's nonsense.' And I'll always remember how she looked at me and said, 'Well, get my lipstick,' I told her, 'Forget your lipstick. Just get your shoes and robe on.' I practically carried her to the car, and as I drove her over to the hospital, during that short drive, she didn't know me from that time on.

"I often have blamed myself for not remembering about the arteries in her neck which had closed. A long time ago every one of her brothers but one had died of the same thing. The doctor said the initial cause of death was pneumonia. If I had been thinking, who knows, maybe she could have been saved. I'll never forgive myself. All I kept thinking about was how she said she was hurting all the way across her chest. I guess that's what was wrong when they performed the autopsy on her. They discovered the artery problem. You think the doctors would have diagnosed something other than pneumonia. It's a disgrace.

"I went over to see her and her feet were swollen up. They were so round and so swollen, and they felt just like ice. I took my socks off and put them on her feet. I thought maybe it would warm them up."

The day before she passed away, in her last coherent moment, we were at her bedside. She opened her eyes, wondering if we were all there. She looked at all of us and said, "Where's your brother?" My brother was always the apple of her eye, right up to the last words she ever spoke. I turned around. He was standing behind us. She didn't see him.

She passed away around midnight. We were all destroyed.

Someone had to take the reins. So I went and found the cedar chest she had had ever since I was a little boy. We carried it from coast to coast in our U-Haul trailer. It was all beat up. There I found the dress she wanted to be buried in. We took it to the funeral parlor and buried her at two the next day, which was also my opening night at the MGM Grand. My dad was so devastated, I had to handle the funeral arrangements. As I did I thought to myself, *There would be nothing better that I could do than go to work.* In a strange way I felt it would be a tribute to her.

Everyone was waiting to see if there was going to be a

show. So I called my secretary, Mona, and said, "The show will go on." I also explained to her, "I want you to tell my good friend and conductor, Don Vincent, and everyone else that I do not wish to discuss it. I don't want people coming in and telling me how sorry they are. I appreciate it and I'm not insensitive, but that will not help me through this time." So I did two shows that night. And there wasn't one person in the audience who could have known what had happened. I know that would have pleased my mom.

She loved life. She had a great wit, was extremely sharp, and liked to laugh a lot. My dad loves to tell the story about the time they were driving through Oklahoma City in a mobile home. She didn't drive, so Dad seemed to spend all of his time behind the wheel. When they arrived in Oklahoma, it was one o'clock in the morning. My mom took one look at my dad and said, "Why don't you just get us a room tonight and we'll get a good bath and have a good night's sleep?" So they pulled into the hotel parking lot and went in. When they arrived at the front desk they were told there wasn't a room in the building. Just as they started to walk away disappointed, the manager shouted, "Wait! The only thing we've got's a suite and it's a bridal suite." Well, my dad didn't hesitate. He stated, "We'll take it!"

The next morning when they went down for breakfast and were checking out, the desk clerk smiled and said with a laugh, "Oh, we were in the bridal suite last night, were we?" My dad was embarrassed, but my mom said, "Yes. You can rent a ballroom but you don't have to dance."

She had a great sense of humor. One time, during dinner, I told my mother that I had just received the Indian Entertainer of the Year Award. Without looking up from her plate, she asked, "Who else was in the running?"

The thing I remember my mother saying most is, "Wayne does not care which way the wind blows as long as it doesn't hit him."

My dad didn't go to the funeral. He just sat on the couch and stared in disbelief. He couldn't believe that there could be a life without her. They had been together so long.

They had met at a little old dinky carnival in Fredericksburg, Virginia. He asked her if she wanted to knock down some milk bottles. She said, "I can't hit them," and my dad replied, "I can't either." From that moment they started dating and went together three months. They were married in August 1939. She was eighteen and he was twenty-three. And they shared a wonderful life together. Forty-six years of being inseparable.

The day of the funeral, my father talked about her and the life they shared together. He summed it up this way: "I lived a beautiful life with her. I can't complain, not about a thing. Your mother was very special. She wasn't a money spender. She knew where her dollar was going before she spent it. If I wanted to buy something, I'd always talk with her about it. Even moving all over the country we always talked about it and made the decision together. She believed a wife's purpose is to help her man, not to pull you down. I don't think that while we were married I ever saw a paycheck. I'd bring it home, give it to her, and she'd take care of everything. She'd lay my clothes out for me, including my socks. And every morning I knew what to wear. If I got up to go fishing, she'd get up and fix my breakfast for me at three in the morning. I used to beg her not to do it and she'd always say, 'Well, you can't go hungry.' She looked after me just like I was a kid. Spoiled me is what she did. The day she died and I was all alone, I realized for the first time that I didn't know how to run the washer or dryer, even the dishwasher. Without her it was as if the good Lord had taken my very heart and soul."

If I could have avoided it I wouldn't have gone to my own mother's funeral. And while I'm sure many will criticize me for going on with the show the night of her funeral, I did it to snap myself out of the tremendous depression I felt. It was that or go insane. Performing was something I had to do to remain sane. The funeral had fallen totally on my shoulders. My father was incapable of handling it and my brother was not particularly of any help. I knew that it was up to me to hold our world together, and for me to rise above my own grief meant I had to work. It got me through when my mother died, it got me through when Jack Benny died, it got me through when Bobby Darin died, and the same with Elvis.

I made the mistake of attending Jack Benny's funeral. When I arrived, I became totally frozen. I stood outside; I refused to go in. I could hear parts of it as my heart and my insides were being torn apart. I am one of those people for whom paying tribute to the dead cannot be done well in public.

I go to my mother's grave about once a month when all the lights are out and it's just the two of us alone. I talk to her and ask her so many questions. I'm not a good public mourner. I just don't like people to see me cry.

I kept my promise to my mother that she would to be buried immediately. I took a lot of heat from her family. They came down hard. They accused me of being selfish, heartless, and cruel. They said, "How do you dare to do something like that without giving us the chance of coming and paying our respects?" My answer to them remains the same today: You should pay your respects while people are alive. There is nothing you can do for them after that. That's been part of my philosophy toward my parents my whole life. I never wanted to look back at any time and say, "I should have"; I wished I had"; "Why didn't I?"

I believe that the body in the casket is nothing more than a shell. I think the real soul has gone on, and to sit around and pray and hold a funeral service and have your friends show up seems almost barbaric to me. While I'm a religious man, there is no religious foundation to public viewing, where people walk up to the casket and say things like, "Look how nice she looks. It's like she's sleeping." I want to believe they're gone. That's why we closed my mother's casket. Those are the things you remember last.

No matter how many wonderful memories you have about anybody, that picture of them lying in a coffin is what sticks in your mind. I want to remember them alive.

Close friends have often asked me if I'm prepared for death. I guess I'm as prepared as much as anyone can be. I have a premonition that I will be buried on my plantation, Casa de Shenandoah.

I do believe in reincarnation. I don't think you come back as a dog or a bird or that kind of thing, but I believe in the evolution of the soul. I believe I've lived before. The reason I'm convinced is that I have certain interests and compulsions for no rhyme or reason. There's this strange calling and a bizarre affinity for the South. I can't explain it, but I recently bought a house there and it's doubtful I'll be able to spend much time in it. But it was something I had to do.

Sometimes I hear Indian voices. That has to do with the fact that I'm Indian—much more so than one would imagine. Look at the name of my ranch. It's just never very far from my thoughts. And then, too, I often have dreams of the Civil War and the great joys I experienced during that time. I can't explain it, but I know I lived through that war. I have feelings which I can't explain that send a chill up and down my spine. Anytime I visit Gettysburg, I feel as if I'm coming home.

CHAPTER 23

I leaned my head against the wall and began to cry uncontrollably. This was more than a horse. This was a soul that I loved deeply.

EVERYONE HAS PASSIONS in life. My two have been music and horses. As long as I can remember, I've always wanted to sing and I've always wanted a horse. My mother's uncle was always promising me a pony. As I was growing up, I'd beg my parents to see him because I was sure that on one of the trips I would walk into his barn and there would be a pony waiting for me. It never happened.

When I moved to Arizona as a kid, I finally bought my own horse. It happened this way: I discovered that the horse was going to be killed and used for dog meat, so I traded my parents' movie camera and my entire life savings of fifty dollars so that I could save him. My parents had no idea that I had traded in the movie camera, and when I told them, my dad just shook his head. "You traded our movie camera?" And I looked him direct in the eye and said, "We don't use it a lot." My father was in shock. He held up his hand and said, "Wait a minute. You traded our movie camera." Before I could respond, he looked at me and smiled. "Did you take the film out of it first?" When I told him I had, he just winked. "Okay, as long as you kept the film." I don't think I ever loved my father more than at that moment.

Years later, Aramis galloped into my life. He was the horse of my dreams. He was the kind of horse you only see on the big screen at the movies. Along the way I had gotten interested in Arabian horses. Until then I had bought racing Thoroughbreds. Horses made me realize something about myself: I discovered that I am not a spectator by nature. I don't really like to watch sports. I like to play. I like to be a part of it.

I brought the Thoroughbreds home from the track, kept them for a while, and then started to give them away to people who wanted them and would take good care of them. It was a special kind of horse that I was looking for, and Thoroughbreds just weren't it. It's kind of like your first girlfriend. Once you pass that first time, you become a little more selective.

But even though I was disappointed with Thoroughbreds, the dream did not die. As a child I imagined owning a big ranch where people could bring their old horses that they didn't want anymore, where I could turn them loose and let them live out their final days happily. Every kid has those kinds of dreams about something or other. For me, they were about horses.

Then it happened. I went to Phoenix to do a show and stopped by an old stable where I used to ride as a kid. There I saw a black Arabian stallion. My legs weakened. It was as if I had been hit by a ton of bricks. This is what I was looking for in horses all my life. But I didn't know it until that moment.

When I was a child, I had in my bedroom a painting of two horses. One was white, the other was black, and they were crossing their necks in the wind. They appeared to be in the middle of a storm. When I saw this black Arabian stallion, that picture flashed in my mind. At once I started to look for Arabian horses. I wanted black Arabian horses, not knowing that they were mutants. The Arabian horse is a horse of the desert. The reason God gave them white or gray hair was so that they would reflect the sun.

I was convinced that I could raise the perfect black Arabian horse. Well, I found myself buying twenty horses before I realized that you cannot breed a horse for color.

You have to breed for conformation. You have to let the animal be what it is.

My horse trainer said, "I saw the most incredible horse in my whole life. He's in Wisconsin. Wayne, you won't believe it; he's snow white." The trainer added, "He was just imported from Poland and we might be able to lease him, but he's not for sale. His name is Aramis."

As I turned to walk away I said, "Get me a picture!" Weeks later, he showed me a picture of the horse and I couldn't believe it. Aramis was indeed incredible. As I looked at the photo I realized that I had to own him. I felt like a kid at Christmas. I kept saying to my trainer, "We've got to lease him!"

Three months passed and each day I became more jittery about Aramis. Finally the good news came. My trainer announced that the lease had been worked out and that we'd be able to pick him up in about four months because they wanted to keep him through breeding season. I honestly believe that those were the slowest-passing months in my life. There wasn't a day that I didn't look at the photo and think to myself, *This horse can't be like the picture.* It's kind of like looking at a picture of a beautiful woman. You keep thinking she can't be that pretty.

Well, the time finally arrived. My trainer went back to Wisconsin. He called me from there and told me, "If you think he's pretty in the picture, Wayne, wait till you see him in person. He is a looker. The picture can't even compare to this animal."

Then there was a long pause. For a moment I thought we had been disconnected, but when his voice became a mere whisper, I knew we had a problem. "Wayne, I don't know how to tell you this. The horse has klebsiella."

I was in shock. I didn't know what to say. Klebsiella is a venereal disease that is absolutely devastating to a stallion. Once a stallion has it, he can never be cured and you can never breed him because he will pass it on to the mare.

I didn't even pause. I told my trainer, "You've got to

bring him home. I've got to see him.'' The trainer hesitated. ''Wayne, you're nuts.''

I asked, ''Who diagnosed this?''

He said the vet from the University of Wisconsin diagnosed it. ''Well, that's not enough for me to give up on Aramis,'' I said. ''You're going to bring him home and you're going the long way. You'll go by way of Kentucky and have the University of Kentucky check him. Then you'll go to New Mexico and have the university give him a going over. And when you're finished there, you'll go to Colorado. I don't care what it costs. But I'm determined to try and save Aramis. And I won't settle for anything unless we've made sure that we know positively that this horse has it.''

When my trainer said that Aramis should be put to sleep, I said, ''Not a prayer.''

From university to university Aramis went through a battery of tests. Each time I got the results, they all proved positive that he had klebsiella.

One morning I pulled aside the drapes and saw the trailer coming up the driveway to the house. Aramis was finally home. I threw on my bathrobe and ran out the front door and watched him being unloaded from the trailer. This animal was the most gorgeous creature I had ever laid eyes on. It was love at first sight. We became instantaneous soul mates. I know that sounds strange, but it's true.

The next day I telephoned the people who owned him and said, ''I want to buy the horse.'' The guy laughed at me and said, ''Buy him for what? You know his condition.'' I said, ''I'll tell you what I want to do. I'll make you a deal at two prices. One price will be if he can never be cured.'' The man laughed again. ''Wayne, you don't cure klebsiella.'' I said, ''I know. But what if I cure him?'' The man chuckled. ''He's not for sale.''

He obviously heard the desperation in my voice. I said, ''Will you sell half of him?'' He said, ''I feel badly about taking advantage of you.'' I said, ''Take advantage of me.''

He seemed choked when I asked what he'd sell half-interest in the horse for. He said, "Make me an offer."

Without hesitation I said, "Seventy-five thousand dollars if he's cured." In those days, the highest-priced stallion that was ever sold at public auction was in 1967 for $25,000. Then I added, "If he's not cured, I'll give you twenty-five thousand dollars for a half-interest in him." With happiness in his voice, the man said, "Put it in writing."

We signed the papers. I called my trainer, and in a last desperate attempt I told him I wanted to take Aramis to the University of California. I had met Dr. Don Wheat, who was the head of the veterinarian department there, and I was so impressed with him. I was willing to put my fate in his hands. Before I sent the horse there, I called him. I said, "Doc, tell me about klebsiella." Dr. Wheat was very candid. He didn't pull any punches. "Wayne, why do you want to know? I won't fill you with any horse tales. If the horse has it, and it's a mare, she'll be barren. She'll never be able to produce. If it's a stallion, you must geld him because the worst thing is to have him breed. The disease is very contagious." Then I asked the doctor the question that I dreaded most. I said, "Is it absolutely incurable?" Dr. Wheat said, "Absolutely!"

When I told the doctor that I'd be sending him a horse and that I wanted him to do all the necessary tests on him, he asked for the horse's name. The doctor seemed surprised when I told him, "That's not important. Let's just call the horse Firewind." The doctor laughed. He knew that I had made up the name at the spur of the moment. Dr. Wheat said, "Wayne, you're trying to pull one over on me. I know that's not his name." I explained to Dr. Wheat that I didn't want him to have other horse people see his real name on the stall, because then all the rumors would start. Now, as strange as all this sounds, those were exactly my thoughts: Protect the horse's name because God was going to protect Aramis.

Two weeks later I was appearing at Lake Tahoe, and as

I was taking my final bow, I heard a whisper from the side of the stage. Mona Montoba, my secretary, was standing in the wings waving at me and telling me, "It's Dr. Wheat. He says it's important." I don't think I've ever run to a dressing room that fast. When I picked up the telephone, I didn't even bother to say hello. The doctor spoke first. "Wayne, God likes you, doesn't he?" I knew at that moment what he was going to tell me. Dr. Wheat said, "Your horse has no trace of klebsiella."

At first I was hesitant, and, like an impatient parent, I couldn't believe his words. "Are you sure you've run enough tests?" I asked. Wheat joked, "Trust me. When you get the bill, you'll see we ran all the tests we needed to run." When I asked the doctor how that can happen, he said, "Well, veterinarians don't like to talk about it, as medical doctors often steer away from the subject, but the fact is that horses, or any animal, will contract something that is absolutely incurable, and before it's diagnosed the horse will build its own immunity to it. This is evidently what has happened in the case of this horse. You might not have ever known that the horse had a problem except that he was checked at those times when the disease was prevalent and before he could build his own antibodies to it."

I sat down at the makeup table, put the phone down, put both hands over my eyes, and thanked God. Through the receiver I could hear Dr. Wheat talking. Those words still echo in my ears: "Your horse is absolutely clear and free of any problems and he is magnificent. Good luck with Firewind." He laughed and hung up.

The day Aramis came home it was like a welcome-home celebration. I never felt so good and so thankful for God's blessings. I called his former owner and said, "I'm going to have to send you the rest of your money now." The guy was in shock. We started to show him and he won more national championships than any horse in the history of the Arabian breed. He became the standard for

what the Arabian horse should look like. He was the
sweetest animal God had ever put a breath of life into.

Aramis sired more than 420 foals in his life. The horse
was so good he had won the national championship, beating out a horse that had won four different times in prere-
gional shows. They had a show in Reno, Nevada, called
the Supreme National Championship Class. The only way
a horse was eligible for that category was if he had won a
national championship. Once they've won a national
championship, they can't go back and compete again the
next year in that same class. They're done forever. It's like
winning the Triple Crown. So when I was told about this
Supreme National Championship Class, and was asked if
I wanted to put Aramis in it, I was also told that the last
three national champions were going to be there. I raised
my fist in the air and shouted, ''Let's go for it!''

The contest was under a three-judge system. Aramis
had that special something that set him apart. The grand-
stands went nuts when they saw him enter the ring.

After the judges had made their decisions and turned in
their cards, the horses were standing in the ring. My trainer
was on the rail and had his back to Aramis, talking to his
son. Everyone was waiting for the judges to tabulate all
the points to see who had won. One of the judges, Billy
Harris, who had already turned in his card, wanted to go
back to look at Aramis again to see how magnificent he
was. The horse was just standing their looking around.
When the judge walked down the center of the arena, Aramis saw him out of the corner of his eye. My trainer was
busy talking to his son on the rail and was oblivious to the
fact that the judge was headed his way. Without a moment's hesitation, Aramis stood up, placed his feet where
they should be, and struck the pose. The place came apart.
There were cheers from the showgoers because the horse
was literally showing himself at that moment. I could have
burst with pride. He knew that's what he was supposed to
do for the judge. That's the kind of horse he was. He won
on a unanimous vote.

I had made a deal with the previous owners to alternate keeping him for breeding season. It became such a love affair between us that Aramis was devastated when he had to leave me. The first year it was very difficult for me to see him go. Even though he was there for only three months, when he returned I could tell that he was not nearly in the condition he was in when he left. When he came back to see me after one of his trips, he had lost about 300 pounds. It saddened me so much that I knew I could no longer take it. I had put into the contract a buyer-sell clause. That meant that if either of us were unhappy with the other's partnership, whatever they offered for sale, they also had to buy. If they said, "I want another seventy-five thousand dollars for the second half," they had to be prepared to pay that or sell it for that. So I said, "Buy me out or sell, because I can't take it anymore."

When they replied, "Send me your check," I jumped with joy. Aramis was totally mine.

One day I hopped in my helicopter and flew up to my ranch in Logandale, which is 218 acres. I wanted to see what was going on up at the ranch. I had hired a guy who had come highly recommended as a breeding manager, and at that point we were breeding a lot of horses. A mare's cycle is every 18–22 days. You bring the mare out and bring a stallion to face her. If she gets excited and starts to show that she's in heat, then you lead that stallion away and bring out another stallion you're going to breed her with. You never use the breeding stallion as a teaser. Most of the time ponies and miniature horses are used. I heard that the new breeding manager used Aramis one time as a tease, and I flew up to Logandale and sat him down for a heart-to-heart discussion. He wasn't too delighted with what I had to say. Eyeball-to-eyeball I told him, "Never go near that stallion again unless you're breeding with him. And you're never, ever to use him as a teasing horse." I really chewed him out because he was messing with Aramis.

About six months later, I went up to the ranch and had

the trainer bring out Aramis. He was always food for my eyes. Then I'd personally bring him back to the stall and feed him an apple. He was always as happy to see me as I was to see him. However, that day I noticed when they brought him out of his stall that he didn't have that fire; he didn't have that attitude he always had. I instantly recognized a problem. I said to my trainer, "Did you work him today?" Whether he did or not I'll never know. But he said that he had. Obviously, if a horse is worked, and maybe even bred to a mare, that day he's not going to be as arrogant and as up as he would be if he had been resting. So I pressed the issue. "Tell me, did you work him today?" He hemmed and hawed and finally said, "Yeah." I remember thinking that maybe he didn't and maybe he did.

About a week passed and I got a call from my veterinarian in my dressing room. I could tell that the vet was holding back bad news. He didn't have to tell me. I knew. I said to the vet, "Aramis is sick." The vet said, "You're right, Wayne, he's ill." Even as we spoke, Aramis was on his way from Logandale to Vegas, which is about seventy miles. The vet had already made telephone calls to other doctors who were rushing to the ranch.

"What's the problem?" I asked. He had to clear his voice. "We think it's hepatitis." I said, "Hepatitis? How the hell could he have hepatitis?" Even the vet had to admit that it seemed impossible and that they were still trying to find out how it could have happened. When the vet suggested that he meet me at the ranch, I was out that dressing-room door so fast I was a blur. I hit the gas pedal and didn't let up. I was going. All I could think was, *Oh, my God, Aramis.*

All of a sudden I saw flashing lights. The police pulled me over and I got out of the car and pleaded with the officer. "I've got a horse that's ill. I realize that I'm speeding. You know where to find me, but I've got to go." The police officer tipped his cap. "Mr. Newton, go right ahead. But be careful."

Aramis's love for me was so great that the moment he saw me he acted happy and began to prance. I looked at the doctors as if they were nuts. "What makes you think he's ill?" Then the moment of truth. The vet pulled up Aramis's lip and he was already yellowing. Then he pulled back the whites of his eyes and they too had begun to yellow. "Tell me about this," I said, hoping against hope.

"Wayne, we have bad problems here. A horse doesn't have a gallbladder like a human does. The poisons will attack the liver and the kidneys, and they do it directly. There is nothing to absorb the poisons. The reason he's yellowing is jaundice. Aramis's body is so full of poison that we're going to have to do something and we're going to have to do it quickly."

My feet didn't touch the ground. Every telephone in the house became a hot line. I started calling everybody. We called all around the world. We got the best vets in the country on the phone. My plane was constantly ready in case we had to bring them to Las Vegas in what was our only hopes of saving Aramis.

Someone recommended a young veterinarian in California by the name of Doug Herthell. I sent the plane for him and he came to Vegas, where we spent fifty-three hours without sleep with Aramis. We had a special telephone line installed in the barn and he was even on the phone to Europe constantly.

I was holding Aramis's head in my arms. Doug walked over to me looking drained and exhausted. He put his arms around me and whispered, "Aramis will probably die."

I pleaded, "Doug, you must try something." He said, "Could we have a donor horse?" I didn't understand what he meant. He said, "Could we take one of your other horses and use it pretty much the same way as we would with dialysis with kidney patients?" We would actually pull the blood out, run it through another horse and take out the toxicity and run it back. The doctor stated that perhaps there was a chance that we could get enough oxygen into Aramis's blood that the dialysis treatment could save his life. A long shot, but a shot.

At this point Aramis wasn't living for himself but for his love for me. If I left the barn and went to the house to get something to eat, Aramis would start to fail tremendously. Doug would run up to the house and tell me to get to the barn immediately. I'd go back out there and the horse would perk up as if nothing were wrong. Doug said to me, "I've never seen anything like this and if anyone told me that a horse could react this way and could show such strong emotions, I'd call them a liar. Aramis does not want you to see him this way."

Being totally exhausted and worried sick, I debated whether I should cancel my show. When I asked the doctor if I should go to work, he said, "Yes. It's the best thing you could do for yourself. There's nothing more you can do except give Aramis moral support."

So I went onstage, and between shows I would rush home. After the second show I would stay up with him all night and let Doug get some sleep. Aramis would actually stand there with his head in my arms and go to sleep. All of a sudden he would jump. He'd wake up, look at me with those sad eyes, and fall back to sleep. I could sense he was failing. Doug didn't even want to tell me how bad it was, but I didn't need to hear the words from him. Just one look at Aramis pretending for my sake to be healthy and I knew.

For months a recording session had been scheduled. Neil Sedaka had cleared all of his engagements so that the two of us could record "Hungry Years." Sedaka was doing a duo with me on part of the tune. Of course I wanted to cancel the session, but everyone advised me against it. So I went to Doug and asked, "How long have we got?" He shook his head, thought for a moment, and said, "We've got another forty-eight to, possibly, fifty-six hours." He advised me to go to L.A. He said, "I think it would be best for you emotionally if you lived up to the commitment and recorded." I looked down at the ground and confessed, "I don't know if I can record. I don't know if I have it in me. I have this lump in my throat and I don't know if I can do it."

Doug put his arm on my shoulder. "Look, you go ahead. But come right back after the session because the horse's will to live is totally dependent upon your being here. The minute you leave, he really will start to go downhill. He'll only fight if you're with him."

I only wished I had followed my gut reaction not to go. I went to L.A., and it couldn't have been six hours when the call came. Aramis had died. To this day I'll never know how I finished the session. I hung up the telephone, leaned my head against the wall, and began to cry uncontrollably.

This was more than a horse. This was a soul that I loved deeply.

When I arrived home Elaine met me at the door. It was one of the most tender moments of our marriage. She was crying. She threw her arms around me and said, "I don't know what to say." She didn't have to say anything. I could feel her heart breaking against mine and I knew that we had both lost something very precious. The silence was broken when Elaine told me that the veterinarians wanted to do an autopsy on Aramis. Even Doug was adamant on the subject. "The other vets that I've talked to and spoken to in Europe went me to post this horse." I said, "He's not to be touched!"

I left Elaine and Doug standing in the driveway and slowly walked toward the barn. I opened the barn door, went in and got a blanket, and sat on the floor and groomed Aramis. The entire night I sat there staring at him. I sat with him until we buried him the next day.

He was buried on a bitter-cold January morning. It was dark and clouds filled the sky. The weather reflected my grief. Nobody really understood the relationship that Aramis and I had. If you're a real animal lover, and you've had that one soul in your life that will never come again, then you know the feeling.

Aramis is buried right on the other side of the lake looking toward the main house at the Shenandoah. And there isn't a day that passes that I don't walk by that site and bid him a hello.

I asked everyone to leave once we put Aramis in the grave, and I took a blanket and wrapped his head in it.

A gnawing question kept running through my mind: How did Aramis get hepatitis? I found out that the same breeding manager I told to stay away from Aramis had given him a shot that Aramis should not have had. Apparently the horse was out playing and he had scraped himself with one of his hooves. It didn't even draw blood. But this guy brought him back to the barn and gave him a shot of tetanus antitoxin, which you do not give to a horse that's over a year old.

As I look back, I'm convinced the trainer did not work the horse the day I had asked him if he had. If I had only realized that it was not activity that made Aramis so tired, we might have diagnosed hepatitis and maybe we might have been able to save his life. We will never know.

When I found out the truth about how it happened, I sent a message to Logandale. I told the guy who had given Aramis the shot that it would be best if he left the ranch, and probably, for his health, it would be best if he left the state, because if I ever saw him I'd kill him. Aside from the tremendous loss of this horse to the industry and to me personally, the guy had gone against direct orders. Repeatedly I said to him, "Don't go near Aramis. Leave him alone."

When I left Aramis's grave, Doug Herthell said, "What are you going to do?" I stopped dead in my tracks and announced, "I'm getting out of the horse business." He looked at me. "Wayne, if you do that, then everything that Aramis lived for will have died with him. He will have had no purpose if you don't carry on." I realized that what he was saying was true.

Every horse we have on the ranch today is either an

Aramis granddaughter or daughter or grandson or great-granddaughter. His blood is carried through them all.

There were a few unhappy faces when I announced that I was canceling my appearances and flying back to Poland and try to find another Aramis. It didn't work. You just can't replace a love like him. I was staying in the horse business for Aramis, but there were times when I wouldn't go to the Logandale ranch for months on end. It was too painful. It tore my insides out.

About a week after Aramis's death, I had a lot of mares that needed to be bred. It was breeding season, and I had no idea whom to breed them to. They had, in the past, been bred and purchased for Aramis. A decision had to be made. So I flew to my ranch at Logandale to determine what stallion I was going to use on the mares starting to go into heat.

Without my knowledge, the breeding manager had not left the ranch, and I was totally unaware that he had once again disobeyed my orders.

By the time I had finished my second show and arrived at the ranch, it was three o'clock in the morning. When I finally got there, there was a five-page letter handwritten to me on a yellow legal pad. It was stuck between the screen door and the front door and was signed by the breeding manager whom I had fired after Aramis's death. It took him five pages to explain to me why he went against my orders to stay away from the horse, why he had given him the shot he shouldn't have. In his own mind, he was justifying his actions. The last four lines of the letter are something I will never forget if I live to be nine thousand years old. They said: "Now, I understand that you want me off the ranch. And all I can say to you, Mr. Newton, is that you really know how to hurt a guy." He felt no shame and felt no guilt over the death of a million-dollar stallion. Nor did he care that all the money in the world could never replace Aramis. He only cared about losing his job, and how could I do that to him?

I lost a lot when Aramis died. I didn't have the same

feeling for the other horses. I had a lot of other horses, but I had built my entire herd around Aramis. Aramis had a son by the name of Aristarsa, and when his dad died he was about a year old. Days when I passed the barn, I would look in and see Aramis's empty stall and my eyes would fill with tears. I wouldn't allow anyone to put another horse in his stall. It remained empty for about a year.

Aramis's son just didn't have the spunk of his dad. He was the ugly duckling. He was lanky, and around other horses would always stand in the corner all by himself. He never challenged a horse, even when it came to eating. One day I said to my trainer, "Take him and put him in his dad's stall." The trainer couldn't believe his ears. "Are you sure, Mr. Newton?" he asked, because everyone knew that stall was off-limits. I smiled. "Put him in Aramis's stall." Three months later I walked into the barn and, lo and behold, there had been a total transformation of the ugly-duckling stallion. He was snow white. He looked as if he had just stepped out of the pages of a fairy tale. He looked just like his dad and, more important, he had his dad's attitude. Whatever magic was left in the stall by his dad wound up in him. He's won many championships and is my personal riding horse to this day. He's gorgeous.

It always puzzles me, the mystery of life. Aramis died in January 1976. My daughter was born on July 25, 1976. So every time God takes something away, when I feel I no longer can bear the pain or wake up the next day, He does something miraculous again and restores me. What He takes away, He gives back twofold.

A great highlight in my life was when Aramis's granddaughter won the championship in Scottsdale, Arizona. She's the spitting image of her grandfather. In my soul I knew he was watching and I knew he was proud. Because we had continued, his life had meant something.

Then, in 1984, I was to be spooked. There I was, sitting at the nationals, and a black horse came into the ring. My body began to tremble. The horse looked right into my eyes. I thought, *My God! It's Aramis*. But now, instead of being white, he was black. The moment that horse came into the ring, I knew it was Aramis. It was a three-year-old, just a baby. I stood up in my seat and grabbed someone's program book right out of his hand. Everybody was in shock over my behavior. I was asking, "Who is that horse?" After the horse showed and left the arena, I rushed to the barn to see him. When the horse saw me coming, he perked his ears up and looked at me and I looked at him. Our eyes met and I knew that someone special was back. Yes, Aramis was back.

Aramis,
a final tribute

I have hoped. I have planned. I have striven.
To the world I have added the deed.
The best that was to me I've given.
I have prayed, but the Gods did not heed.

I have dared and reached only disaster.
I have battled, but broken my lance.
I am bruised by a pitiless master.
That the weak and the timid call chance.

I am tired. I'm bent and feel cheated,
of all that youth urged me to win.
But name me not only with the defeated,
for tomorrow again I begin.

CHAPTER 24

*My philosophy: Friends and relatives,
after five days, like fish, smell.*

WITHOUT SOUNDING LIKE a boasting Englishman and
friend by the name of Robin Leach, and talking about
Lifestyles of the Rich and Famous, I have seen the American dream come true. It has been hard work and plain,
old-fashioned sweat. It can hardly be called an overnight
success story. It was one cinder block after another, and
today, there stands the Casa de Shenandoah on fifty-two
acres. The main house is 13,600 square feet under the roof
and has three bedrooms. There are nine two- and three-
bedroom homes on the property, and that's not counting
the trailers where some of the barn help stay.

Friends have asked me why, with the house so big, I
only have three bedrooms. I'm not fond of a lot of company.

I have never been one to enjoy staying at a person's
home. There are lots of reasons, but the primary one is
my own privacy. I like to get up when I want to get up,
and if I want to go to the refrigerator at three in the morning, I don't want to feel like a burglar stealing a glass of
milk. Most people don't take those things into account.
But I was raised in such a way that you wouldn't dare go
into another person's refrigerator. When I visit friends,
I'm always happier and feel better if I stay at a hotel and
visit their home in the daytime.

That's my philosophy: Friends and relatives, after five days, like fish, smell.

My dad has to chuckle and makes fun of the fact that I didn't build more than three bedrooms, and now I'm forced to add two rooms on either side of the house. When I built originally I was married, and Erin didn't need a governess. Now, with Sister Barbara, a dear friend and Erin's governess, I needed another bedroom.

I have been building this home my whole life. I'm proud to say that I designed it myself. But, not being an architect, I didn't count on little things like storage and lots of closet space. We have simply run out of both. I own a 13,600-square-foot house, and the winter and summer wardrobes are all shoved together like a Macy's bargain-basement sale. One of the new additions to the house that I'm excited about is that I'm taking my gym and my workout room, which now exist at the end of my father's home, and moving it to right off my bedroom. Now, don't laugh; in terms of distance, my current gym is only a city block away from the main house, but it may as well be nine miles. To get out of my house is impossible sometimes. The minute I start to head out the front door to work out, there always seems to be an emergency phone call or some problem that has to be dealt with immediately. I was going to build my garage and workout room in the basement. We went down six feet and hit water. Here I am, sitting in the middle of the desert with an underground river real close.

Often, late at night, when I drive past the lights and off into the desert, I pass my dad's house on the property. It seems like a million tears and years, a million rounds of applause, as I pass that little house built on the prairie. I often pause and think that some of the best memories I have are of watching the ranch develop into what it is today.

My other ranch in Logandale is run by a top horse trainer, Alfredo Ortega. It has a three-quarter-mile race-track on it and we even have a horse swimming pool.

While there are those who feel that a swimming pool for horses sounds kind of ostentatious, it's not that at all. For a horse, swimming one time around the pool is equivalent to five miles at a hand gallop on the track. So you can condition a horse much easier in a pool, with no stress and strain on his legs. If we have an injured horse that can't go out to run and play, we can exercise him that way. We have ninety stalls in four different barns on that property. We raise all of our own hay and oats.

Many performers enjoy going on tour. But for me, touring is a lonely life. It's not because I'm not surrounded by friends; it's because I miss my home and my family. I stay in good hotels and eat in good restaurants and have my own plane. But that doesn't make up for being in my own home. That's kind of a nice feeling.

Yes, I enjoy performing. But I'd be lying to you if I told you that the man *Newsweek* magazine called the King of the Strip is not a slave to his life-style. Between the two ranches in Las Vegas and Logandale, we employ 125 people. That varies between summer and winter.

It isn't just horses I care about. There must be one hundred peacocks roaming the grounds. I started out with three that happened to come with the sale of the property. When I was purchasing the place, I asked about the peacocks. The lady said, "The male is sterile. We've had him for four years and the females will lay every year but they won't hatch."

The day I moved onto the property I told my people, "Turn the peacocks loose." My ranch manager said, "They'll fly away." And I said, "Well, let them. I don't like things caged." Well, from those three peacocks, I have well over one hundred, and 40 percent of them are pure white. We probably have the largest collection of white peacocks around.

I'll admit that at times I haven't exactly been the hit of the neighborhood. You see, the peacocks often parade up and down the street. They love to sit on the fence at sunset and watch the traffic go by. It's amazing to watch them, and you can't imagine how many people come to the front gate and tell me that they've seen one of my peacocks strolling up the street and I might want to go get it. But I know, as does everybody else, that they'll come home.

We have kangaroos, we have eagles, and we are set up with the state of Nevada as a raptor rehabilitation center. If birds have been injured in the state of Nevada and can no longer take care of themselves, even for a brief period of time, they're brought to the Shenandoah to recuperate. When they're well enough to leave, we let them fly away. But if not, they have a place to live for the rest of their lives.

Easter is not one of my favorite times of the year; not because I don't love the meaning of the holiday but because people throw Easter bunnies over the fence. Every year, without fail, when parents buy their children bunnies and the kids lose interest in them, we end up having more bunnies than Hugh Hefner.

Years ago, when I started building, it was just a two-lane road that the house was on. Now they're planning a four-lane highway. I'm fighting with the city to stop the other two roads by my property from becoming four-lane highways. I don't know how I'm going to react to that as years go by. That's why I put up the high wall that I have now, in hopes that I can maintain my privacy—not from my fans but to have the feeling that I'm somewhere peaceful, quiet, and serene, because the ranch is all of that.

I have two lakes, a swimming pool and waterfall, a flamingo fountain, and, by the time I'm finished building, I'll have my own private penguin island that could also house dolphins.

Frank Sinatra gave me a puppy that we named Thor. It's a Rottweiler. I'll admit that it's a tremendous responsibility, but I can't imagine not having pets in my life. Each one has its own individual personality and is special. Two weeks ago a lady brought up a little puppy. She had raised it and it was the pride and joy of her breeding dogs. She had named it Danke Schoen. She wanted me to have it because she was a fan. And one of the members of my staff handled the situation very badly. If I'm asked in advance if I want a puppy, then I generally tell the fan, "Why not consider giving it to someone else?" simply because it might not get the attention that it should from me because I'm on the road so much. But my staff member took it upon himself to tell this lady that she should not have brought the puppy, that this puppy will not have the wonderful life she thinks it will because I have nine other dogs and all of them are bigger. To further scare her, he told her that all nine dogs are big and will either tear the puppy apart or eat it.

The woman was destroyed. Now this guy thought all of that was very funny. When I found out, I was not pleased. I was very angry and explained, "You have no right to do that because you painted a picture that is not true. And in doing so you demoralized this lady. That's wrong. So I will accept the puppy." Well, she brought the puppy down and it's the cutest thing that ever lived. We named it Ferris Bueller after the motion picture, and he has become Marla's dog.

When I go on tour it should be "Wayne Newton and Ringling Brothers and Barnum & Bailey" combined. This past tour was just like a three-ring circus. I had my daughter, Erin, and Sister Barbara, plus Erin brought along two girlfriends and three dogs. When we travel it's a circus. We have traveled with ferrets and Arctic foxes. The only reason why I travel with the animals is because I think it's important to keep my daughter surrounded by the things that she loves in her normal everyday life.

Some of the hotels are not particularly thrilled, except that all the dogs are housebroken and they are all very well behaved. Every dog should be like these dogs. I'm proud that we've never had a complaint anytime, anywhere, from any hotel when we've moved in with our traveling zoo.

Imagine landing at the airport with my JetStar. We call it *The Eagle*. I must put 250,000 miles a year on that plane. It's very roomy for my flying menagerie. When the plane comes to a stop and the stairs are pulled down, the first thing off is Thor. You should see the expression on the limousine drivers' faces. Usually the limousine doors are open and Thor picks the one he wants and gets in it. Well, the driver hasn't met any of us yet because we're gathering the other stuff to get off the plane. It's not uncommon to come off the plane and see the driver's face just drained of blood. What chauffeur is going to tell a 140-pound vicious-looking dog that he can't sit in the backseat?

CHAPTER 25

*The Pittsburgh Hilton will never be the same after
Wayne Newton's musicians turned it into
"Nightmare on Elm Street."*

SHOW BUSINESS is two words. There's the show part, in
which you get out onstage and give it your all, and you
receive the gratification and the love that you've done a
job well. Then there's the business part: the contracts, the
negotiations, the planning of tours, the designing of sets,
the writing of orchestrations, the lawyers, and the meetings. Definitely not one of my favorite parts of show business.

My heart is in entertaining, not in sitting in a lawyer's
office. But don't get me wrong. There's a fun part of show
business that no one, not even your closest fans, ever
knows about, hopefully. So, for the first time I'm going to
take you beyond the footlights, past backstage, and recall
for you some of the funniest, hilarious moments that could
ever happen to an entertainer. It's a combination of the old
TV shows *Laugh-In* and *TV's Bloopers and Practical
Jokes,* only those shows had to be censored, and what I'm
about to fill you in on is uncensored.

Over the years, working the Copa Room of the Sands
Hotel was always a very enjoyable experience. There was
an intimacy about the room; you felt like you could reach
out and touch the audience. It's incredible that so many
musicians can fit on such a small stage.

We had an interesting violin section. They were very
conscientious. They'd stay up all night practicing, then

come and try to do the show. Their eyes always looked beet-red. One night one of the violinists called my conductor, Don Vincent. He was very polite and explained to Don that he had had some cosmetic surgery done on his behind. He explained to my conductor that he hadn't quite yet healed, and would he mind if he played the show kneeling on a pillow? You have to understand that this violinist was the sweetest guy who ever took a breath of air. So Don Vincent didn't want to hurt his feelings, but explained to him that he might look a little conspicuous, especially on a small stage like the one in the Sands. But the violinist was very convincing. He said, "I'll use a pillow when I'm on my knees."

Well, my conductor told him that he would discuss it with me. Needless to say, I was the last to be informed. I never heard anything about it. I walked out onstage, and I was singing in the spotlight, and I'd just sung my fourth song, and I looked over and saw that one string player was about a foot taller than the rest. My immediate reaction was that the violinist had to be sitting on something. I glanced over at Don Vincent, who just raised his eyebrows and went ahead with the show. Out of the corner of my eye I noticed that when the rest of the string players stood up, this guy didn't stand. The band began to laugh, and I was the only idiot who didn't know why this guy was a foot taller than everyone else. And when the violin section stood he looked like a midget.

So when I came offstage I was irritated. I turned to my conductor and snarled, "What the hell is it with that violinist?" Vincent admitted that he had wanted to tell me about him but that he hadn't gotten around to it. "Tell me what?" Don looked me straight in the eye and whispered, "He's had an ass tuck." I said, "He had his ass operated on? You mean for hemorrhoids?" Don just shook his head. "No, Wayne. He wanted it to look better."

I'm still not sure what it is with violinists, but they are definitely a special breed of musicians. We had a concert master violinist, originally from Budapest, Hungary. Elix always loved to jam with other musicians. If we were in a several-hundred-mile radius of a jazz club, he would drive all night just to get there so that he could have a good time drinking and jamming.

One night he was in New York City at the Village Vanguard. The very next morning we had a rehearsal in Valley Forge, Pennsylvania. He was getting ripped. So with his heavy accent he told the owner of the Vanguard that he had to protect his violin and needed to put it in a safe place—a pizza oven. The next morning, on his way to Valley Forge, he started screaming in his heavy accent, "My violin! My violin! Oh, my God, I forgot my violin!" When we reached Valley Forge, we called the Village Vanguard, where they had put it in a safe place overnight. There it was, toasted to a crisp, in the pizza oven, the last place anyone would have looked for a violin.

He was incredible. No matter how much he drank, he could still sit up there and play because he was such an incredible musician. He was a Hungarian gypsy man, and when he was on the juice and started to play, he could make you cry. Once, when we were asked to play at the White House, they requested passports from all the musicians. He gave us six. All of them had a different age and a different place of birth. Needless to say, both the CIA and the FBI found themselves very busy.

When he got drunk he wanted to be your best friend and cry on your shoulder. Sometimes he would get on these binges where he didn't care how the orchestrations were written: He was going to play it with his own jazz style. I finally got so irritated with him that I walked up to my sound man during rehearsal and said, "I want you to only record him playing and isolate the rest of the microphones in the band. This way when the song is over, I can play it for him and he can't say—which he did on every other occasion—that it was the person sitting next to him that played that jazzy style." The tape was perfect. With the one microphone, it was a masterpiece. It captured every note and he was really jamming. When it was over

I gave the band a break except for Elix. I said, "My dear Hungarian friend, I want you to sit right here and hear something," and I played it back. He sat there with his eyes rolled up in the air, and he listened and he listened. By this time I was furious. I turned the tape recorder off and stated, "What do you have to say for yourself?" Elix shrugged his shoulders and said, "I loaned my violin to the person next to me. That wasn't even me playing."

I had to let him go. I mean, of all the excuses in the world, when a guy is caught plain dead cold and comes up with such a preposterous story, I just had to laugh. As I was firing him, he said, "She liked my violin. So I loaned it to her on that song, Wayne. Trust me. It wasn't me playing."

He really was a character, and I will always have fond memories of him and his heavy accent, and I miss him. You could never understand what the hell he was saying, and it was laughable to watch him at the Grand Ole Opry in Memphis trying to explain to the violin section how to play the music. His accent always seemed to get him in trouble.

One of the most famous stories about him took place in Harrah's in Lake Tahoe. He was very hungry and called room service. He wanted a waffle. But with his accent he sounded like Bela Lugosi. In his Hungarian vampire voice he said to the room-service lady, "Darlink, let me have a vaffle." The lady couldn't understand him, and after the third try thought he was making fun of her. When he couldn't get her to understand that he wanted a waffle, he asked for porn cake instead of pound cake. She explained to him that she didn't understand a word he was saying and that she had no time for his practical jokes. That's when she clearly understood him. He told her, "Go fuck yourself." He got himself in big trouble.

The violin section isn't the only section in the orchestra that's had its magical moments. One time we were in White Plains, New York, and we hired some additional musicians for the engagement. Now, in my act, the trumpet section stands up quite a bit throughout the orchestrations, and they're even asked to take bows on certain songs.

During rehearsal I saw this one trumpet player limping a little bit. But I didn't pay much attention to him, thinking, *The guy's got a little limp, no big deal.* Well, we had a jam-packed house. So I invited the trumpet section to stand up and take a bow. As the orchestra began to play "Daddy Don't You Walk So Fast," the trumpet player with the limp leaned back and went backward and fell off the stage. There, in front of thousands of people, he fell off the high platform. I looked over and was worried, thinking that this guy had just killed himself. Several of the trumpet players stopped playing, and they yelled down to him, "Are you all right?" He nodded and shouted back up, "I'm all right."

Two orchestra members decided to lift him back up on-stage when he told them that they couldn't; the reason was that when they tried to lift him they found out he had a wooden leg. There was a brace on it, and when he had fallen off the stage the brace had broken and the leg was left in a permanently bent position. No matter how hard they pulled, the brace remained stuck. I finished the song, and while the audience was applauding and laughing at the same time, I turned to my conductor and said, "I don't care what the problem is, just get him up there." I didn't know anything about the leg; I thought he had had one too many. So he played the rest of the show sitting on one leg.

I am told, and it may come as no surprise, that musicians are legendary ladies' men. When they're not playing an instrument, they're usually checking out the scene, trying to find the lady of their dreams, or at least the lady of their dreams for that night.

I knew none of this next story till much later. The Pittsburgh Hilton will never be the same after Wayne Newton's musicians turned it into "Nightmare on Elm Street." After the show, some of the musicians got nice and mellow and decided they were a little lonely and needed some girls to party with. They called the bellman, and he sent up a bona fide Pittsburgh hooker. Well, before long this girl was downing one drink after another, and after a few bottles she passed out.

One of the musicians decided that he would become the Salvador Dali of creative hooking. He announced, with his finger raised in the air, "Let's put her on a room-service tray and finger-paint her with food." There was this, uh, lady, totally nude, lying on a room-service tray as they proceeded to add rasberries, strawberries, and yogurt, with finishing touches of whipped cream, and the decorative touches of a hot fudge sundae and several bottles of ketchup. They wheeled her out the door at six in the morning, pushed her onto the elevator, and pushed the lobby button. To this day you can still hear people screaming in the lobby of the Pittsburgh Hilton. We have not been invited back.

Let's get one thing straight: Wayne Newton and his congregation do not throw chairs out the windows, demolish hotel rooms, or indulge in drugs. I've always given my musicians strict orders about their conduct. After all, it is a reflection on me. But we all know that boys will be boys, or, in this case, Newton's kids will be kids. Sometimes I feel like a high school principal having to call them into my office for a lecture, or, tougher yet, having to expel them from school.

Good drummers are not the easiest musicians to find. And when you find an incredible one, you're willing to overlook almost anything. Almost, that is! One night, after completing my second show at Harrah's, I was sound asleep when I received a telephone call from security. The voice said, "Is this Mr. Wayne Newton?" Sleepily I responded, "Yes." And the gentleman said, "I'm the director of security at Harrah's and we realize that you really have a conservative group." Before he could go any further I asked, "And what did my drummer do now?" "Well, it seems he found himself a lady of the evening at one of the casinos. He had talked her into getting into the shower with him in the dressing room. He was unaware of the fact that security guards check the dressing rooms every few hours. Well, my drummer and his lady friend were yelling and screaming and carrying on in the shower. Repeatedly the security guard banged on the door, but because of their loud screams nobody answered. Finally, the security guard, using the passkey, let himself in. The dressing room looked like a steam bath as he worked his way to the shower. When he opened the shower door, my drummer looked at him and said, ''Well, damn it, if you're going to join us, take off your clothes.'' That incident I overlooked. I got him off the hook with his promise that he'd never do it again.

But he quickly went back on his promise in Reno. This time he found himself another lady, and once again he got around to finger painting. But this time it was with three large pizzas and all the works. There she was, stretched out on the bed, and pizzas were flying all around her body. It looked as if there had been a massacre.

But the problem came the next morning when the maid went in to clean the room. She thought there had been a murder in there. It looked like blood all over the sheets. At seven in the morning the maid went screaming through the hallway, ''Murder! There's been a murder!'' Fifteen minutes later, the hallway was filled with police.

This is one drummer who would never get the lead in ''Little Drummer Boy.'' We were appearing at the Frontier Hotel in Las Vegas. Christmas holiday was coming up and Don Vincent said to me that he was going to drive back to Los Angeles after the show. His family was there and he was going to pick them up. Once he got to the City of the Angel he'd catch some sleep, and they would drive back in time for the show the following night. As Don was leaving the dressing room I told him, ''Have a safe trip; give my love to your wife and kids.''

Well, the hotels were packed and three stewardesses I know who came to see the show came backstage and announced to me that they could not find a room. I immediately picked up the telephone and, sure enough, the town was not only jam-packed but overbooked. Just as the girls were about to panic and nearly in tears, it popped into my mind that Don Vincent would be gone that night and the next day. I asked the girls, "What time is your flight?" They said, "Well, we're going to leave about six o'clock tomorrow night." I told them their problem was solved. As they each gave me a big hug, I told them about how my conductor was out of town and asked them just to be kind enough to get out of the room by four to give the maids time to clean it up. So I got a key from the desk and put the three airline stewardesses into Don's room.

Well, Don drove all the way to L.A., and once he arrived, he wasn't tired anymore. He announced to his wife and his three boys, "Grab the hamsters. Let's climb into the car and drive directly back to Las Vegas." They all arrived back at the Frontier. Don put his key in the door, and of course it was dead-bolted from inside. There was Don, one tired wife, three kids, and two hamsters standing in the hallway, unable to get into their hotel room. Don's wife said to Don, "Why don't we all go around to the pool side? That might not be locked." Well, it was locked, but his key worked because the girls hadn't dead-bolted the glass sliding door. He put his key in the door and pulled back the curtain. And, being the gentleman that he is, said to his wife, "Please, sweetheart, you go first."

She went in and there were three gorgeous girls stark naked in bed. The girls sat up and didn't even notice his wife. All they saw was Don, and they said, "Oh, hi, Don." With that his three sons let out a scream. "All right, Dad! All right!"

I swore that Don had no idea I put those three girls in his room. But to this day his wife still does not believe my story. Don remembers it too. Laughs Don, "There they were, completely nude, and I kept thinking in the back of my mind that I had better get my list of reasons and excuses out. The kids thought it was swell. My wife didn't say a word. The whole family just stood there paralyzed; even the hamsters. I swear to God that they weren't even moving. Because of Wayne Newton's wonderful generosity, it was one of my most embarrassing moments.''

Musicians aren't the only ones who have been the targets of practical jokes or experienced Wayne Newton's wild side. Stars, and one in particular, Robert Goulet, became the brunt of lots of good humor. Although Goulet may not look at it that way.

One night when Robert Goulet was headlining in Las Vegas, I decided to sneak onstage and become a part of the string section. While I am an accomplished violinist (jokey jokey), here was my chance to have a little fun at Bob's expense. Just as he started to sing ''If Ever I Would Leave You,'' his big hit from *Camelot,* I started to play real loud and horribly out of tune. Robert Goulet was trying to sing, but he just couldn't. His face was becoming redder by the moment, and he had a look of anger that made the whole orchestra freeze in fear. He stopped the band and said, ''Hold it! We can do better than that, can't we? Let's do the song again.'' Well, the orchestra began to play and Goulet started to sing and I waited until Goulet thought everything was cool. Just as he hit the last sixteen measures of the song, I started to make horrible noises. Talk about angry, Goulet turned around, looked at that orchestra, and there was ''kill'' in his eyes. Once again he insisted that they replay the song, and told the audience, ''We are going to stay here all night if necessary until this, uh, orchestra plays it right.'' He sang that song four times in a row before he realized that someone was putting him on. Bob has a wonderful temper, but little sense of humor in those matters.

I've always enjoyed getting at Goulet. One night, to Goulet's surprise, I walked onstage. And I could tell by the twinkle in his eyes that he knew he was about to get it, but he couldn't figure out what was going to happen. I told Goulet, ''I have a friend here from France. He is your biggest fan in the world.'' Goulet looked at me suspiciously and whispered, ''Newton, what are you up to?'' I looked at the audience and said, "Bob, trust me." Goulet just shook his head. "I wouldn't trust you as far as I can see you."

I went in to my best pleading act in front of the audience. "Bob, just let me introduce you to this fan. He's come all the way from France. The audience will understand." So I walked to the side of the stage and the audience went wild as I walked back onstage hand-in-hand with a chimp dressed in a tuxedo and a French beret. What I didn't realize was that Bob was afraid of animals. I announced to the audience, "Don't you want to hear Bob sing a song to one of his fans?" Well, the audience went crazy, leaving Goulet in a very embarrassing situation. If he said no the audience would think he was stuck up, and if he said yes, he would be scared just standing next to the chimp. Well, the orchestra played the downbeat and he started to sing to the chimp. The chimp reached up and grabbed Goulet by the cheeks. Bob didn't know whether to crap or go blind. While the chimp was holding his cheeks and Goulet was doing his best to sing to him, the chimp started to pee all over him. Goulet didn't speak to me for months.

So Goulet, in his own humorous way, was getting back at me every night onstage at the Frontier Hotel. He'd have the audience laughing as he'd tell them, "I've known Wayne Newton since he sounded like a girl. But now he's matured. He sounds like a woman." So I figured, "You SOB, I'll start taking some cute swipes from the stage." I would tell my audience, "I saw Bob Goulet the other day and he was really depressed 'cause he had cut himself shaving and his legs were still bleeding." So this went back and forth and we were both like teenagers having a dart-throwing contest to see who could come up with the best one-liners.

9One night I invited three showgirls to come over and visit with me backstage at the Sands. I told the girls of my plans and they immediately wanted to be a part of them. I told them, "I want you to take off all of your makeup."

Now, they didn't know that I had called the stage manager of the Frontier and the maître d' and asked if there were any gaming junkets in that night. The maître d' said, "We've got a junket in from Buffalo." I said, "I want you to hold three ringside seats for me for three nun friends of mine who are coming in from Buffalo. The maître d' said, "Oh, yes, Mr. Newton. We'd be honored to have the sisters join us. What convent are they from?" "St. Mary's," I quickly announced. Every town has a St. Mary's. I'm not even Catholic, but you can always count on a St. Mary's. I even called the spotlight men and told them that three nuns from Buffalo wouldn't be there as the show started but most likely would walk in on the second song, and to shine the spotlight on them so that Goulet could see them making their entrance.

I flew in three nun's habits from Los Angeles Central Costume Company. They all looked like "the flying nun." Now, if Goulet had been the Catholic that he pretends to be, he'd have known that nuns don't wear those anymore. But then, being the guy that we all know and love, Goulet was certain that these three nuns really cared about Robert Goulet. Even the audience was impressed when the three girls with the nuns' habits made their way through the crowded showroom to the ringside table.

Goulet fell for it hook, line, and sinker. After his third song he leaned down over the footlights and told the audience, "Oh, sisters, how proud I am to have you with us tonight. This is an honor for me." He handed them the microphone and asked the nuns, "Where are you from?" The showgirls, in their best dramatic voices, timidly announced, "We're from St. Mary's in Buffalo." The gaming junket from Buffalo cheered. Well, the place went up for grabs. Now I got him by the *culliones*. He really believed, because of the applause, that they truly were three nuns from St. Mary's.

So there he was as they handed him the first note. I wrote five of the filthiest notes you could ever imagine. They were all written on the lyrics of his hit song "On a

Clear Day.'' One note read: ''On a clear day I would like to _____ you forever.'' Each note got progressively more filthy. Each time he opened the note he became more embarrassed and couldn't even read it to the audience. At one point, in desperation, he even stopped and tried to explain to the crowd that these were not nuns. The audience would not accept it. Each time he read a note he laughed robustly because he was so nervous. By now he knew he'd been had, but he was stuck between a rock and a hard place. He couldn't tell the audience; he tried to, but they wouldn't believe that they were not nuns. He could not read the notes out loud, and as they handed him each note, they became filthier and filthier.

Goulet's expression turned from nervousness to meanness. He looked at the three of them with a glare like, ''I'm going to kick your _____.'' It so surprised Goulet and threw him off guard that by the fifth song he said, ''Good-night, ladies and gentlemen,'' and turned and walked offstage.

Within a half hour Walter Kane, my grandfather and the entertainment director of the Summa hotels, which Robert Goulet had a contract with, was standing in my dressing room. He asked me, ''What's happened to Goulet?'' I looked at him with surprise. I said, ''What do you mean?'' Walter replied, ''Well, we can't figure it out, but he's over in his dressing room yelling and throwing things through windows, screaming about nuns. Everybody thinks he's flipped out.''

Goulet has been a gem of a sport when it's come to having some fun at his expense. But here's one last Goulet story that I hope will make you laugh, because it sure made us laugh when we pulled it off.

The KGB would have been proud of us. Goulet was appearing at the Frontier Hotel and his dressing room was a beautifully decorated trailer. We were sitting around with my friend and chief of security, Bear, and Parsons, the lighting engineer, and Joe Schenck. I said to the group, ''I want to really get that damn Goulet.'' So we put our heads together and thought. We figured out that Goulet always came to work late. If his show was at eight o'clock, he wouldn't arrive any sooner than seven forty-five. He'd change clothes, put on his makeup, and walk out onstage.

It was then that I came up with the "Let's Get Goulet Plan." We figured out how long it took the security man to go backstage to make his rounds on the stage and then lock the gate and go out. I knew that if I walked over to the Frontier Hotel and sat in the lounge and established my presence, the word would quickly get out that Newton was in the building and all the security guards would follow me around and keep their eyes on me. So while I sat in the lounge, Bear and the guys went to work. I then took a special hallway to join them, pretending to go to the men's room.

Sure enough, we had precise timing. The security guard went by and we watched him lock up the gate. As soon as he left, we had forty minutes to do what we had to do. We went into the trailer, took the light bulbs out, took the furniture out, took the mattress out, took the chairs out. If it wasn't nailed down, it disappeared. We even rolled up the carpet. The trailer was stripped bare. We put all the stuff on the elevator and sent it down below the stage. I realized that it wasn't good enough just to get the stuff below the stage. We still had another fifteen minutes before security made its rounds. We took all the furniture, everything, off the elevator, and hid it where all the props were stored, underneath sheets and blankets where nobody would notice. Sure enough, the security man came just as we were ready to leave. We hid behind the wall, holding our breath in hopes that he wouldn't catch us. He walked right past us, never noticing for a moment the four images hiding in the darkness. We went back upstairs, sat in the lounge, listened to one song, walked out the front door, got into our car, and left.

The next night, when Bob Goulet got there about fifteen minutes before show time, he walked up, put the key in the door, and opened it. He turned on the light switch, but there were no lights. He was feeling his way around in the dark. Bob started to walk his way around the dark trailer and couldn't find his makeup table, his couch, not even a chair. Finally Goulet came storming out onstage, screaming for security. He demanded a flashlight. In the meantime, the security guard checked the electricity and it was still hooked up. So they couldn't figure out why the dressing room was in total darkness. Goulet started to get mad. "What the hell is this? I've got to get ready." One of the security guards told him he could make up in one of the dressing rooms downstairs.

When the head of security arrived, Goulet was totally out of control. When he demanded to know what had happened, he called the head of security. Goulet went nuts. When I tell you nuts, he went nuts! He wasn't going on. He called Walter Kane, who was having dinner, and, ranting and raving, said, "I can't prove it. But I know that smart-ass Newton did this."

The Frontier's director of security was pretty smart. And Goulet was determined to find out what happened. "Did anything in particular happen that seemed unusual?" asked Goulet. Then he asked, "Was Wayne Newton on the property?" When the guard said yes, Goulet shouted, "I knew it, I knew it!" He pounded his fist. "They did it. I can't prove it, but I know if Wayne Newton was on this property, and those things were taken out of the dressing room, he did it!" Goulet wanted the security man fired. He was so angry he threatened to walk out on his contract. Needless to say, Walter Kane, as entertainment director, was duly upset.

Goulet demanded an investigation, and one went on for a week. But we never admitted to anything. Finally, it just blew over. But Walter Kane always had a twinkle in his eye when he told the story about the bandits who robbed Goulet's dressing room.

Back in the early days, before the tour buses, we used to travel on Greyhound buses. We'd play a gig, hop on a bus, and off we'd go to the next stop. One time there was a heat wave in upstate New York. It was 110 degrees and the air conditioning was out in the bus. All of us were unhappy. The musicians were on the verge of a mutiny when we decided we had to stop the bus to get something to drink. We drove into a little community where all the houses were white. And we noticed that everyone was dressed in white.

Al Longo, my trumpet player, got off the bus because he couldn't stand the heat, and he drifted off. Several of the musicians decided to cool off and they disembarked. We drove a little bit farther until we reached a gas station. As we stood around the station drinking beverages, we saw several of the musicians running down the road screaming at the top of their lungs, "Get in the bus, they're crazy! Get in the bus, they're crazy!" We had driven smack into the center of a mental institution and one of the patients had tried to attack the trumpeter!

Ten minutes out of the little white town it was unbearable. It was like driving in a giant oven. It was 110 degrees outside and 130 degrees in the bus. We happened to pass a bus depot. So my security chief and road manager at the time, Bear, looked at the bus driver and said, "Listen, guys, you promised us a nice air-conditioned bus. This group cannot make another six-hour ride in this inferno. They've got to play tonight. So I am insisting that we stop at this bus depot and you call the company and get us another bus." Well, we arrived at the depot only to discover that there was not another bus available. The supervisor admitted that they had only one bus available and that it was leased out to the girl scouts.

It was noon, and the girl scouts' trip wasn't till two o'clock, so Bear convinced the driver to let us use the bus to take the musicians to the airport so they could catch a plane. The girl scout bus pulled into the depot and it was in A-1 shape. The air conditioning was working and we loaded all of our equipment and gear into the bus in ten minutes. Everybody was on board and Willie, our driver, thought we were headed for the airport. As he was driving away, his supervisor lectured him to be sure to pick up the girl scouts at two o'clock because they had been planning this trip for a month.

All the musicians knew that Bear was up to something, but they just couldn't figure it out. The bus driver was totally unsuspecting. He thought he was going to drop us off at the airport. So Bear walked up to Willie and sat beside him as we were driving down the highway, and he opened up his bag. Right there on top, in plain view, was a nine-millimeter gun. The driver looked over and swerved into the other lane. Bear whispered, "Guess where you're taking us?" The driver nervously responded with a stutter, "To the airport." Bear smiled, pointed to the gun, and said, "Do you know what this is?" The frightened driver said, "It's a g-g-g-gun." Bear looked eye-to-eye at the driver. "I'm going to ask you only once. When you get on the freeway, you just keep going. There's no stopping at the airport and there's no picking up the girl scouts at two o'clock."

We were on our way and we had just hijacked a bus. So the group by now was convinced that the highway patrol was going to pull us over any minute and haul us off to jail. Everybody on the bus kept looking back, waiting for the sound of sirens.

We arrived just in time for the show, and of course had no idea that Bear had hijacked the bus. The bus driver was frightened that he'd be fired, but by now he was kind of enjoying all the excitement and he'd become one of the guys. He was our friend and loving every minute of it. After the show we got back on the bus and the driver smiled. "Should we keep going?" The bus driver's boss finally caught up with him three days later, along with our hijacked bus. To make sure that we didn't get caught, we didn't stay at the hotels we were supposed to, and we ran in and out of the auditorium as if we were Bonnie and Clyde on the run.

Well, the girl scouts found out, and when they were told the story about the guy with the gun it got quite a laugh.

The bus company got all the notoriety, and they even let the driver take us on the rest of the tour. As a result of that story, the girl scouts voted Wayne Newton "Role Model of the Year for the Girl Scouts of America." And I've been buying cookies ever since.

CHAPTER 26

☆

*If I were offered a chance or a job to be a critic,
I would flatly turn it down.*

I'M NOT A a gambling man. But I'll bet I'm the only performer who carries a card in his wallet with one of my epigrams about critics written on it. On the back of the card it says, "It is easy for a critic to tell the big man how he might have done it better or to point out how the king stumbled. But the accolades belong to the man in the arena, never to the man who explains how it should have been better." It's quite a nice saying and it exemplifies my history with critics. There's never been a gray with me when it comes to critics. It's either black or white. They either understand what I'm doing and respect it or I'm a total enigma to them.

Some entertainers wouldn't be truthful enough to admit it, but I am hurt by reviews. Nobody likes to be torn apart. There are shows I've done that, deep down inside, I knew I bombed. Sometimes it was through no fault of my own. There were equipment problems, sound problems, things just didn't work and the whole performance just went in the toilet, and, would you believe, I got rave reviews? Then there are times when everything goes just right. It's the perfect show. You couldn't do any better if you had rehearsed all night. That's when I'm shocked that a critic would tear me from limb to limb.

Early on, when I performed with Mr. Benny as his opening act, I noticed that the critics were afraid or didn't want to rip apart a legend like Jack Benny. But they felt that they had to do their job as critics, so they looked to me to criticize. God forbid their readers should think they enjoyed the show! There's a certain mentality that exists among critics that I don't understand. There has to be something wrong with the show, otherwise they feel they haven't earned their paychecks. Then there were critics who sometimes liked me and bombed Mr. Benny. But that's one thing I'll always remember about how secure Mr. Benny was: It never presented a problem for him. It never disturbed him in the slightest. In fact, during many press conferences there was a reporter who was quick to suggest that "Wayne Newton has really been stealing the show. How do you feel about that?" Uncle Jack would give one of those great Benny expressions, put his hand on his cheek, look at the press, and smile. "Well, if Wayne could not steal the show, I wouldn't want him on the bill." It usually drew both applause and laughter by the surprised members of the media.

Because of Jack Benny's attitude, I learned a great lesson about show business. And I'm grateful for having had such a wonderful man teach me about ego, truth, and honesty. I have no problem with featuring people who are tremendously talented during my show. If people walk out having enjoyed the show, it's ultimately going to be better for me. What's sad is that many times the "critic cycle" repeats itself. Rather than taking me on and giving me a bad review, they will tear up the talented performers I feature in my act. It bothers me.

While critics will have you believe they have much influence, I don't believe they do anymore. Jackie Gleason once likened a critic to someone who tells an eyewitness to an accident what they just saw. Most of the reviews are after the fact. So they don't even sell tickets anymore.

In Las Vegas, the critics have a tremendous effect on a new production show that's planning on having a long run. But by and large, when a performer is on tour, it's a one-week stand in Las Vegas. By the time the reviews come out, the performer has left town and it has had absolutely no effect on the showroom or the performer's career.

Pittsburgh will always have a place in my heart when I think of a certain critic and his review. It read: "Wayne Newton opened last night at the Pittsburgh Arena. And I personally did not enjoy the show. I am not a fan of Wayne Newton. I did not like his singing. I did not like the pacing of his show, I did not like the orchestra. In fact, I found very little that I enjoyed. But I must tell you I was the only one in that room who did not enjoy the show. The man got four standing ovations. People were yelling and screaming and I have to tell you that the audience left totally entertained." The critic finished his review by writing, "I have no doubt that if he came back tomorrow night, it would be a sellout like it was last night." I called the reviewer, and when I reached him in the newsroom I said, "Hey, this is Wayne Newton," and there was dead silence. Finally, he responded with a timid, "Yes." I said, "I've got to tell you that I've been reviewed lots of times in my life, but never have I been reviewed more fairly than in your column. And I want you to know how much I appreciate your total honesty." He was in shock. But I meant it.

So many writers feel that they have to kill the lion. The British press is the most famous for accenting the negative rather than writing about the positive. In 1967 I was asked to perform for a Royal Command Performance. The British press picked it up and lashed out with, "Who is Wayne Newton? Never heard of him."

When we arrived in London I was actually in bed sleeping when there came a knock at the door. My brother answered it, and there were six press guys standing in the hallway wanting to interview me. My brother came into the bedroom and woke me up. Jerry said, "I think you'd better get up. There are six press guys and they're not going to leave. So we can either do it in the comfort of the living-room suite or they'll be waiting outside and they'll hound you when you go out." I said to Jerry,

"Well, invite them in." I pulled myself together as much as I could and went out into the living room. One member of the press cracked, "Mr. Newton, I presume." I knew instantly that I was in a jungle and the hunt was on. Before I could even answer, he sharply announced that he would be the spokesman for the press and that he only had about three questions to ask me. He rattled them off with a superior tone in his voice: "What are you doing here? Who invited you?" And his last question: "Pardon our ignorance, but we have never heard of Wayne Newton before." That was my welcome to Great Britain.

As I sat down I told them, "I'll answer your questions in the order in which you asked them. Number one, I am here to entertain at the Royal Command Performance tomorrow night. Number two, I'm sure you are aware the invitations come from Buckingham Palace. So it should not be difficult to figure out who invited me." Then I looked at the six of them as they wrote in their notepads. "It does not offend me that you've never heard of Wayne Newton before. Because two years ago I had never heard of the Beatles." The spokesman smiled and said, "Jolly good. I appreciate your candor. Thank you very much." And with that they all got up and left.

I was the only American performer in that show who got a good review.

If I were offered a chance or a job to be a critic, I would flatly turn it down. Because even though I have seen shows that I have not enjoyed, I have always felt that the performers were doing the best they were capable of doing. And how can you find any possible good purpose in criticizing that? I don't need critics to criticize Wayne Newton because I'm more critical of myself than anybody else can be. I've never done a show in my entire career that I was totally happy with. But I can come offstage feeling 90 percent good about what I've just done, and that's good enough for me until tomorrow night.

CHAPTER 27

☆

*While my heart may have caught fire, my mind told me
that the last thing in the world I needed
was another relationship.*

WHEN ELAINE AND I decided to separate, it was one of
the saddest days of my life. I felt a loneliness come over
me that was impossible to describe. And just when it
seemed the darkest, Marla Heasley, co-star of the TV show
The A-Team, entered. From the moment we met, something magical happened. Our romance caught fire and it
gets better and better every day. She's terrific. She's got
beauty, sensitivity, and a wonderfully bright mind.

I guess it's when you're not expecting it that you fall in
love. Or perhaps it's when you're not looking for love that
it leaps out and engulfs you. I met Marla in Lake Tahoe.
I had been separated from Elaine for about four months
and we had decided it was going to be a permanent separation. Elaine was going through a lot of changes at that
point. Marla was in Lake Tahoe with her parents, and had
bumped into my former associate Alan Margulies. She
knew Alan from one of her girlfriends, and knew he was
my manager, and came down to the dressing room to say
hello to him. That's how we met.

When I look back at it, I can remember that my heart
did skip a few beats. But while my heart may have caught
fire, my mind told me that the last thing in the world I
needed was another relationship. As you can imagine, my
brain was still reeling, trying to figure out what was going
on with my marriage. I would toss and turn every night

thinking about my daughter, my separation, and all that was going on.

Marla and I had dinner once, and then she flew back to Los Angeles. It took me a week to realize that I had to call her. I asked her to come up for the weekend, and she did.

Marla was very supportive through the divorce. A divorce, no matter how amiable, and this was amiable by certain standards, is devastating. What Elaine and I went through because of the NBC reports had a terrible effect on our marriage. My attorney told me that it would, and he had spoken the truth. Elaine and I were married on June 1, 1968, and my divorce became final on June 6, 1985. My mother died on June 13 of that year. My brother was in jail. Those were some rough times.

Marla, who is much older spiritually than she is chronologically, truly helped me. I don't know what I would have done without her. If it hadn't been for her and Erin, who said prayers for me daily, my life would have had little meaning.

While Marla had all the ingredients that I was looking for in a woman, she also had a drawback—she was an actress. I had always told myself that I would never become involved with anybody in the entertainment industry. It was a wonderful rule, but, unfortunately, my heart was unable to follow it. I didn't really think that anything would come of Marla and me because I knew I didn't want it and I knew she didn't need it. As our relationship grew I became very protective of her and her career.

I realized that as an actress on an NBC TV show, she was playing Russian roulette. I sat her down and said, "Marla, you're asking for trouble. You're in the big leagues now and I think it's important that you realize the price you could pay for being in love with me." Little did I know, later on my worst fear for her career would become a reality. NBC did let her go from the series. I didn't even want her in the courtroom because I knew how NBC would react to her presence. If they can't hurt Wayne

Newton for suing them, they're going to hurt anybody they can because that's how small-minded they are.

Even my lawyer, Mort Galane, didn't want Marla in the courtroom. His reason was that she was too pretty, and her being there would only spell trouble. Marla, bless her heart, was willing to do anything that I wanted her to, but she wanted to be by my side. So I told my attorney that Marla was going to be there.

After my first day on the stand—and I was on the stand for seven days—Marla gave me some advice. That evening she said, "Wayne, you know I love you, right?" And I answered, "Yes." She continued, "Well I have something I must tell you and you're not going to like what I have to say. You're coming across as being angry and arrogant."

I looked at Marla and laughed. I said, "You're right. I'm angry. I've had seven years to be angry." Marla smiled and whispered, "I don't think it reads well to the jury."

After giving it some thought, I realized that she was probably right. So Marla would sit where I could see her every day when I was on the stand, and if I started to lose my temper, I would glance up at her and her smile would break my tension long enough to calm me down and maintain my cool while I was answering the questions.

It became even more interesting to me after I got over the initial anger and dislike for the NBC attorneys, for obvious reasons. Marla told me one night, "Why don't you think of it in terms of playing word games?" She was right. I realized what word games the NBC lawyers were playing, and it became interesting to see how many ways I could lead them down the garden path. It wasn't as if I were lying. I was just playing their game with them. When the attorney would say, "Have you ever heard that Guido Penosi was a member of the mob?" I'd look at Marla and answer, "Yes." Well, the NBC attorney would get all excited and he'd say, "Who told you?" And I'd smile back and say, "You just did."

It would be misleading to tell you that our relationship has been one without its ups and downs. It's been like a soap opera. And we've broken up at times. Marla has quite a temper, but so do I. Once we broke up for six months. I can't remember exactly why we split because I block out unhappy memories, if possible. Most of our fights have had to do with rumors.

I do admire the fire and sparks that she can make fly. I probably couldn't love her as much if she weren't that way.

Women have always fascinated me, and sometimes it's been impossible to figure out their logic. I think one of the funniest nights I can recall was after Elaine and I were divorced. I was appearing at the MGM Grand and Elaine telephoned me backstage and said, "I want to come to your show and we're going to bring Erin, and we'll all have dinner afterwards." And I asked, "Who is 'we'?" Elaine responded, "Well, Lola Falana's coming with us and we'll have dinner together."

Now, there was a time when Elaine was accusing me of having an affair with Lola. So it seemed bizarre that they had become pals. Quite frankly, I wanted to go to dinner with the two of them like I wanted another hole in my head. But Erin was going to be there. So I said to myself, *Elaine is a wonderful woman and she's my former wife and I'll get to see my daughter, so why not,* although I believe in not opening a door once it's closed. I'm not one of these guys who can take out his former wife and spend the evening together. There are those who can do it, and Elaine has the ability to be one of those people. Unfortunately, I do not share those feelings.

So I accepted her dinner invitation, realizing in the back of my mind that time would be limited because I would have to do a second show. The dinner consisted of Elaine and Lola throwing barbs at each other. It finally got so bad that Erin looked up at me, rolled her eyes, and said, "Daddy, don't you have to go to work?" I laughed out loud. And to this day I get a chuckle when I remember having dinner with two women with bright-red nail polish clawing at each other. That fact that Lola and Elaine are close friends is just mind-boggling. Maybe women know something that we don't know.

Women have an incredible way about them that men don't seem to have. When Marla and I had a tiff and weren't seeing each other for a month, I had to do a double take when I went to a horse sale. Who showed up but Elaine, which was shocking enough. But next to Elaine was Marla. The two of them greeted each other with hugs and kisses. I couldn't believe my eyes. All of a sudden the two of them were bosom buddies and had something in common. I couldn't understand it. As soon as Marla and I made up, Marla and Elaine no longer talked to each other.

One thing Marla must learn is that a career is a real mistress. That was one of the problems with my marriage to Elaine. My career became the mistress and she couldn't handle that. If it's another woman, that's body and soul and hair that she can scratch and kick, and they can call each other names and get their attorneys on the phone. But when it's a career that's your mistress, it's another story. I find I'm wading through the same syndrome almost in reverse with Marla. I'm waiting for her to decide whether I'm her life, or her career is. Both seem impossible, at least for me.

I've been in love a lot of times, but it never lasted. But if the moment could last forever, that's the moment I'm looking for. I found some of the moments with Elaine. And, more than any other woman in my life, I've found those moments with Marla.

CHAPTER 28

☆

*Every entertainer should be required to watch Sinatra
from the side wings.*

DESPITE WHAT SOME people may think, my friendship with
Frank Sinatra does not go back to the Rat Pack days. I
was working in the lounges while Sinatra had already established himself as a headliner. The first time I met Frank
was in Los Angeles when I was asked to take part in a
benefit show. Mr. Benny had requested my presence, and
on the bill was Frank Sinatra. I was standing in the wings
watching him sing and felt this enormous presence behind
me, and I turned around and this giant of a man absolutely
dwarfed me. It was John Wayne, and he said to me in his
famous slur, indirectly, because he was mostly talking to
himself, "Kid, now that's a real professional. Take a good
look, 'cause you'll never see anyone like him again."

As a youngster, I could never understand why Sinatra
was such a big star. I didn't understand his kind of music.
I grew up in another era. And so when everyone got so
excited or made comments, my attitude was, "So he's a
singer. He's Frank Sinatra. So what's the big deal?" I
quickly learned, playing Vegas, why Frank Sinatra was
such a big deal.

While we didn't actually meet that night backstage, he
did leave a lasting impression on me. Watching him from
out front is one thing, but to watch him from backstage is
a totally different experience. Every entertainer should be

required to watch Sinatra from the side wings. There's so much to learn about the way he performs.

After he had his fight with the Sands Hotel and moved to Caesars Palace, I went to see him on a number of occasions. The fourth time I got the surprise of my life. Sinatra, when the applause died down after a song, put me into total shock. He said, "There's a guy in our audience. I'm sure he's a nice enough guy, but I'll say one thing. He sure is interesting 'cause he looks like a truck driver and sounds like a girl." Then he introduced me. Sinatra, perhaps, doesn't even remember it, but I always will. It was one of those kinds of introductions that I didn't really know how I should take. Was he complimenting me or was it Sinatra rudeness? I didn't know whether I should be mad; I didn't know whether I should have been grateful that he introduced me at all.

So when I went backstage, I didn't know what to expect. He couldn't have been nicer, which threw me off even more. Sinatra said to me, "Kid, why don't you come over and have a drink with me one night?" And I said, immediately, "Okay," and I left.

A year went by and I was having a little get together at the Sands with some of my close friends. It was three in the morning and the phone rang. The operator said to my head of security, "Would you tell Mr. Newton that Mr. Sinatra is on the phone." So Bear came over to me and said, with a big grin on his face, "It's Frank Sinatra on the phone, boss." I laughed, "BS!" I told Bear to take the call because it was someone putting us on. Bear got back on the line and the voice said, "Is the Injun there?" Bear growled back, "Who is this?" In his unmistakable voice, he announced, "Frank Sinatra." Bear practically dropped the phone and rushed over. "Chief, I swear it sounds just like him. I'm telling you, it's Frank Sinatra." So I was still convinced that it had to be a put-on and someone was pulling a practical joke. I downed a drink and went to the phone and said, "Hello." Then I realized it was Sinatra the minute he said, "Hello, Injun. What are

you doing?'' I answered back, "We're just having a few
drinks." Sinatra then said, "Well, why don't you come
over and have a drink with me?" I don't know why, but I
asked Sinatra who was on his guest list. "Who's there?"
I asked. Sinatra's voice sounded surprised, but he said,
"Rich Little's over here and Tony Bennett and most of the
guys up and down the Strip. We're just having some drinks
and we realized that the Injun was missing, so I thought
I'd give you a call and invite you." Now, I don't know
what possessed me to be so bold. Perhaps the Injun had
too much firewater, but I said to Sinatra, "Well, why don't
you call me when there's less people?" Sinatra said,
"Okay, I'll do that sometime."

The next day when I came to work, I said, "Did
we . . . ?" and before I could even say Sinatra's name,
Bear shook his head. "Yes, we got a call." As Bear started
to put together the pieces of my side of the conversation,
all I thought was, *Oh sh—*. Just at that very moment the
phone rang. The operator said to Bear, "Mr. Sinatra calling Mr. Newton." I realized that I was in deep trouble
because he had to be livid. My hands were shaking along
with my voice when I said, "Hello, boss." Sinatra, hearing the nervousness, said sternly, "Injun, is my wife and
me too many people?" I laughed, "When?" He said,
"How about between shows?" I said, "I'll be there."
Elaine and I went and it was just the four of us. From that
point on we became friends.

I'm not good at being one of the guys. I never have
been. I have never been good in crowds. I'm uncomfortable. I'm always very aware of feeling like a nuisance, and
it's a feeling that I don't like. Star parties and hanging
around stars' dressing rooms just isn't my scene. I handle
it infinitely better when people visit me in my dressing
room. It's on my turf and I feel more comfortable about
that. But to be one of the guys and visit another star's
dressing room always makes me feel kind of like a free-
loader. Since I don't like the feeling, I'd be an idiot to put
myself through it. So I just don't do it.

My show-business peers and I get along fine. But not in a group. One-on-one I'm comfortable. But there's nothing I hate more than show-biz stories in a group where each person is trying to top the others. Nothing can get me to clear out of a dressing room faster.

Ol' Blue Eyes is quite a guy. No one has shared his talents more than he has. He's raised more money for charitable organizations than anybody I can think of. Look at what he's done just to help his wife, Barbara, with her children's abuse center in Palm Springs. It's always a pleasure when he telephones and asks me to help out.

One funny moment that he always kids me about to this day occurred years ago, right after I met him, when we were doing a fund-raiser in Washington, D.C. It was Danny Thomas, Dinah Shore, Frank, and me. We did four shows over a period of time as a fund-raiser for Danny Thomas's St. Jude's. Over that year-and-a-half span, all of us performed the four benefit shows. The first show was in Washington, and when I got there I was told, "Sinatra wants you to close the show." Well, my God, what an ego booster that was. I thought, as I put my makeup on, that it was the greatest compliment Frank Sinatra could pay me until I realized that the three of them wanted me to close the show because they wanted to get out of there. It became a standing joke every time I saw Sinatra. I'd say, "What time is your flight?" Sinatra would laugh.

One of the things that surprised me when I tuned in the 1988 Republican convention was that Tom Selleck, not Frank Sinatra, was delivering a tribute to First Lady Nancy Reagan. I guess what surprised me even more was that they had telephoned me two weeks before and asked if I would be available for the TV tribute. It was going to fall on a Monday, so it worked out nicely with my performing schedule. But two days after they asked me to do it we received a call that they had changed the entire idea of what they were going to do and had decided they weren't going to use performers. The 1988 Republican convention, from a celebrity standpoint, was pretty strange. There was

Charlton Heston and Pat Boone, but in terms of the people who surrounded the Reagans, they seemed to have been pushed out. Obviously, the Bush steering committee wanted the convention to highlight Bush's VIP friends and not the Reagans'.

Of course the gossipers and the supermarket tabloids always come up with their version of what the "inside story" really is. The gossipers had it that Frank Sinatra had been cut off by Nancy Reagan because he didn't call her up to defend himself when Kitty Kelly's book came out. Kelly claimed that Sinatra called Nancy a woman with fat ankles, along with a few other derogatory remarks. Personally, I don't believe the gossipers. I can tell you that the Reagans are not that petty and neither is Frank Sinatra.

It is very conceivable that the reason why Frank Sinatra did not deliver the tribute to Nancy was the same reason why I was first asked and then not: because the Bush group did not want themselves surrounded with the same people who surrounded President Reagan.

The more they gossip, the more the *National Enquirer* and the *Star* and all the other rag sheets knock Frank, they only serve to make him a bigger legend, if that's possible. Every time the media has attempted to attack Sinatra, he has fought back like the true champ that he is. I think that's a direct tribute to Frank Sinatra, because that kind of adversity can do one of two things: It can destroy you if you let it—and 99,000,000 people out of 99,000,001 would let it—because it comes at you from every direction; or it can motivate you. Those people stand up on their hind legs and say, "I'm not taking that sh—." Frank Sinatra has survived it and is a survivor because he will not take anyone's crap.

Looking back at his bouts with the media, I realize how much Frank Sinatra has taught me. You have to fight back, and if you don't, then it is an admission that what they're saying is true. The media leaves you no options. The only position you have to decide is whether you're going to crawl under a rock to get out of the heat or fight them, because there's no middle ground. Sinatra can attest to that. I admire the way Frank Sinatra has handled himself.

You hear all the rumors about Mickey Rudin and Colonel Tom Parker. What I'm about to say is not meant in any derogatory sense about either of them, but I'm afraid that people will all too often not give the credit where the credit is due.

I believe that Elvis should be given a lot more credit and deserves a lot more than he has been given, and I think the same holds true for Frank Sinatra. Any manager of Frank Sinatra or Elvis is going to be directed more than he directs.

I believe that Frank Sinatra deserves accolades for his courage and should get most of the credit for having maintained his stature. While he has an enormous amount of talent, it plays only a small part in Frank Sinatra, the living legend. Sinatra is one of the few entertainers who truly has said, ''We're going to do it my way.'' Sinatra is a man made of a lot of guts and a big heart. The Italians call them *culliones*. He's got big ones.

CHAPTER 29

*If anything, my ESP powers are a gift from God. It
might have been the Indian part of me that aroused
the sensitivity . . .*

STRANGE, ALMOST EERIE things that cannot be explained
happen to all of us from time to time. Many believe such
phenomena could be examples of extrasensory perception,
or ESP. Personally, I feel that everyone has ESP or will
experience it sometime during their life. I've had it quite
a few times.

I used to scare people to death with it and I used to use
it when I was younger because it was fun for me. I have
found that the mistakes I have made in judging people
were due to not following my first instincts. I had a woman
walk up to me downtown at the Fremont Hotel years ago
and ask, "You don't know me, do you?" Now, I had never
seen the woman before in my life. I paused for a moment
and then correctly identified her by name. I also told her
where she lived and how she was related to a mutual
friend. I don't know how I did it. Something came to me
and I knew exactly who she was. These kinds of things
happen to me frequently.

Eerie things sometimes happen between me and others
I'm close to. This was especially true with my friend
Bobby Darin. We were on the same wavelength. One
Christmas I looked around for a nice gift for a married
couple. I knew that two of their favorite songs were "Only
You" and "I'm Confessin'." I had never recorded either
of these old standards. I took a few musicians into a re-

cording studio and sang the two songs, and ordered one copy of the record pressed—a gift for my friends. It would be a rare gift, because they would have the only copy in existence.

The next time I went to Los Angeles to confer about an upcoming recording session, Bobby handed me two pieces of sheet music. "I think," Bobby said, "that it's time you recorded these two oldies." When I looked down at the titles I began to laugh. He had handed me "Only You" and "I'm Confessin'."

My ESP might be inherited from the Indian part of me. I have always had it and I consider it a gift from God. I was born with those gifts and sometimes it can be frightening. In many instances I know what will happen, and it turns out exactly that way. There were times my parents actually got angry at me at Christmas because I would tell them what they had gotten me without even opening a present. It became a running gag with my family. It seemed natural to me as a child; I didn't realize then that it was a gift.

There was a time when I thought that I had lost it. It came right after the NBC broadcast attacking me. I became so preoccupied and so distraught that everything and every feeling became clouded. Because I was so emotionally numb and drained, the ESP went dead for three years. It's like that portion of me just shut down.

For me, ESP is a mental picture. I've never heard the third eye totally explained, only because so many people attach voodoo to that kind of stuff. I think if I had to define my ESP, I would tell you that I am a receiver. I tune in and receive people's emotions and thoughts. Anybody who knows me, anybody who has been around me, will tell you that it scares them at times.

I've watched channelers and find them humorous. I'm not sure they're using ESP, but people have a great tendency to throw all that in one barrel. Of course, I do believe fortune-tellers, by and large, are just a hoax.

I don't believe I'm clairvoyant in the same sense as Ed-

gar Cayce, but I do have strong feelings that I cannot deny.
I have impressions that are instantaneous and beyond my
control. When I get these impressions they are not always
right. There were times in my life when I resisted them
because I really thought I was some kind of freak. I don't
do that anymore. I also don't talk about it a lot. It's such
an unknown science that I don't know where the natural
ends and the supernatural begins. I do know there's somebody up there guiding me; call it a guardian angel, call it
God, call it whatever. I just know my thoughts are not
necessarily my own.

I believe ESP and reincarnation are deeply connected.
I didn't realize how my life would become intertwined
with Edgar Cayce. The man who had his own psychic
institute died in a Roanoke, Virginia, hotel in 1944—in
the same city where I lived. I had no idea who Edgar
Cayce was, but when I was playing the Copacabana in
New York in my late teens, an odd sensation that seemed
bizarre came over me over a two-month span. I must
have had twenty people come up to me and say, "Do you
know of Edgar Cayce?" I'd say no. It wasn't like he was
a star on Broadway. What I didn't realize was that one of
the networks was teaming up with a motion-picture company to produce a movie of Edgar Cayce's life. They
didn't know whom to get to play the part of this genius
of ESP. One of Cayce's aides who worked at the institute
asked the network executives if they had seen this kid
named Wayne Newton on *The Jackie Gleason Show*.
When the executives confessed that they had not, Edgar
Cayce's assistant said, "Go see him because he's the one
to play Edgar Cayce." When Cayce's assistant came to
the Copa to see me, he said he knew that I was Edgar
Cayce's soul mate.

Now, I was born in 1942, not 1944 when Cayce died.
But I believe that reincarnation can overlap like that. I've
also experienced it with horses. I don't have anywhere
near the gift that Edgar Cayce had, but there's a strong
bond between us.

Cayce's assistant came to see me and told the executives from the network, "I will know the minute that I look into Wayne Newton's eyes." He walked up to me at the Copacabana and stared right through me as if he were in a trance. Within seconds he stated, "You're the one!" The movie never came about.

With Al Jolson, it was pretty much the same thing. Everybody gave me records of Jolson. I was always being compared to him, but I brushed it off. Then I saw the movie *The Jazz Singer* on television. The tears poured down my cheeks and I remember thinking that it was the saddest story I had ever seen. If you remember the end of that movie you may recall that his wife couldn't understand why he needed to perform and told Jolson, "It's me or your career."

I can't tell you how many times in my life I have gone through that. Although I didn't realize it while I was watching that film, I knew later on that Jolson's life was a mirror image of my own. If Jolson gave up his music, he would lose a part of his life. If he let his wife go, he would also lose half of himself because he loved her very much. I could never understand how people who love you can hand down ultimatums. You can't win. You lose either way. That's why I let my ESP powers guide me. I have learned to go with it rather than resist it.

Now I go with my gut feelings, my first instincts, but it took me a long time to trust them. Once I thought about trying hypnosis to see if I could develop it in any way. I've only been hypnotized once. The hypnotist couldn't hypnotize me, but while she was attempting to hypnotize my brother, I went under. I'll always remember the feeling and it was strange. A euphoric sensation came over me and I started to cry. I cried for about twenty-five minutes, the hypnotist later told me. To me it seemed like maybe a minute. Then I felt very relieved, which I'm told is not uncommon. I'm told that when people are under hypnosis their emotions are tapped. They either cry or laugh.

Hypnosis interests me. I think it would be quite an experience to be hypnotized and go through a form of regression and be taken back through past lives. But I don't know what good that would do me, so therefore I've never done it. I'm interested, but I don't know if I believe it all because I know the mind can do wonderful things.

Reincarnation is another issue. I do believe in it; however, I don't believe that you or I will come back as a bull in Montana, which might not be a bad job except that I hate cold weather. Jokey jokey. I believe in the evolution of souls. I feel that we're drawn to the same souls in this life that we were in another. Moreover, you pay for the crimes in a future life that you commit in this one. The soul simply keeps coming back until it has fulfilled its higher destiny, which is to become the master and the teacher, and then the soul has reached its peak.

It's those feelings that serve a great purpose for me. That's how I can intelligently understand why a baby would come to earth already suffering some disease. Or a child would die. It seems cruel, but if God is a loving God, and I truly believe He is, it's the only answer that I can deal with. From that standpoint, I'm a great believer in destiny and reincarnation.

My mind tells me I've never known my brother in another life. I believe we were put together in this life to learn some great lesson from each other. I know my mother's soul and I know that I've known my father's soul. But I've never known my brother before. We are brothers in this life to learn something very dramatic from each other, and perhaps atone for something that each of us did in another life.

There are people in your own family that you know you've known from the time you could remember. And yet, deep inside, your gut reaction is that you're never going to know that person. There is a wall, a barrier that you can sense, and it's always there. Then there are other people whom you feel you've always known when you meet them for the first time. It doesn't mean you're going to like them, or even dislike them. But you experience that, deep down inside, they are not strangers. Almost everyone has felt this, but most people seldom examine those reactions.

I'm not one to share my psychic experiences with other performers. I wouldn't sit down with Shirley MacLaine backstage and share my ESP experiences with her. But I think that one of the reasons is because anytime performers come in contact with each other, it's usually not on a one-to-one basis. It's either at a party on a social level or backstage after your show; it's never just kickback time where you each express your innermost thoughts about life.

However, Bobby Darin's soul I knew intimately. I also knew Elvis's soul. There are other performers whom I don't know even though I know them very well. Sammy Davis's soul is another that I've experienced, and I think I know Frank Sinatra's soul. The reason why I say "I think" is because it has become clouded. I have only been close friends with Frank Sinatra in the last twelve years. It was difficult for me to get over who Frank Sinatra is and has been. You have a preconceived idea of a person, and that idea, if it's strong enough, will cloud the natural experience that babies and dogs have instinctively.

I confess that if my dog Thor, the one given to me by Frank Sinatra, doesn't like somebody consistently, and continues to growl, I really take a good, hard look at that person. I know Thor is picking up something on a much higher level than my own awareness can sense. Dogs have a wonderful sense. It's the same with babies and young children. They are taught hate. And they're taught fear. But they are not born with those things. So what they react to from birth till the age of about six is what they are. And how they react to things they are taught and things that are natural to them are totally different.

Imagine that somebody had masterminded Elvis's death, then found out that Elvis was truly living a happy, useful life somewhere. Some people seem to believe this. But

I'm afraid the chances of Elvis being alive are a billion to one, only from the standpoint of knowing the true medical problems that Elvis suffered. That wasn't made up; he was slowly but surely dying. Even if Elvis had been able to mastermind his own "life after death plot," how would he be able to deal with such things like the government, and especially the IRS? . . . Little, insignificant things!

When the world thought Howard Hughes was dead, one of the great comforting assurances for me that he wasn't was that the government would be the first ones to know if he were dead. Of course, that's exactly the way it turned out. So all of these things about Elvis's casket weighing too much, the misspelled name on the grave, I'm afraid are the result of someone making a lot of money for the sake of making a buck. I've listened to the tape and certainly it sounds like Elvis. But I'm also smart enough to realize that electronics are so good today that you could feed somebody's voice into a synthesizer and make it sound any way you want it to sound. You could match Elvis's voice identically. They could have even taken some old TV and radio interviews and edited them together. There are a million ways they could have brought Elvis back from the grave. The whole thing reeks of flimflam. I would love to think that he were alive and well and happy somewhere. I honestly believe that he is, but not on this earth.

When you die you pay the biggest price for fame. The thing that incenses me beyond words is what exploiters are able to do once a person is dead. I'm talking about books. Look what they've done to the memories of Errol Flynn, Tyrone Power, and Clark Gable. They're not around to defend themselves. It's not right. Wherever I end up, should they do something like that to me, I'll come back. Houdini won't have to worry where I'm at!

I especially envy the free soul of Errol Flynn. I mean, any guy who can go into a morgue and take his best buddy out with three or four guys and sit him up and have a party, that's my kind of guy. He definitely was a free spirit. He had a freedom about him that I don't have. He had an irresponsibility that I don't have. There's a lot about him, though, that I do know, and I think that I possess some of the same feelings. Flynn's was a free spirit and mine is not.

Flynn had a basic mistrust for women, which I also have. I love and respect them, but it's hard for me to trust any woman totally. I think there were things in Flynn's childhood that disturbed him: I think he wondered if his mother was faithful to his father. That I understand. That's not peeping any hold cards. I'm just saying that I understand those things.

If Errol Flynn wanted to go to Spain and fight in the revolution, he got on an airplane and went to Spain. I have always been too disciplined to do something like that. My soul has always felt too much responsibility, but God knows I would love to be able to act so spontaneously.

Sometimes those ESP feelings scared even me. My father would be the first to tell you this story: As a young child, when we were traveling from Virginia to Phoenix, I used to play a game using my ESP talents. We would be traveling across the desert without a cloud in the sky and I would say to my brother, "I'll bet you a dime that it will be raining in fifteen minutes." On my father's life, on my daughter's life, within fifteen minutes there would be a downpour. It wasn't just one instance of child play; there was something going through me that made me foresee these things.

One year at Christmas my father said, "You're never going to guess what we got you this Christmas. I mean, all this ESP crap of yours and you're always doing these things and giving us all headaches with it, you tell me what we got you for Christmas and I'll believe it now." My father just stood there and I said, "Dad, you really don't want me to do that." He laughed and said, "Yes, I do!" I looked him straight in the eye and mumbled, "I don't know why this picture comes to my mind but all I see is baby shoes."

My dad got up from the table and left the room. He wouldn't talk to me for the rest of the night because, in fact, my Christmas present was my baby shoes, which he had had bronzed.

I think my ESP powers got to him. My mother was always more curious about my ESP talents. She would often bring them up in conversation because it was fun for her. She thought of it as mind reading. She'd remember things that I'd forgotten over the years because they were insignificant to me. It seems so natural to me, until someone thinks it's strange. Then I think it must be strange to others, but it's not strange to me. My mother would say, ''Don't ever let Wayne Newton want for anything because he'll get it. There's no stopping him.''

I can walk into the room of an ill person and 95 percent of the time can tell you whether they are going to recover, because it's a feeling that comes over me. I have walked into hospital rooms and immediately become saddened because I know the person is never going to leave. Mine is a mental picture, and when I tell you that I can't control it, I can't control it. It's just a picture that I get. It's an instant flash and I don't know how it's going to work out. I don't know why it happens, but it always does. I foresee the future and I know, as I'm writing this, that I am going to own another hotel, maybe even two. I'm going to do motion pictures and I will have maybe three top-ten records. I mean, it's pretty scary, but I've been telling my crew of this vision. However, it isn't a completed picture. It's fragmented. It's like a polarization of things. I'm picking up things from audiences, for example, that I've never picked up before. I'm a receiver of thought waves. That's the only way to describe it. Call it ESP or whatever.

I look at what's in front of me and who's going to be gone. I realize that in the next five years many of the great saloon performers will no longer be with us, as we know them as performers. I look at what's behind me and I realize that nothing is coming. I think that there is a path the size of a freight train opening up.

When I look at the great souls I've come in contact with in my lifetime, it's frightening. I've often asked, "Why me?" From Howard Hughes to Jack Benny to George Burns to Bobby Darin to Elvis and on and on. Why were we soul mates? It's because I'm being prepared for something. Could it be the preparation of another life and not necessarily this one? That's a possibility. I might be fulfilling the top end of this ring too. I don't feel that it is the end because there's too much that keeps spurring me on. There is too much that's within me.

Everybody I've talked to who has achieved that "position" of elder statesman has said there's a certain calmness that comes with it. From the teacher to the master, from the student to the teacher, there's a certain order that we must live during our lifetime. We see it in the Oriental arts and all the Oriental movies. The master, the teacher, has nothing to do with the chronological thing. There is a calmness that comes with that. I don't have that calmness. While I have the calmness in some areas of my life, I can't find it where my work is concerned. In fact, I'm wondering at times if maybe the reality is never going to be perfect. Although the one thing that spurs me on is trying to make it as perfect as I can, and maybe that's what makes me happy, because when I finish something I have a tendency to move away from it.

Being named Entertainer of the Year and being initiated with a star on the Hollywood Walk of Fame were thrilling moments for me. But there was a point of sadness in them too, because they left me with two less things to strive for. It's a strange phenomenon, but from the day the star was put on the Hollywood Walk of Fame, I have never seen it again. At the ceremony, I uncovered it and that was that. I don't know why. Maybe it comes from the realization that something I worked for a long time ago was taken away from me, because it's there.

It's almost spooky the way songs I have recorded have been almost like crystal balls, telling what was about to happen in my life. Whoever would have thought that the song that had five million sales, "Daddy Don't You Walk So Fast," would become the story of my personal life? I lived it almost verbatim, which is kind of scary.

When I first heard "She Believes in Me" I felt as though the writer must have been looking through a keyhole into my life. I'm sure I'm not the only singer who has felt that way. I think any singer who loves a song and sings it well goes through lots of those kinds of emotions. I always sing my love songs to a special woman. I put a mental picture in my mind and sing to her alone—one-to-one. And maybe it's ESP—or something—that goes out to my audience and makes them think of someone they love too.

It's funny—I never thought I'd be writing about my life because I've been too busy living it. But once before I go I wanted to set the facts straight, and tell my fans *danke schoen*.